W9-CSL-684

STILL *Sexy*

STILL *Sexy*

How the Boomers
Are Doing It

SUSAN CRAIN BAKOS

ST. MARTIN'S PRESS ⌘ NEW YORK

Book design by Ellen R. Sasahara

Library of Congress Cataloging-in-Publication Data

Bakos, Susan Crain.
    Still sexy : how the boomers are doing it / Susan Crain Bakos.—1st ed.
       p.   cm.
    ISBN 0-312-20591-0
    1. Sex instruction.   2. Middle-aged persons—Sexual behavior. I. Title.
    HQ31.B237   1999
    613.9'6—dc21   99-13299
                                          CIP

First Edition: June 1999

10 9 8 7 6 5 4 3 2 1

FOR BARBARA AND MICHAEL,

the sexiest couple, the very best friends, with love

ACKNOWLEDGMENTS

Thank you to the following people, who helped turn an idea into a book:

Dana Albarella, my editor, and Joe Rinaldi, St. Martin's dedicated publicity manager.

Richard and Tamm Bakos for help with research.

Barbara Haigh, Jane and Wesley McCune, Carolyn Males, Marilyn Dorfman, Linda Stern, Patricia Corrigan, Bob Berkowitz, Harper Barnes—friends and fellow writers who contributed suggestions and encouragement.

Ellen and Dick Shepherd, my sister and brother-in-law, for installing me in the guest bedroom and asking daily, "How many words did you write today?"

Our darling Iva for the joy she brings.

To everyone at Blueberry Hill, the ultimate Boomer shrine.

And most of all, to the men and women who filled out questionnaires, distributed more of them, and consented to be interviewed, often for hours. Thank you for sharing a part of your lives with me.

Sex, Drugs, and Rock 'n' Roll

Seventy percent of Baby Boomers still listen to rock 'n' roll music, but the drugs they take are more likely to be Prozac and Viagra than the kind once scored in the park. The question is: Are they having sex? That question was seldom asked of preceding generations at life's midpoint. One just assumed: They weren't. Don't make the same assumption about the Boomers.

Who Are the Ubiquitous "Boomers," Anyway?

Four out of every ten adults belong to the Baby Boom generation born between 1946 and 1964—or, seventy-seven million men and women. In the decade of the nineties twelve thousand people turned forty every day. The median age for Boomers is now forty—and counting. By 2006, it will be fifty. From 1996 well into the twenty-first century, another Boomer will turn fifty every 7.6 seconds.

The Boomers can be more accurately defined as two subgenerations, the Vietnam (born between 1946 and 1954) and the Watergate (1955–1961). Eighteen years is a long stretch, encompassing almost two generations measured in any other than Boom years. Every generation is shaped in part by the history of its times. For early Boomers, the Vietnam War, the assassinations, political activism, sex, drugs, and rock 'n' roll were as significant in shaping them as the sheer force of their numbers. And for later Boomers, Watergate, recessions, the national malaise, the women's movement, the self-actualization movement, and the steep rise in the numbers of sexually transmitted diseases (STDs) formed the environment in which their own personal dramas were played out.

Collectively, the Boomers established the market power of the teenager in movies and music, rearranged the timing of traditional life markers like marriage and childbirth, and took sex out of the shadows and into the headlines. Our contribution to modern society's obsession with youth is immeasurable. Yet both groups are rapidly moving into and cruising through midlife, a period never before considered "sexy." A generation that didn't want their parents' stodgy automobiles certainly doesn't want Mom and Dad's middle-age sex appeal. Have we fashioned an alternative?

I traveled the country talking to dozens of Boomers about their sex lives, past and present. Hundreds of other Boomers from all parts of the country received detailed questionnaires on their sexual behavior and attitudes. I wanted to know the specifics, like how many times a week they have sex, how many orgasms, how much oral sex, how many lifetime partners, how many sexual variations they practice. I also wanted to evaluate the intangibles, like how satisfied they are with their sex lives and their lives in general.

Did those who were sexually active at an early age maintain a greater-than-average level of activity into middle age? Did the promiscuous pay? The late bloomers catch up? Does sex ever really get "better" in midlife for anyone? For whom? And what do they know that other people don't?

Is Sex Still Important to the Boomers?

I had to go on a road trip to get the answers to the questions not asked in those ebullient articles on aging Boomers featuring interchangeable quotes by Cher, Michelle Pfeiffer, Susan Sarandon, or Goldie Hawn. By planes and Amtrak trains, in rental cars—that white Chevy Malibu was my favorite—and, yes, for the sake of diversity, a Greyhound bus, I traversed America from her sea to shining sea talking to Boomers about their sex lives. (If the midterm Congressional elections of 1998 taught us anything, it's that the pundits and other so-called experts know far less about what the people are thinking and doing than they think they do. You have to go out there and ask and pay attention to the answers.) Driving west at dusk behind the wheel of the Malibu into the setting sun with a bottle of water, a bag of M&Ms, and one of the nation's 3,500 or so "classic" rock radio stations booming, I thought I understood at last the meaning of life somewhere between Columbus, Ohio, and Indianapolis, Indiana. Sex is as important to my life as drums are to rock 'n' roll.

And sex is still important to the Boomers, including the ones who tell you it isn't. Many of the happy and sexually active claim they are having "the best sex" of their lives. The women are more orgasmic, the men capable of greater emotional expression and able to make love for longer periods of time. If Boomers aren't "having sex," however, they define their lives in part by that absence and report less overall life satisfaction than the sexually active. Discontented singles and unhappily marrieds are more likely to live in urban areas than not. Manhattanites, for example, reported having fewer sexual experiences in the past year than men and women the same age and marital status who live in any other place. They also expressed the most dissatisfaction with their sex lives.

"Are the Baby Boomers still having sex?" joked a Philadelphia woman, fifty-two, born in 1946, the official Year One of the great American boom in births. Her mouth, outlined expertly in a deeper shade of coral than her lipstick, was twisted into a wry grin. "It's fashionable to deny all knowledge of sex these days, and fortunately, few single women in my age group have to fake it," she said, her hand covering her vivid mouth in mock shame. She was copping an attitude, and the attitude was a condescending one: At midlife, the best single women can't find comparable partners among the men who are "left."

She was not, she said, "having sex," unless masturbation "counts." Strip away the pseudo-sophisticated acceptance of the sexual status quo and you see a woman, lonely, brave, and vulnerable, willing to reach out a hand to grasp another's if only one were there. She was not having sex, but she felt the beat in her soul. She wanted to be having sex, but simply admitting that, without placing the blame on the men who aren't there, was too painful.

"Is sex dead?" asked a thirty-nine-year-old Manhattan bachelor, whose recent failed attempts at finding commitment would qualify him for a guest role on the HBO sitcom about disconnection *Sex in the City*, "or merely slumbering? Is sex dead because the Boomers are too old to do it?" On the rainy winter evening he posed those questions, in a restaurant in the Flatiron district of Manhattan, thousands of long-married Boomer couples were getting it on across the land.

The people who are having the most sex are not the people I expected them to be. Couples who married young, before age twenty-five, and stayed married to high school or college sweethearts, spouses to whom they have remained largely faithful, report having sex most often in the most varied ways and experiencing the greatest satisfaction with their partners. If you're looking for where the love is, cancel the appointment with the cynical urban sophisticate and drive out into the suburbs, the countryside, the small towns where the married live.

But, after all the complaints have been made, single Boomer women are less interested in commitment than single Boomer men. And Boomer women are almost as likely to have had extramarital affairs as the men. That aging Boomer women can't find partners among aging Boomer men is a familiar female lament. "The good ones are gay," women say, and many know from firsthand experience, having been involved with or married to men who were secretly gay, openly bisexual, or in the throes of discovering their true, gay, identity. That straight men can't "commit" is also an old complaint. The big surprise, according to many men, is that some women can't commit either. The power balance between the sexes has shifted yet again. After forty, men are more interested in getting married than women are. "I'd rather be alone than settle for what's left" was a comment I heard from financially secure women nationwide while men spoke longingly of the desire for a loving partner.

There was an almost wistful quality to the happiness of a slender, attractive forty-year-old bride I met in Cleveland, as if on some level she regretted the sudden absence of romantic possibility. Commitment closes doors. Marriage later in life seems to lock them. Her bald, chubby husband, on the other hand, looked as though he was ready to pronounce himself King of the World in front of a large audience. Perhaps she had reason to look askance into the future.

The unhappily married, more often urban than not, were more likely to have married later—after age thirty, often considerably after—and have had more lifetime sexual partners than their sexually satisfied married counterparts. Most of these couples accept the prevailing Boomer wisdom that marrying later, after having more experiences, sexual and otherwise, increases the odds of happiness and success. Yet it hasn't for them. One factor: It is simply harder to juggle two careers, a home, a marriage, and children after age thirty-five than it would have been a decade earlier. Only a Boomer could find this surprising. The discontented marrieds were also less likely to define themselves as "religious," meaning anything from regularly attending services to having an abiding belief in God.

But the remarried are often very happy. "Love is lovelier the second time around" is more than a song title for couples who found each other after a failed marriage. More surprising, many who weren't faithful to their first wives or husbands are monogamous in their second marriages. Mama was wrong when she said, "Once a cheater, always a cheater."

The unhappy, single or married, harbor the belief that something (someone) better is out there, somewhere. Call them jaded, hard to please, or eternally optimistic, they believe they haven't met the right one, that ideal partner tantalizingly just out of reach. The more lifetime partners they've had, the more inclined they are to imagine the best is yet to come.

The "promiscuous" didn't necessarily pay the expected price for their behavior. Heterosexual men and women who have had in excess of twenty-five lifetime partners suffered only slightly higher incidences of garden-variety, non-life-threatening STDs, no higher rate of HIV infection, and had no more unwanted pregnancies than their virtuous counterparts. The women were no more likely to have been raped, sexually abused, or harassed.

Both generations of Boomers, married and single, happy and not, have a common rallying point: the past. It is our youth, the salad days of Boomers older and younger, that is deemed to have been the best of all possible youths, even by the younger-than-us generation, the twentysomething Generation X.

"Free sex"—which presumably we and only we truly had in the glory days after the pill and before AIDS—like classic rock and "good drugs," i.e., pot and pure LSD, is mythologized. The orgasms flowed as easily as jug wine, their crescendos as high as the highest notes of the Queen of Rock 'n' Soul, Aretha Franklin. Lies and exaggerations are rampant whenever Boomers reminisce. I interviewed a forty-five-year-old man, a confirmed bachelor, a low-level bureaucrat in the State Department, who told of an orgy that had supposedly taken place in the seventies. "The condoms were flying," he said, proudly. I didn't believe him. Condoms weren't standard issue in the seventies. If they had been, the STD numbers wouldn't be as high as they are now. That wasn't the only reason I didn't believe him. His story didn't resonate. He was talking about a time and place where he thought he should have been but wasn't. No, he was not there when the condoms, like magic carpets and elephants with big ears, flew by. Orgies were a small part of the sexual history of Boomers, attended by a handful of devotees of Studio 54 and similar places.

Our collective past, though remarkable when compared to that of our parents or grandparents, is really not as interesting as our present. When I hit the road, I wanted to learn what "sex" means to the members of the Boomer generation, both publicly and privately. What role has it played and does it continue to play in our lives? Are the Boomers still having sex? Yes, they are. I can close my eyes and see in the rearview mirror couple after lively couple, arm in arm, waving good-bye as I drove away, his hand sliding down toward her ass.

As often happens when one undertakes a journey alone, frequently dependent on the kindness of strangers and occasionally in need of rescue by

American Express, I learned more than I thought I would. The Boomers I met, whom you will meet in these pages, are single, married, divorced, re-married, heterosexual, bisexual, satisfied, and discontent. They lost their virginity at thirteen, at thirty-one. They've had one partner, a hundred partners. Their stories form an erotic patchwork quilt, a generational memoir, of how it was and how it is.

For most of them "is" is better than "was."

PART 1

The Way We Were

Some people really do reach not only their physical and social peaks but also their erotic peak in high school or college. Others start early but continue to blossom sexually for many, many years. These chapters examine the lives of people who bloomed early, sometimes briefly. What factors make the difference?

1

The Mythmakers

The way it was isn't always the way we remember it being. In the moon-glow of memory, we didn't have pimples buried in coverstick, sweaty armpits, or tissue stuffed in the stiff ends of our cotton bras. No. We danced at the prom as light on our feet as John Travolta and Olivia New-ton-John in *Grease*. The girls in gossamer, the boys in starched white shirts and neon pastel cummerbunds, we danced, without missing a backbeat, without experiencing a heartbeat out of tune with our partners. Our eager, firm young bodies sought and found succor in the other's embrace. Hands were not sticky. Elbows and stick shifts did not get in the way.

Sex, drugs, and rock 'n' roll are the natural elements of the Baby Boom generation's cherished myths. We did them, we had them, we experienced them all in our youth. Well, some of us really did. If everyone who lists "Woodstock" on his or her personal bio had actually been there, the state of New York could not have contained the overflow crowd. Considerable socioerotic revisionism has occurred among Boomers "remembering when." Yet a core group of Boomers in both generations did live a credible version of the exciting life. The mythmakers were sexually active at an early age and led their peers in everything from number of partners to variety of experiences. Being a pioneer was not without its drawbacks.

For older Boomers, particularly women, becoming sexually active at an early age is more chic in retrospect than it was at the time. We can be smug in our retroactive hipness. Then we were "fast," "loose," "wild," and in danger of unwanted pregnancy, the wrath of parents and other authority figures, and the harsh judgment of "good" girls and the boys who loved them. Even boys could be too fast. The members of the Vietnam generation were reared under a set of sexual values that were already considered outmoded by the time they reached their twenties. Younger Boomers reached puberty under the new rules. They had more latitude, but by no means lived in the permissive society that we collectively recall as "the Sixties." Orgasms weren't as easy to come by as 45-rpm vinyl disks.

A fifty-one-year-old woman who lost her virginity at fifteen says, "I was the first girl in my rather upscale social group to go all the way. The other girls were fascinated and scandalized at the same time. I got away with a lot because my parents were screenwriters. We lived in the Valley, which was more conservative than you would imagine, but their status as 'creative people' gave them and me and my brother more leeway than we would have had otherwise. If my mother had been a waitress and my father a truck driver, I would have been a slut."

Blooming before one's perceived time was not without its hazards. Some were cut down by early pregnancy, parental discovery and punitive response, or social ostracism by their peers. But most, like the fifty-one-year-old Valley Girl, probably got away with it. If you're looking for stories of biblical punishments, you'll be disappointed here. How has the early-blooming Boomer held up over the years? Most would say very well.

LET THE LITTLE GIRL DANCE

"She never danced before . . . she wants to give it a try."
(Recorded by Billy Bland for Old Town Records)

"I discovered sex in high school, really discovered sex, but I was smart enough not to go all the way until I graduated," Patricia says. "I wasn't beautiful, but I had thick wavy hair, nice breasts, big eyes—and I really *liked* boys, which I realize in retrospect scared off several of them."

Patricia graduated from high school in 1966, a year on the cusp of the sexual revolution, half in the land of *Leave It to Beaver* and half in the world of the Beatles, in East St. Louis, Illinois, a town on the verge of annihilation via white flight. Motown stars like the Supremes were featured acts on *The Ed Sullivan Show*. Nancy Sinatra released her big hit, "These Boots Are Made for Walkin'." The Monkees were on television and on vinyl with "I'm a Believer." Hemlines were short. Political idealism was high.

By 1976, when Patricia's class might have held a tenth reunion, the town was a virtual lost city, inhabited largely by blacks on welfare. What happened to inner-city neighborhoods in Detroit, Chicago, Philadelphia, and other big cities happened to the entire city of East St. Louis. For Patricia and the other far-flung white members of her graduating class—about two-thirds of the total—"home" was no longer the kind of place people visit at the holidays, much less plan reunions around. Everyone's parents had moved away, typically after the last child graduated from high school, sometimes sooner. The boys she first kissed are lost forever, their lips never to be spotted through the greenery while picking out a Christmas tree on the discount store parking lot with Grandma. Price's, a drive-in hamburger hang-out, like Arnold's on *Happy Days*, is gone. Reidel's, a "better" restaurant, where Patricia had her first mixed drink, a black Russian, when she was seventeen, gone. Jone's Park, the tennis courts, the riding stables at Holten Park, Siedel dress shop, gone. Barry Manilow wrote the songs and Eric Clapton shot the sheriff, but it's unlikely anyone left in East St. Louis took note.

"I don't remember black boys," she says, "not at all. There were two black girls in my classes senior year, very bright girls. Those were the waning days of segregation, when whites and blacks were kept largely separated by academic 'tracking,' supposedly by intelligence. I didn't think of black as sexy until I saw Sidney Poitier in *Guess Who's Coming to Dinner?* in 1967. For months I had fantasies of him making love to me."

If no black boys made it onto her sexual radar screen, plenty of white boys did. Phillip, Jewish, tall, lean, and angular, with a prematurely receding hairline; Sid, shorter, more fair, one of the "cute" boys, probably destined to inhabit a larger waistline, a smaller life than the one he had in senior year; David, "very ethnic," Eastern European, short, with curly hair, and a sturdy bulge inside his trousers; Sonny, older, tall, sophisticated, the college boyfriend; Bobby, tall, gangly, but a good dancer. And more.

"I liked slow-dancing best. We swayed back and forth, in time to the music, our bodies plastered against each other, his crotch pushed against me, my breasts smashed into his chest. Oh, very erotic. Dancing has never been so hot. I was a hot babe, but those boys didn't know what to do with a hot babe. Fortunately, the ethics of the time had unexpected benefits for me. If I hadn't felt compelled to preserve my so-called virginity—actually my hymen broke when I was climbing a tree at age twelve—I would have gone straight to intercourse in my early teens as girls do now, forgoing all that delicious petting. I regularly petted to orgasms. More than one boy marveled at the contractions he felt through our clothes while dry-humping on top of me. It was the golden age of foreplay."

At the end of senior year, Patricia decided she wanted to lose her virginity. David, the boyfriend of the moment, balked. What if he hurt her? Damaged her marriageability? Got blood on his clothes and had to explain that to his Hungarian Catholic mother?

"We didn't," she says, "which was lucky for me. The summer before college, I met Roger, my first lover. He was one year older and slightly more experienced, enough to know about buying condoms and about inserting one, then two, then three fingers into my vagina before thrusting his penis there. We made love the first time at his grandmother's house. She was away for a week, and he had the keys. There was a heavy cream-colored chenille spread on the bed, crocheted doilies on the dresser, chest, and bed tables, the stale scent of lilies, lavender, and lilac in the room. It was the middle of the day, but we had the drapes closed. Straight sharp lines of sunlight delineated their edges. The room air conditioner hummed on high. I didn't have an orgasm, but I was enormously proud of myself when it was over. I was a woman. The third or fourth time we made love, I did come. He was passionate and playful and very concerned about pleasing me. I couldn't have had a better first lover."

He was killed in an automobile accident that fall. After him, there would be three more lovers—most of her orgasms achieved during foreplay or the "after-play stroking" rather than intercourse—before she met her future husband, Rick, when she was nineteen and he was twenty-five. The courtship was "whirlwind," the petting prolonged, the precoital orgasms abundant. She also learned how to have an orgasm via intercourse alone by delaying penetration until she was on the verge of orgasm, then adjusting her hips and controlling the thrusting to get the stimulation she needed. They were wed, weeks before her twentieth birthday.

"Really, it was all a downhill sexual slide after the wedding," she says. "Once our son was born, Rick put me on the madonna pedestal. I was a mother, and mothers should adhere to a different code of conduct. We had perfunctory marital sex, a little foreplay followed by a minute or two of him on top. I alternated between faking orgasms and telling him I'd been faking orgasms. Once I got him to go down on me; after a few minutes, he went into the bathroom, spit, and gargled. Fortunately, I had no hang-ups about masturbating when I was home alone and the baby was napping.

"In the last years of our marriage, I had affairs and made sure he found out about them. I was trying to make something happen between us, divorce or some kind of dramatic improvement. One of my lovers, a twenty-two-year-old poet, actually came to the house and asked him for my hand in marriage. Rick sent him away. Another time he drove me to the airport to take a flight to meet my lover for the weekend. What madness. Our marriage actually ended on the New Year's Eve following our tenth wedding anniversary. We had a big party. He had sex with one of the female guests on our bed—and left the door open. After everyone had left at four A.M., he said, 'You aren't going to divorce me over this, are you?'

"It was clear to me then that we could go on having tit-for-tat affairs, each trying to force the other into making a decision about the marriage— or I could take charge. I got the divorce. It was more difficult than I thought it would be. Husbands of friends hit on me. I had an affair with an older man that wasn't serious, but I invested it with meaning out of a need to have someone to hold on to. He did give me my first oral orgasm, however. The irony: It happened on another chenille bedspread, this one orange and worn in spots, at a Howard Johnson's Motor Lodge in south St. Louis. Some female friends and acquaintances were actually quite hateful to me. I think many of them were jealous because I was dating—and they were married to men who weren't as good as the wives pretended they were.

"My friends thought I was wild and liberated, but I didn't come into my own again as a sexually powerful woman who could command the kind of erotic attention she wanted from men until I was into my thirties. In my forties, I had affairs with younger men, black men, a Puerto Rican. I tried anal sex, a little bondage, sex in semipublic places. That hot little girl finally grew into one libidinous woman."

Like Patricia, many of the Boomer women, at both ends of the age spectrum, found that early sexual exploration led, if not immediately then eventually, to adult satisfaction. They were more likely to masturbate than later-blooming women and unlikely to be deterred by early disappointments—chiefly, difficulty in reaching orgasm during lovemaking. "I had the drive," one woman explained. "I didn't discourage easily."

The Survey Says
- 20 percent of younger Boomers, the Watergate generation, were sexually exploring (no intercourse) at age thirteen or younger. The average age for sexual exploration was fourteen for both sexes. Men lost their virginity at fourteen and women at fifteen. Three-fourths of this group remain sexually active with a partner or through mas-

turbation and are satisfied with their sex lives. Another 13 percent expect to be sexually active again.

- Slightly more than 10 percent of older Boomers, the Vietnam generation, were sexually exploring (no intercourse) at age thirteen or younger. The average age for sexual exploration was fifteen and a half for women, fifteen for men. Men lost their virginity at sixteen and women at seventeen. Approximately 72 percent remain sexually active with a partner or through masturbation and are satisfied with their sex life. Another 16 percent expect to be sexually active again.

- In both groups, the men and women who became sexually active at later-than-average ages reported less activity and less satisfaction with their sex lives. Only 38 percent of Watergate-generation men and 35 percent of Vietnam-generation men who did not lose their virginity until age twenty-one or older remain sexually active and say they are generally satisfied with their sex lives. They are the least active and satisfied group in the survey.

Other Surveys Say

Other surveys, including *The Janus Report on Sexual Behavior*, a comprehensive report done in 1993, also report that younger Boomer women had earlier sexual experiences than older Boomer women, and that the nature of the experiences differed somewhat. For older women, the initial sexual experiences were more likely to have been prolonged and heavy petting, including dry humping and stroking each other to orgasm. Younger women had intercourse sooner.

In fact, the age of first intercourse has been steadily declining since the first Boomers reached puberty. It was not uncommon in the supposedly swinging sixties for boys and girls to do everything short of intercourse, either to "save" the girl's virginity, still perceived as having value in the marriage market, or to prevent pregnancy when condoms were harder to get and conceal and high school girls weren't routinely taken to their mothers' gynecologists for prescriptions for the Pill. Today many young girls have intercourse before they've masturbated.

"Girls had more control over when intercourse would take place when I was in high school than they did when my younger sister was," says Kate, fifty. Her sister is forty-two. "She came to me for advice when she became sexually active. I was surprised at how quickly she moved to intercourse with a new boyfriend. She was afraid of losing a guy if she didn't. Often girls my age would not have intercourse for the same reason. They'd lose him if they *did*.

"The pressure on younger girls to have intercourse earlier cut down their opportunities for pleasure. Lowering the age of penetration wasn't a good thing for girls. The boys were getting off, the girls were getting fucked. When I was in high school, we benefited from the sexual rules more than boys suffered from them. We got more of the kind of erotic attention we needed. I had orgasms before I had intercourse. It was the other way around for my little sister. She was more experienced, but she knew less about her own sexuality than I did at her age."

The rush to intercourse has been cited by many women as a factor in delaying the experience of orgasm for young women. But regardless of how quickly they moved from petting to intercourse or whether orgasm preceded or followed intercourse, both men and women who experienced early intense sexual desires are likely to have maintained an interest in sex well into midlife and beyond. Many researchers, including David Rubin, author of *Everything You Always Wanted to Know About Sex, But Were Afraid to Ask*, and Dr. Eric Pfeiffer, an influential early sex educator and researcher who published studies in the seventies, have concluded that there is a significant positive correlation between high levels of sexual activity in youth and greater sexual activity in later years. That may be dismaying to the parents of teens, but hardly news to early-blooming Boomers.

SOUND BITE

From a conversation with a forty-five-year-old woman: "If only I'd appreciated the joys of virginity while there was still time. I look back now at those fleeting days when my body was the temple the devoted male was trying to enter. All the delicious kissing, touching, caressing, licking, entreating. Why was I in such a rush to 'do it'?"

BOOMER SEX TIPS

I'm Gonna Do Something Good to You
(Recorded by K. C. & the Sunshine Junkanoo Band)

Initially, attraction between lovers is strong, in part because obstacles abound. When we were young, even the sexually precocious Boomers endured a period of longing before consummating a relationship. Would the slow dance have been popular if we hadn't?

Take it back to the golden age of foreplay when the Beatles sang "you're sixteen," and you really were.

Kiss

Start with the Essential Kiss

With one hand gently holding the back of your partner's neck, caress his or her cheek with the other hand. (Alternately, take the face in both hands.) Kiss playfully at first. Lips only, mouth loose. Brush lips. Pull away. Make eye contact. Lick your partner's lips with the tip of your tongue. Brush lips again. Don't kiss harder until you feel your lover's response.

Add Some Riffs

Tickle. Run the tip of your tongue around your lover's lips, inside and out, and then back again.

Rub. Kiss softly, then rub your lips back and forth against your partner's. (Try the rubbing kiss later on your lover's erogenous zones.)

Feather. As passion increases, make your kisses hot and fast. These repeated urgent but light kisses are effective on the neck, too.

Suck. Lightly suck your partner's lips one at a time. The operative word is "lightly." No slurping noises.

Lick and Bite. Alternate the top and underside of the tongue when licking. Lick lavishly, without leaving a trail of moisture. Bite gently. A love bite is a mere closing of the teeth around a lip, nipple, or other body part—not an actual bite.

Add a foreign language. A French kiss is not the shoving of one's tongue into the other's mouth. It is a passionate, yet delicate, erotic exploration of the lover's mouth and tongue. Lead with the tip of your tongue. Pull back. Circle your lover's tongue with the tip of yours. Pull back. Lick the sides, underside, and top of the tongue. Repeat, repeat, repeat. When you are both very aroused, thrust your tongue in and out in rhythmic, thrusting movements. Only when your partner is very aroused should you search the recesses of his or her mouth with your tongue.

Flirt

Have you forgotten how? Flirting is not complicated. Lightness is everything.

Make eye contact. All flirting begins with eye contact. Seek your partner's eyes. Hold the gaze a second or two longer than you normally do. You don't have to gaze soulfully. Let your eyes convey affection, a hint of amusement, an erotic suggestion.

Speak low. Lower your voice a bit. Banter. Be witty if you can. Praise your partner's appearance. Make suggestive comments. Tease, if you can do it in a lighthearted way that won't give offense.

Use your body. Convey your admiration and desire through open, inviting body language. No crossed arms—or legs for men.

Touch. Run a finger down his or her cheek. Stroke your thumb across a hand. Brush a leg under the table with your foot. Lightly.

Pet

When teenagers pet, they stroke each other with fingers and tongues. He touches her more than she touches him. They each have one foot on the floor. Petting is done in an upright position. When the feet come up and the bodies go down, it isn't petting anymore.

Particularly for the older Boomers, petting was a competitive game with more than one goal: He tried to "get," while she was determined not to "give" too much, too soon. Playing games can make you both feel young again.

Dry Hump

Take petting to the next level. One lies flat out on top of the other. Leave your clothes on. Blouses and shirts may be unbuttoned in the frenzy to touch skin to skin, but the pants' zippers stay zipped. Skirts can be hiked to the waist. Move together simulating intercourse. She can have an orgasm, but he should stop the rocking motion when he feels ejaculation is imminent.

Take it higher yet. Pull down the pants. Remove every item of clothing except underpants. Rub her clitoris through her panties. Take his penis in her hand, but only if it falls spontaneously out the slit in his shorts or briefs.

Go Almost There

To preserve her virginity and prevent pregnancy, you can't "go all the way." He can penetrate her vagina, but not fully. Shallow thrusts protect the hymen. He must withdraw before ejaculating. It's acceptable, of course, to ejaculate between her breasts, on her stomach, in her hand or his.

Can't get in the mood? Put on some oldies. Imagine you're in the backseat of a Mustang convertible or the carpeted living room floor—the parents are asleep upstairs—or on the sofa in the home where she's babysitting after the little ones have been tucked in.

Other Surveys Say

Studies show that 90 percent of women close their eyes while kissing. Only a third of men do. Are they shy?

Researchers say that men find the visual stimulation arousing. Women, on the other hand, use the closed eye time to fantasize.

A reason to open your eyes, women: Men bond with greater intensity by looking into your eyes during kissing and other forms of love play.

TRY A LITTLE TENDERNESS

"You know she's waiting, just anticipating . . . "
(Recorded by Otis Redding, for Irving Music Inc., B.M.I.)

"I had sex when I was fifteen, but I didn't have an orgasm until I was twenty-five," Elizabeth says.

Typical of a subgroup of female early bloomers, Elizabeth had the sex without the pleasure, just like women of previous generations, only at a younger age. Some young women were too inhibited to communicate their sexual requirements to their partners, while others weren't familiar enough with their own sexual responses to know what they needed. Propelled by curiosity, desire, or the desire to please, they formed sexual relationships.

By age twenty-five, when she experienced her first orgasm, Elizabeth had been married and divorced and was married again. She was the mother of a seven-year-old daughter. That pregnancy had led to her first marriage at eighteen. Now forty-four, she is midway between the oldest and the youngest of her Boomer cohorts. At her high school graduation party, one of the girls brought Helen Reddy's "I Am Woman" and a copy of the premier issue of *Ms.* magazine. The boys brought alcohol, tried to get the girls drunk, and mostly succeeded. Richard Nixon was president, though not for much longer.

"I was probably one of the fast girls in high school," she says, "but I wasn't part of the 'in' group, so I can't be sure that anyone paid enough attention to me to categorize me at all. I was a strange combination of shy and belligerent. I wanted to be a social activist but didn't have the courage to do anything except sneer at people who had shallow, materialistic values. A friend I made in my late twenties said I was probably the kind of girl the good girls secretly envied. They interpreted my sneering demeanor and sexual availability as indicators that I was really getting it on. I guess she knows what she's talking about. She was one of the good girls—prom queen, cheerleader, scholarship, the whole nine yards.

"I lost my virginity to a boy named Chuck while a Fifth Dimension album played in the background. To this day I can't hear 'Aquarius/Let the Sun Shine In' without remembering how he smelled. He was actually repulsive—fat, a little stinky, breath like bananas and oatmeal cookies. When he took off his shoes and socks, his feet stank. I didn't exactly say yes to him. I just didn't know how to say no. My parents liked him for some reason, probably because my father is fat, which makes my mother a chubby chaser. She actually flirted a little bit with Chuck, in that harmless way mothers do flirt with suitable young boys dating their daughters. Maybe I took my cue from her. Whatever the motivation or lack of it, I had sex with him, and it was very disappointing. The next boy was Todd. The sex was better. At least I liked it. I got pregnant right away because I wasn't using anything. I wish my liberal parents had suggested an abortion, but the word was never mentioned.

"I love my daughter. She's turned into a beautiful young woman, very intelligent and impressive. I never had any other kids. I got the hang of birth control. It's funny that it took me an unplanned and unwanted pregnancy to figure out birth control and ten years of having sex with men to have an orgasm. I never masturbated. Why didn't I at least do that?"

Elizabeth grew up in a southern Illinois community not geographically distant from East St. Louis but socioeconomically light years away. Lush green lawns were as well manicured as the fingernails of the neighborhood's housewives. The school system was 95 percent white. Barbie and her pink dream house, G.I. Joe and his equipment were the toys of choice. In her bedroom in the split-level ranch style home that was popular there in the sixties she could sometimes hear her parents arguing about sex.

"My mother was hot for him, but he disappointed her a lot. I remember her yelling at him because he couldn't last long enough or couldn't get it up. I knew they had a bad marriage. I just didn't draw the right conclusions from the obvious lessons in the room next door. I've been married three times and had long living-together arrangements with two other men. Sex always felt good to me even when I didn't have orgasms. I liked sex. Having sex with a man validated me. Sometimes I picked up strangers in bars, that old cliché. If I went out with a guy twice, I thought I was in love. That kind of thinking led to bad choices in men, of course. My daughter can separate sex from love, and I admire her for it. To be so smart in your twenties is a very good thing. I don't know if she has orgasms, but I'm betting she does and has had them for a long time. The first time I came it was because Steve, my lover, was just so good and lasted so long. He was patient. I was a weird combination of experienced and ignorant—ignorant about my own sexual responses as well as his.

"Really, I believe I was addicted to sex or to having a man in my life. I was possessive and very jealous of every man, no matter what a jerk or a loser he was. I alienated a friend or two by accusing them of coming on to my boyfriend when they weren't. Now I have a man without being possessive of him. We've lived together for seven years. At first the sex was really good. I impressed him with my skills, but he was easily impressed by little things like basic fellatio. He had little experience. And he felt like *wow!* when I went down on him and stayed there for more than fifteen seconds. He was in a similar place to the one I was in when I met Steve at twenty-five. But we don't have much sex.

"Part of the problem is herpes. You have to keep up with sex at this point in life or you lose the momentum. We've lost it. I am a herpes carrier. I passed it along before I knew I had it. My outbreaks are rare and mild. My partner, on the other hand, has prolonged and frequent outbreaks that have all but killed our sex life. Recently we had sex three times in one week, because it was a good week for him, no outbreaks—but that's rare.

"In spite of three failed marriages and two attempts at forming life partnerships before this one, I still believe in true love. Though I've had a strange, some would say promiscuous sex life, I'm a little bit prudish and old-fashioned. Do I think I've found true love now? I don't know. I do know there's a lot of my mother in me—clingy, jealous, denying reality and projecting a fantasy.

"What's real is what happens between two people in bed. A lot of what we tell each other happens isn't true just as a lot of what we tell ourselves isn't. Much truth is never spoken, even between best friends. In our thirties, all my friends talked about sex, about how they liked it, how often they were getting it, or how much trouble they were having getting it, but I really don't know anything about what my friends actually do in bed. Do they come? Have a lot of oral sex? Go in for the kinky stuff? I don't know. Now, in our forties, we never talk about sex. Most of my friends are married. They seldom mention sex, and then only in passing. Everyone I know has had more to say about Clinton's sex life than about their own in recent years. I sense we share relief that our hormones have cleared and we can think again. We can stop asking, 'Is this true love?' and behave like intelligent, powerful women who can make a difference in the world.

"Sometimes I look at the man beside me and think he is nothing like my fantasy of my true love. Maybe it's time to grow up and accept reality. In a real relationship, the sex isn't so important after the beginning. At first you need the sex to bond. Later, other things matter more, like dependability and shared interests and goals. When I met him, he was suffering from clinical depression and anorexia, a rare condition in men. He's better now, except for the herpes, which I gave him. I think he's better because of what we have together, because of love. When we have sex, we make love."

STDs proliferated in the wake of the sexual revolution. After the birth control pill became the most widely used form of contraception in the late sixties, condom usage plummeted. That dovetailed with other social trends—delayed marriage, earlier sexual experimentation, living together before marriage, more frequent divorce—to create a society in which people were having more lifetime sex partners and protecting themselves less against the spread of disease. The seventies exuberance and sense of freedom was exemplified in disco and other popular music and those wacky fashions we find embarrassing today. Many people didn't think about consequences. They led sexually careless lives until the decade ran out on them.

The explosion of genital herpes was the subject of a *Time* magazine cover story in 1981 that called the disease "the new scarlet letter." The implications were obvious: STDs were the visible stigma of sexual sin. Some social commentators view the *Time* herpes cover as the end of the sexual revolution. Then came AIDS, which was accompanied by exaggerated fears of disease and public moralizing.

Non-life-threatening STDs such as herpes and genital warts can be managed or contained but not entirely cured. They have certainly inconvenienced many Boomers and put out, at least temporarily, some of their sexual fires. Some STDs, like chlamydia, which is often asymptomatic yet easily treated by antibiotics, can leave women and sometimes men sterile. How an infected person deals with an ongoing STD depends both on the severity of the outbreaks and his or her underlying sexual attitudes. A disease can be an excuse for shutting down just as extreme fears of contracting an STD can be the reason one gives for leading a sexless life.

The Survey Says
- 21 percent of the Vietnam generation and 24 percent of the Watergate generation have had an STD.
- In 75 percent of the cases, the STD was chlamydia.
- Of the remaining 25 percent, 11 percent had herpes and 10 percent had genital warts, with gonorrhea, syphilis, and other STDs making up less than 4 percent.
- Only two questionnaire respondents, both gay men, said they were HIV positive.

Though it would seem that the more promiscuous members of the Boomer generation would be more likely than others to have contracted STDs, that proved to be not necessarily the fact. Boomers reporting the greatest number of sexual partners had only a slightly higher incidence of STDs than those who'd had more than one lifetime partner but fewer than five. One incidence of exposure can infect someone, so that a man with one or few partners can be infected by a woman with one or few partners or vice versa. More partners doesn't have to mean a bigger risk. Since many STDs are asymptomatic, an infected person can spread a disease without knowing he or she is doing so. Symptoms may suddenly appear long after infection. Many couples discover after they've made a monogamous commitment to each other that one or both have an STD. Often people with multiple partners are more careful about practicing safe sex and getting tested regularly than those who've had fewer partners. Urban singles expressed the most concern about STDs though their likelihood of infection was no greater than that of a person the same age with the same number of lifetime partners living in a suburb, small town, or rural area. In fact, only one in ten New York City residents surveyed has ever had an STD. Go figure.

For the most part, the surveyed Boomers who took foolish risks with their sexual health have learned to live with the consequences without surrendering their erotic rights. And many have avoided consequences altogether. A thirty-eight-year-old woman who estimates she's had fifty or sixty partners in her lifetime says, "I didn't always use condoms, though I have used them more in the past several years than I did when I was young. I'm very lucky I've not contracted something. I never had an abortion either. Many of the women I know have had either an abortion or an STD or both."

Other Surveys Say

According to a study by the New York City Health Department, women accounted for 7 percent of the 11,820 new AIDS cases diagnosed in the United States in 1985. By 1996, they made up 20 percent of the 57,200 new cases diagnosed nationwide.

A small but growing percentage of the total number of AIDS cases are aging Boomer women.

Women may actually be more at risk of contracting HIV as they age for these reasons:

- Either as a result of sterilization or menopause, they are no longer concerned about contraception and may not use condoms, reasoning that their partners are "safe."
- Other STDs, especially herpes, make them more vulnerable to infection.
- The natural thinning of vaginal walls that accompanies aging (unless a woman is on hormone replacement therapy) increases the risk of damage to tissues during intercourse. The HIV virus is transmissable via two routes: blood to blood and semen to blood. A break in the vaginal wall gives the virus entry.

The lesson here? Safe sex is not just for kids.

BOOMER SEX TIPS

Get Ready
(Recorded by the Temptations for Motown Records)

Playing like a teenager is fun, but is not a practical way to handle adult sexuality in a new relationship or an affair, unless you are one of those fortunate Boomer men who has convinced a young woman that sex equals blow job. *Condoms are essential.* Some STDs are spread by contact with bodily fluids or mucous membranes, which means condoms alone won't protect you fully against potential exposure. Since it is unlikely you will opt for latex body suits, evaluate the risks, use the condoms, and get tested for STDs as often as you have a routine physical exam unless you're in a monogamous relationship.

LIGHT MY FIRE

"Come on, baby, light my fire."
(Recorded by the Doors for Elektra/Asylum Records)

Most men, one might argue, are early bloomers, but that's not necessarily true. Boys tend to masturbate earlier than girls. They are expected to play the role of sexual aggressor. But girls in high school date older boys. The sixteen-year-old boy loses his virginity with a fourteen- or fifteen-year-old girlfriend. Unless their mothers worked outside the home—and only 25 percent did in the sixties—Boomer men didn't have good opportunities for sex until they were old enough to drive. Only the adventurous few overcame that handicap.

"I swear to God I was trying to put my little wienie inside a playmate when I was nine years old," Robert says. "I know I was nine, because I remember it was 1967; my parents were constantly playing the Doors and 'Mrs. Robinson,' the Simon and Garfunkel song from *The Graduate*. I certainly wasn't forcing her. She was into it. We were taking doctor one step beyond. I don't know how common that is, but it seemed like the most natural thing to us. We didn't exactly know what we were doing, but we knew the parents wouldn't think it was a good idea. We were discreet.

"Her parents and mine were neighbors and our fathers were business associates, but they were not a regular part of my parents' group. Those couples got together nearly every weekend at someone's house, had big dinners, drank a lot of wine, smoked some grass, and flirted with each other's spouses. I don't believe there was anything like swapping—that wasn't my parents' generation—but I do think there were some affairs within that group. It was Updike country in spirit, if not in geographical locale."

Robert, who recently celebrated his fortieth birthday, grew up in suburban Chicago. His father was a successful executive, his mother an occasional painter. Their friends were exclusively couples in which the man made a better-than-average living and the woman dabbled in the arts and performed volunteer work. The women's movement and all the discontent that phrase implied lurked around the edges of their glossy existence like specks of scum in the corners of the backyard pool. But by the time Robert turned thirteen in 1970—the same year Kent State students were shot down by the National Guard—the lives of his parents and their friends had changed as much as he had. The sixties were over.

"When I was nine, none of my father's contemporaries had cashed in his wife for a trophy bride," Robert says. "None of my mother's friends had begun spouting quasi-feminist rhetoric. They'd been to college, but not to one of the Seven Sister schools. They didn't talk about Sylvia Plath sticking her head in the oven when they got sloshed the way my wife's mother's friends did when she was the same age. While I was playing penis games in the family room with Leslie Lynn, my wife was eavesdropping on adult female conversations about literary suicide. Her mother's little group was a lot different than the couples group. My parents seemed to me to have it all together when I was nine and ten. But the year of my thirteenth birthday, the divorcing began.

"I officially lost my virginity when I was fourteen, to an older girl. She was sixteen and she called my penis her ding-a-ling, after the Chuck Berry song. We met at summer camp, where we were both counselors. My parents were fighting all the time, often about sex. I was glad to go to camp. I'm pretty sure Dad was cheating on Mom. I asked him to add a year to my age on the application form so I'd qualify for counselor, and he did. I was the youngest counselor. I never told the others how young I was. I told the older woman I was three months short of my sixteenth birthday, which neatly explained why I didn't have a driver's license. She was sixteen and four months and felt like she was cradle robbing, but she overcame her principles and robbed.

"I have to say it was a great first time. I'd played around enough to have some knowledge of where I was going. And I had trained myself by using the stop-and-start method during masturbation to last slightly longer than the average mad-out-of-his-mind-with-hormones adolescent. My parents had two sex books under the bed: *The Sensuous Woman*, by J., and a big book by Masters and Johnson that had the stop-start directions in it. My sixteen-year-old honey had a little experience. We had an entire sunny afternoon by the lake alone together. She was the first girl to take my dick in her mouth. What an awesome experience. I came a dozen times between noon and six P.M. She came half a dozen times. I really wanted to see her after camp. She wrote and phoned, but I had to brush her off because I couldn't let her know I was fourteen. I still think about her sometimes and wish I knew where she was so I could tell her why I 'dropped' her. She probably wouldn't blink at the age difference today."

Robert continued his sexual exploring in high school—he had nine partners senior year—and in college. "I'm not proud of the way I treated some girls senior year," he says. "With six other guys, I talked two girls into 'pulling a train' "—a euphemism for a group sex situation in which one or maybe two girls service several boys, one after another. "They were drunk and so were we. Afterward they looked sad. One of them told me later she was sore for days."

Robert's wife, Sugar, was not an early bloomer. While some of her classmates at the exclusive private high school she attended flaunted their sexual experience and others quietly pursued their erotic development, she hid behind her shyness, her braces, her twenty extra pounds. Robert met her at the University of Illinois when both were seniors, after the braces and the pounds had come off. The shyness appealed to him.

"On some level, I was the classic son of a bitch who'd had his way with a lot of girls and wanted a virgin bride. I was having sex with four different women on a more or less regular basis and banging the occasional one-night stand when I met Sugar. We saw *Annie Hall* on our first date. She was a little embarrassed by it; I didn't ask her out again for months. Then I saw her one day in the library and knew I had to have her. The sun was shining through a window on her blond head bent over a heavy book. 'She's going to be mine,' I said.

"Everybody told me she wouldn't stand for my philandering ways, wouldn't have sex with me if I didn't marry her. She was a challenge. Sugar held out. That was a new experience for me. No matter how hot and heavy things got, she stopped the action when I put my penis near her vagina. She was a natural 'Rules girl.' And she had me tied up in knots. I proposed in a state of sexual agitation. We moved up the wedding twice, because I couldn't wait any longer.

"I remember walking down the aisle in a stupor. The soloist was singing one of those songs by the Carpenters. I think it was 'Close to You.' Here I was, the guy who'd scored bigger than big at the age of fourteen at summer camp, marrying a woman I'd never had sex with, a virgin. How was this going to work from the sexual perspective? I had no doubt she'd be the wife I needed in every other area of our life together, but how would the sex work?"

Not well, as it turned out. Initially, Sugar threw herself enthusiastically into the experience of sex. He thought she was "having a good time." Within four years, their two sons were born. And then she told Robert she'd faked every orgasm he thought she'd had. *Faked.*

Robert was one of those men who are supremely confident in their ability to "give" their partners orgasms. Initially, he didn't believe her when she said she'd been faking. When he did, he got mad—and then even. Would their marriage have turned out differently if she'd followed the confession with a plea for joint counseling or a challenge to him to "make" her come, leading both of them to discover her path to pleasure?

The Survey Says
- 87 percent of older Boomer women and 83 percent of younger Boomer women say they have faked an orgasm at least once.
- 44 percent of Boomer men believe (or were told) that their partners have faked an orgasm.
- And 27 percent of Boomer men have faked one themselves.

"Sugar's faking confession freed me to have affairs," Robert says. I should have known when I met Sugar that she was never going to live in the hot zone. She's not a passionate woman. I'm content with the split in my personal life, getting sex in other places, having my other needs met by my wife. As long as she doesn't catch me, she's fine with it too. I hadn't had a sweaty, heart pounding episode with her in years. I know part of that is the aging factor, but not all of it. I have some pretty torrid sex with my lovers.

"Frankly, I think Sugar let me know she was faking so I wouldn't bother her very often for sex—and she had to know where that would lead. If I could have anything I wanted, I'd have everything with her. We probably shouldn't have married so young. In a few more years, we both would have known better than to marry each other."

When early bloomers married late bloomers, the result was often something less thrilling than the story of the prince (or princess) awaking sleeping beauty's passion. The early-blooming male/late-blooming female relationship was far more common than the reverse. It was also more likely to succeed, perhaps for obvious reasons. Men were expected to lead and women follow, men to teach and women learn. A forty-six-year-old woman who married a former seminarian says, "We were twenty-five when we met; he was a virgin and I was experienced. After the initial passion subsided, we discovered we were poorly matched. If a man can wait that long, he is never going to be a sexual dynamo."

BOOMER SEX TIPS

(I Can't Get No) Satisfaction
(Recorded by the Rolling Stones for ABCKO Music)

If you are a man who believes you can always tell if a woman is faking, let me disabuse you of the notion. Any woman can fool any man anytime. The supposed indicators of orgasm—chest flush, heavy breathing, dilated pupils, swollen genitals, hard nipples—are signs of strong arousal, not orgasm. The contractions can be faked so well they fool even a man performing cunnilingus, supposedly the one position in which a man can be sure he's "given" a woman an orgasm.

No man, especially an aging Boomer, should waste time worrying about The Fake. Generally, women have orgasms more easily as they get older. (They are also less inclined to say, "Lovely sex, dear," if it wasn't, which is why the midlife faking confession is not something Robert alone has heard.) If your longtime partner fakes occasionally, so what? If she fakes often, it's her problem, not yours.

No woman should be satisfied with a sex life that isn't replete with orgasms. If you're faking more and enjoying it less, have a hormone work-up. Hormone replacement therapy can help. Then shake things up in the bedroom. Change your lovemaking patterns. Improve your sexual skills. Technique does matter.

THE KEYS TO FEMALE ORGASM
Attitude

A man doesn't "give" a woman an orgasm; she takes her own. Touch yourself during lovemaking if you aren't getting enough stimulation. Most women who have trouble reaching orgasm during lovemaking can find satisfaction simply by taking matters into their own hands.

Kegels

If you don't exercise, your muscles grow flaccid. When the pubococcygeus (PC) muscle, part of the pelvic floor in both sexes, loses tone, orgasms don't feel as strong as they did. Locate the PC muscle by stopping and starting the flow of urine. Then do the following exercises:

A short Kegel squeeze. Contract the muscle twenty times at approximately one squeeze per second. Exhale gently as you tighten only the muscles around your genitals (which include the anus), not the muscles in your buttocks. Don't bear down when you release. Simply let go. Do two sessions twice a day. Gradually build up to two sets of seventy-five per day. Then add:

A long Kegel squeeze. Hold the muscle contraction for a count of three. Relax between contractions. Work up to holding for ten seconds, relaxing for ten seconds. Again start with two sets of twenty each and build up to seventy-five.

When you're doing a total of three hundred a day of the combined short and long, add *the push-out.* After releasing the contraction, push down and out *gently,* as if you were having a bowel movement with your PC muscle. Don't bear down. Now create *Kegel sequences* that combine long and short repetitions with push-outs. After two months of three hundred sequences daily, you should have a well-developed PC muscle that can be kept in shape by doing a hundred and fifty sequences several times a week.

Cunnilingus

Many women who don't reach orgasm during intercourse do so via cunnilingus. The basic technique for a woman's partner:

Don't go straight to the clitoris. Lick the line of flesh between her pelvis and thighs. Kiss and lick up and down one inner thigh to the area behind her knees. Use your hand to caress her vulva and the perineum, the area between anus and vagina. Use your fingers to part her outer lips to make her clitoris accessible. Lick and suck the area surrounding the clitoris.

Cover her venus mons, the point where the clitoris begins. Suck, using *gentle* pressure. If her clitoris is well back inside the clitoral hood, exert minimal pressure with your fingers along the side of the hood to lift and expose the clitoris. You may need to keep one hand in this position until she reaches orgasm.

Indirectly stimulate her clitoris by putting your lips around the sides. Hold them in a pursed position as you suck. Alternate the sucking with licking of the sides of the clitoris and surrounding tissues.

When she is nearing orgasm, cover the clitoral area with your mouth. Suck around the sides of the clitoris. Stimulate her labia with your hand or stroke her inner thighs or tease her nipples—or alternate these stimuli.

The Boomer Facts

• Early experimentation didn't necessarily lead to pleasure, especially for women. There are many reasons for that. Neither women nor men understood the critical role of the clitoris in female sexual satisfaction prior to the 1966 publication of *Human Sexuality*, the masterwork of Dr. William Masters and Dr. Virginia Johnson, the founding parents of sex therapy. Masters and Johnson dethroned the penis as the ultimate source of erotic power and pleasure. They reported that nearly two-thirds of women do not reach orgasm by intercourse alone but need direct clitoral stimulation. When the Boomers, particularly the Vietnam generation, were young, nice girls did not touch themselves during sex. Many of them didn't masturbate. Cunnilingus wasn't yet a part of the good lover's repertoire. Unless a young woman was exceptionally savvy, she likely didn't know how to get the pleasure she wanted from sexual contact.

The Survey Says

Ninety percent of Boomer men in both age groups say they had masturbated by their eighteenth birthday. Only 60 percent of younger Boomer women and 55 percent of older Boomer women had.

• Nor did early experimentation necessarily lead to a punitive conclusion. Early-blooming Boomers who enjoyed their first experiences, orgasmic or not, are not much more likely than their counterparts who experimented later to have had an unwanted pregnancy, contracted an STD, or suffered another negative consequence of their sexual behavior. Rather than linking pleasure to punishment, *studies show a positive correlation between early activity and continued lifelong interest in and enjoyment of sex.*

For girls especially, the motivating factors that led them to have sexual relations at an early age affected the outcome. Did she consent to intercourse to please a boyfriend? Flaunt her lack of respect for parental and other adult authority? Or because she craved sex, was curious about what it would feel like, or simply had an adventurous spirit? If the girl was expressing her own sexuality rather than using her sexuality to attract and keep a boyfriend or punish a parent, the woman recalls the early experiences more favorably, viewing them as the foundation for the satisfying sex life she has attained. How closely she linked sexual feelings to love in her teen years may play a role in her life now, too. Girls who forced the fantasy love connection most strongly often made premature marriages to young men who were not good choices for them.

2

The Boomer Effect

Boomers were born cool, and we have lived cool. We are even making middle age cool as we continually push back the aging clock through diet, exercise, cosmetic surgery, hormone replacement therapy, and impotence pills. The mythology has two parts: our glorious past and our glorious, extended futures. The generation who said, "Never trust anyone over thirty" now says, "Let's live to be one hundred and remain active and alert." "Forty is what thirty used to be," we say, and "fifty is what forty used to be." Please don't call us middle-aged. That was an affliction our parents, saddled with inglorious beginnings, had to suffer. We do not. Options still abound for us.

The Boomers aren't the only generation to have a compelling and romantic mythology. Remember "the Lost Generation"? Writers Ernest Hemingway, F. Scott Fitzgerald, his wife, Zelda, and others are the icons representing a generation of people who did not fritter away their languid youth drinking and swapping literate one-liners in Paris cafes. Quite often the generational hype hasn't lived up to the reality as lived by the vast majority. With Boomers, everything is larger than previous life because of our numbers and the technology that exploits numbers. While the myths of the Lost Generation owed their afterlife to books and the film adaptations of those books, Boomer myths have been promulgated by the monolithic modern media, aided and abetted by the national taste for decade nostalgia. Nothing is ever really over. The fat lady never sings. Whenever she clears her throat, someone somewhere puts on a Beatles or Stones record.

The Boomer Effect is created when a man or a woman born between 1946 and 1961 actually believes the myth, and many do. The disconnection between the actual experience of childhood and an individual's perception or false memory of it probably was not possible on such a large scale for the members of previous generations. We all attended the funerals of the Kennedys and King, stalked the Vietcong in full living color, watched Nixon wave that manic good-bye at the helicopter door, and danced to the music, if only in our heads. The Boomer mythology grows like sourdough starter, which multiplied rapidly and spewed out of its containers in the refrigerators of wannabe hippie wives in the seventies. Even men and women born after 1964 pay homage to the Boom years. *Wish I were there* is the postcard message scrawled across the stormy, swinging sixties and the sexy seventies. Why should we castigate those born in the magic time for wishing they, too, had been *there* in the fullest, largest, mega-media sense of the word?

The Boomer Effect can be positive as well as negative. It can enhance the minimal past sex life in the way the Wonderbra creates cleavage from two small breasts. Rather than looking back with wistful regret, some aging Boomers take off their reading glasses and see the past through a rosy haze.

"In my memories, I was Annette Funicello on the beach with Frankie Avalon," an older Boomer says, laughing. "In reality, I was largely dateless in Ohio, miles away from a minor river. There was a glamour attached to the times that rubs off on all of us who were of that time. I do believe this. I have certainly given younger coworkers and nieces and nephews the impression that my life was as exciting as the times. In retrospect, it was. There was an energy in the air, and we all absorbed it. Being alive was exciting then, just like being in New York City is exciting now, even if you're not a full participant."

In the afterglow, ordinary sex can seem like something wonderful.

DAYDREAM BELIEVER

> *"I could hide 'neath the wings of the bluebird as she sings . . ."*
> (Recorded by the Monkees for Rhino Records)

I considered my first meeting with Dan wasted time. A prime example of the Boomer Effect, he attempted to snow me. His lies, as obvious as big wet snowflakes, didn't stick. His only concession to aging he said, was "getting into relaxed-fit jeans" because he "didn't like them so binding at the crotch anymore—but no sexual slowdown." I couldn't bring him around to truth telling by employing the usual journalistic techniques, more subtle than calling him a liar.

"I don't regret my hedonistic pursuit of carnal adventures," he told me in a Kansas City barbecue joint that he said the President once visited. The ribs were delicious, with a smoky, spicy sauce. "It's a phase we all went through back in the golden days of sex. There was no such thing as bad sex, only good sex, better sex, and best sex. I can't recall the names of the girls I did in high school and college, but I can remember their pussies."

Yadda, yadda, yadda. I gave him a phone number and told him to leave a message if he remembered what really happened in his youth and wanted to talk about it before I left town. I didn't expect to hear from him. Surprisingly, he called, but not until I'd left Kansas City for St. Louis, where we eventually met at Blueberry Hill for "famous" burgers. Blueberry Hill, named after the Fats Domino song, is a Boomer shrine. Sitting among the Howdy Doody memorabilia and record album jackets soothes the Boomer soul.

"I'm sorry I wasn't straight with you," he said. "My wife left me last year, and I've had a hard time dealing with it. I was giving you a story. I give everyone a story. The common denominator is the portrait of me as a hip young man. I never was. I never had hair down to my shoulders, never smoked reefer, never had babes in my bed. I was a nerd. A virgin until twenty. That was 1968. I finally lost my virginity between the assassinations of Martin Luther King, Jr., and RFK. I remember watching the television coverage of Kennedy's assassination and thinking, A few months ago he was consoling Coretta and I was a virgin."

Nineteen sixty-eight was a watershed year for Vietnam generation Boomers. The year began in January with the bloody Tet offensive. Walter Cronkite said on the evening news that he doubted the Vietnam War could be won, an unprecedented commentary by a respected anchor. By March, Lyndon Johnson had declared he would neither seek nor accept his party's nomination for President. Eldridge Cleaver's black power manifesto *Soul on Ice* was published. Student riots, cultural upheaval, and political chaos made an impact on people in their impressionable years, the late teens and early twenties. Dan's comment linking his virginity and Coretta King's widowhood is not unusual for Boomers recalling what *Life* magazine dubbed "the Incredible Year." Who did not sometimes feel in 1968 like a minor character in his or her own life?

"My first lover was a pale, serious young woman with a colon condition," Dan says. "Both Washington University [in St. Louis] students on scholarship and in poverty, we met at the old Tivoli theater way before it was remodeled. It showed art house films before the term 'art house' was in vogue. I saw Fellini's *8½* there, and it blew my mind. If you set your pop-corn down on the floor, the roaches got into it. We were both working as ticket sellers, ushers, cleanup crew, such as the cleanup was.

"She had to be careful what she ate or she farted. Since she didn't want to fart in bed, we rarely had meals together after we became lovers. She told me she loved me before I told her. Then, of course, I had to tell her I loved her back. We were outsiders, with our noses pressed against the glass.

"We were together for four years. In the last year we moved to Kansas City together to look for better jobs. St. Louis wasn't happening for us, and neither of us wanted to go back home, me to Virginia, her to Tennessee. I know she had orgasms after the first few months because she worked at having them. It occurred to me one day that she talked about her progress toward The Big O the way my grandmother talked about her digestive system. For a while I couldn't get the comparison out of my mind. I suppose her colon problems made it more obvious. I would lie in bed with her after we'd made love listen-ing to her dissect the session, describing how high up the arousal scale she'd climbed before falling back down unsatisfied, and I'd think of a big family dinner working its way through my grandmother's digestive system.

"Everyone assumed we'd get married, and we probably would have got-ten married because I couldn't think of a reason for breaking up with her. A small incident occurred. An acquaintance of hers, an attractive, sexually alive woman, went to the movies with us one night. She was at loose ends after breaking up with her boyfriend. The friend flirted with me. I was flat-tered and probably blushing like a bride. In the lobby, I left the girls alone to use the rest room. When I came back, I overheard my lover saying to her friend, 'You can have anyone you want. Leave him alone. He's all I can get.'

"It took me a few weeks to tell her what I'd overheard. I was really hurt by it. She shrugged the whole thing off. Later, after the breakup, she ac-cused me of blowing a 'little nothing event' out of proportion as an excuse to dump her. She actually thought that her pretty friend and I might have something going on behind her back.

"On my twenty-fourth birthday, I was alone. I'd had one sex partner in my life. Some of the guys from work—I was managing a retail store be-cause I hadn't been able to find a job in my field—took me to a strip club. They kept paying for lap dances with this same little blonde. She wasn't as well endowed as the others, but she was beautiful, all trim and taut and wholesome looking. Under those circumstances, you probably don't find a lot of girls who look like you could take them home to Mother if you put some clothes on them, but she did look that way. I've never forgotten her. I still masturbate to her memory sometimes. I went back to the club a few times on my own and paid for lap dances with her. Then one day she wasn't working there anymore, and that was that.

"The following year I met Laura. She was pretty, with long brown hair and big brown eyes, a teacher in a private school, the kind of woman I considered a little out of my league. I probably wouldn't have asked her out if we hadn't met through friends. They relayed the word back to me that she was interested, so I called. We didn't have sex until we'd been dating three months; and it was good. She gave me head the first time we made love. After we'd been lovers for a while, she told me she expected me to go down on her, too. I'd never done that and was a little nervous about it. She coached me, which was humiliating, but, if I am honest, necessary. According to Laura, I got to be very good at cunnilingus. She used to tease me by saying that's why she decided to marry me.

"For years we were happy together. I got my own computer consulting firm going and began making decent money before the kids were born. When we moved into the big suburban house, we thought we had it all. A little boy and a baby girl. Two cars, the house, and each other. The sex remained very good for a long time. Then we had the usual problems associated with aging relationships, aging bodies. I had the occasional erection failure. She had heavy periods that lasted for ten days at a time for a couple of years before her gynecologist insisted she have a hysterectomy. After that, she avoided sex.

"I don't know what I thought. I guess I thought she'd get past it. Ignoring the obvious seemed like the right thing to do. When she told me she'd been having an affair—and it wasn't her first affair—I couldn't believe it. I was devastated. She wanted a divorce, not to marry someone else, but to be free to have her affairs. 'I'm tired of lying to you,' she said. 'This isn't a good way for either one of us to live.'

"It had been a good way for me to live because I'd been happy with what I had—a wife, a home, all the accoutrements of marriage. And suddenly I didn't have anything anymore. My friends have been trying to fix me up, but I lie to them and tell them I'm dating around, dating younger women, that I'm involved with a stripper. They seem to be worried about me, but I don't know if it's because they think I'm telling whoppers or because they believe them."

Dan says that divorce has thrust him back emotionally into 1968 when he was an "unappealing" young man who lost his virginity to an "unappealing" young woman while all around him his male contemporaries were dancing to Marvin Gaye singing "I Heard It Through the Grapevine" and the Doors' "Hello, I Love You," having sex with nubile women who eschewed undergarments, and otherwise living the sexual high life as they anguished over the future of the republic. He was impoverished, stuck in a relationship he didn't want, and "living small, very small." The music made him sad.

He says, "Radio stations play 'classic rock,' i.e., oldies, and the soundtracks to commercials are Motown hits. Do you know what that means? Several times a day I am catapulted back to my youth for a dose of pain."

Between the girl with the problem colon and the end of his marriage, Dan describes himself as "happy." The sex, he says, was "very good for a long time." He has achieved professional success, finds great satisfaction with his role as father, and hasn't lost his hair or his waistline. Why can't he concede that life has been generally good and look to a future which might include another love, another marriage?

"I am beginning to see that I have unrealistic expectations," he admits, "but realizing I do doesn't diminish them."

A week after we talked, Dan went to a Rolling Stones concert in St. Louis. The smoke, he said, was mostly legal. Thousands of people grilled meat and seafood on small Hibachi grills off the backs of their oversized sports utility vehicles in the parking lot. The festivities were covered by Boomer reporters from the local television channels. Portly male and softly chubby female Boomer interviewees dressed in clothing from the Gap and J. Crew said, "There'll never be another band like the Stones," implying there would never be another generation like ours.

"A lot of phony, self-congratulatory reminiscing about the old days," Dan snorted. "I didn't run into anyone who hadn't been to several Stones concerts. When I said it was my first, people were astonished. They assured me they had been tripping their brains out the first time they heard the Stones live—and, when the women weren't in earshot, the men would say they'd been balling some hot girl from Kansas State or University of Illinois or Smith the first time they heard 'Satisfaction' on the radio.

"They were ground-zero Boomers. Yeah, sure. And I got it on with that pretty little blond lap dancer."

The Survey Says

- Almost 20 percent of Boomers in both age groups say they are dissatisfied with their sex lives. The most common reason for singles: the inability to find a *suitable* partner. For marrieds: sexual boredom, closely followed by incompatibility in the areas of frequency or sex practices, with one partner wanting more sex or different kinds of sex than the other does.

- Slightly more than 25 percent of Boomers in both age groups say they are dissatisfied with life in general. Reasons most often cited: career and/or money problems, disappointment in marriage or parenthood, overwhelming responsibilities, including care of aging parents. Mentioned by less than 5 percent of all Boomers, including the politically idealistic Vietnam generation: dissatisfaction with the political process or parties or the government in general.
- When questioned individually, nearly two-thirds of the dissatisfied Boomers contacted said they thought their lives, and sex lives, were better than their parents' or those of other previous generations—but they had expected still more.

SOUND BITE

From a conversation with a thirty-eight-year-old woman: "I used to try to have sex two times a week to keep up with what other people my age were doing. Then I realized I probably wasn't having as high a quality sex anyway. That depressed me."

BOOMER SEX TIPS

Game of Love
(Recorded by Wayne Fontana and the Mindbenders for Fontana Records)

Fantasies can get in the way of real life or they can enhance it. Turn your Boomer fantasies into sex dreams and use them to increase pleasure. Many people fear their fantasies because they don't understand them. A fantasy about another woman or man doesn't mean you don't love your partner anymore. Thrilling to the lash in your sex dreams doesn't indicate a desire to be whipped. Read about fantasies if you're concerned. Put your mind at ease. Then indulge.

Play a fantasy in your mind when you need it. Treat a favorite fantasy like a videocassette. Pop it in when you want to increase arousal or speed orgasm.

Share with caution. Your partner is not entitled to your every thought—and may not want to hear them. You should know if she or he will find this an exciting scenario or cause for jealousy or alarm before opening your mouth.

Act with consent. Some couples enjoy acting out favorite fantasies. Others find that even verbally sharing a fantasy robs it of its power to arouse. If you want to act out a fantasy, you must convince, not coerce, your partner to go along. Remember to adapt scripts and props to reality. As books can't be literally adapted to film, fantasies can rarely be acted out exactly as they play in your mind.

Enrich your fantasy life. Get inspiration for new and more varied fantasies from literature, film, art. Be open to the more subtle erotic content of these sources. If you restrict yourself to X-rated videos and magazines, you're limiting your imagination.

Use the power of suggestion to enrich your partner's fantasy life. Leave the book lying around. Speak in double entendres. Be subtle and sexy at the same time. You want to plant erotic seeds, not start a confrontation about sexual issues.

PAPA WAS A ROLLING STONE
(Recorded by the Temptations for Motown Records)

"When my niece asks me what it was like reaching puberty in the late sixties, I smile enigmatically and let her think the worst . . . the best? What is it I'm trying to project here?"

Lisa, forty-two, grew up in the borough of Queens in New York City, in a family one almost needs a *Playbill* to follow. Her mother and her father each had two daughters before marrying and producing Lisa. Then they divorced. Each married again and had yet another daughter. A short stocky brunette "with no neck," Lisa was surrounded by beautiful blond half sisters, ranging from petite and delicate to tall and willowy—six lovely girls with long necks who didn't have her weight problem. They didn't get acne, and she did. Both parents were theater fans, and Lisa and her sisters grew up with show tunes. She could sing "Bali Ha'i" and "A Cockeyed Optimist" from *South Pacific* before she was out of training pants.

"Imagine Cinderella as the ugly duckling and the stepsisters as the lovable beauties, and you have the family picture, as it really was," Lisa says, "but in my fantasies I was Cinderella. The prince did come. He touched me, and I was beautiful. I was Nellie in *South Pacific*, Anna in *The King and I*. There was longing in my love stories."

Fighting the battle of the bulge, she still followed the sexual arc of the younger Boomer. First intercourse at fourteen; abortion at seventeen; seven lovers by her twenty-first birthday; living together at twenty-two, breakup at twenty-four, followed by more lovers and more breakups and marriage at thirty, divorce at thirty-five; and, after a year of trying, a pregnancy at forty. Yet she never felt she was living the Boomer dream. And then the child suffered from profound birth defects, called "anomalies" by the medical professionals.

"In spite of considerable evidence to the contrary, I had myself convinced my life was on a good track before the baby was born with so many problems," she says. "I was an optimist. I saw being a single mother in the most romantic terms until I gave birth. I saw having the baby as the first truly right thing I'd ever done. Maybe the romance would have ended, anyway."

Lisa was only thirteen when she had her first sexual experience, stopping short of intercourse. The boyfriend of one of her half sisters, a sixteen-year-old jock, spent a summer afternoon making out with her on the family room sofa. She thought all the kissing, caressing, and petting meant he loved her.

"I was wildly excited," she says. "I remember my panties were dripping wet. He could have had me then with no trouble, but he was, after all, my sister's boyfriend. He had some standards. Or maybe I was too fat for him to do it with me. He put his penis in my hand and told me to hold it hard and work it up and down. He came in my hand. I can still remember the first time I smelled cum. I felt like a woman."

At her fourteenth birthday party, she "seduced" one of her guests, a "tall, gangly, geeky kid who probably seemed the least likely" to refuse her advances. As soon as he clamped his hand on her breast, she was sure she was in love again. Intercourse was quick, perfunctory, an act born less of passion than a boy's determination to seize the moment. Yet she knew she liked sex.

"I always liked sex. I might have invested every encounter with more meaning than it had. I might have fantasized love relationships where barely like relationships existed. I might have had my share of intercourse leading to no orgasm. But I truly liked sex from the first time. I like the male genitalia. I like the smell, the taste, the feel of everything sexual, including my own genitals. I masturbated, too."

Lisa's exuberant enthusiasm for sex seems genuine. She believes that fat is all that stopped her from experiencing the idealized Boomer sex life. Had she not been fat, she reasons, she would have had the kind of partners who could have given her the pleasure she craved. Fat got in the way and kept getting in the way, causing her to "settle" for "lesser" sex partners, to rule out the possibility of marriage to an idealized man who would be both the love of her life and her parenting partner. Because she was fat, she took what she could get, a man who was willing to impregnate her.

"Michael was a planned birth," Lisa says. "I wanted to be a single mother. Michael's father made it clear that he had no interest in being a full-time father. He didn't want to pay child support. If I wanted a baby with him, that was okay, but he didn't want to be a father. He said he would lend financial and emotional support through pregnancy, be in the delivery room with me, and lend a hand until I had recovered from childbirth. Other than that, he made no promises. I wanted nothing more. What he was offering in addition to his sperm seemed like a nice bonus. I had this vision of myself as the earth mother that was strikingly in contrast with my liberal Jewish background.

"Pregnancy made me grow in sensuality. I never lost interest in lovemaking. I masturbated. I was gloriously fulfilled. Unlike most women in my age group, I didn't have amniocentesis. No ultrasound. I had a midwife and planned a totally natural birth experience. Fortunately, Michael's father insisted I give birth in a hospital birthing room in case of complications. When the baby was born, we were stunned. He had so many problems. For months, his life hung in the balance. There were seventeen surgeries in the first year and more ahead. I didn't think about sex for a long time."

Having a child with multiple birth defects forced Lisa to confront reality—eventually. Before Michael, she liked to think of herself as a sensual, sexually liberated, free-spirited woman. Her personal mythology fit neatly into Boomer mythology. She was a "goddess." Her orgasms were big, bigger, biggest. After Michael, she tried, but was unable, to live in a world, if not entirely based in fantasy, then considerably enhanced by it.

"Before Michael's father, I was involved with a man who owns a small video production company. He produces X-rated videos. His orientation is strictly soft porn from a male perspective. I fitted myself into his ideology. I talked dirty. After a while, I thought in 'cunt,' 'pussy,' and 'throbbing cock' terms. I was desperate to please him, but I didn't recognize that until I was in my earth mother phase, glowing and pregnant. I had moved out of his fantasy and into mine.

"I needed to believe I was having the best sex ever, even if it was sex for one. After Michael's condition stabilized, I crashed. I couldn't cope. Fortunately, my extended family came through for me. They took over at the baby's bedside while I got some rest. They turned on me when I started getting some sex as well as rest."

While her son was midway through the first and longest of many hospital stays, Lisa began an affair with Tom, an old friend, a married old friend. She reverted to schoolgirlish behavior, talking endlessly about him to her half sisters, her eyes growing soft and dreamy whenever she spoke his name. She repeated the litany of a married man's lies to his single lover as if they were sacred truth. He didn't have sex with his wife. The marriage was truly dead. He loved Lisa and would leave his wife for her as soon as his nine-year-old daughter was old enough to understand. Her sisters cringed when his name was mentioned, railed at her "gullible" behavior, lectured her on the immorality of sleeping with another woman's husband while her baby lay in a hospital isolette connected to tubes.

Lisa held on to the myth of her great romance. That myth kept her warm in chilly hospital corridors. Then one of her sisters ran into one of Tom's wife's friends at the supermarket and discovered that the wife was six months pregnant with a healthy baby boy.

"I didn't believe it at first, so my sister dragged me to see the friend who'd told her. Then I lost it," Lisa says. "I went to his office and pitched a fit. I was hysterical. He had security throw me out. I can see now how I must have looked to him, fat, blowsy, unkempt, screaming, and crying. His parting words were: 'You should be with your baby now. What kind of mother are you, anyway?' "

That sounds like it should have been Lisa's bottom point, but it wasn't. She did pull herself back together and resumed her place at Michael's bedside. A month later she'd convinced Tom to see her again. The affair resumed. Periodically she raged at Tom, and more often her sisters excoriated her. After the birth of his son, Tom announced that he would not be seeing Lisa anymore. He was accepting a transfer to the West Coast and moving the family as soon as his wife and baby were able to travel.

"I was bereft. Losing Tom was the best thing that ever happened to me, but I was too stupid to see that. After he left, I was forced to come to terms with my life. I had a child who would never lead a 'normal' life. He was a year old before I came out of the fog of denial and began to face the facts.

"I went into a sexual dead zone again. Oddly enough, a vibrator brought me back to life. I was doing some freelance writing. I hadn't been able to work at a full-time job since Michael's birth. My family had been supporting me, and the government was paying for his medical care. One of my writing assignments for a small women's magazine was to write an article on sex toys. The editor sent over a box of products.

"I decided to try Dr. Ruth's Eroscillator because the product information promised it was quiet. Michael and I were sharing an L-shaped studio apartment in Manhattan. He slept in a crib at the end of my bed. Quiet was essential. I turned on the vibrator and at first couldn't get into it. My fantasies went nowhere. Trying to conjure them was as difficult as trying to read a book at that point in life. I couldn't focus. Gradually the physical sensations took over. I felt a tremendous orgasm building. It was like a huge truck coming over a hill, and I knew it was going to flatten everything. I came and cried and came and cried. When it was over, I was free of tension for the first time in months, since the day I'd found out about Tom's wife's pregnancy. I felt whole and at peace. My soul was restored to me."

Lisa's story, like that of some other Boomers, illustrates the enormous and enduring power of sexuality. A woman who considers herself "too fat" for sex, who has suffered more than a little humiliation in her search for sexual partners and erotic fulfillment, and who has been faced with one of the most painful and challenging situations anyone can ever face, the birth of a seriously handicapped child—this woman still yearns, lusts, reaches out in a darkened L-shaped room for sexual pleasure. She hasn't given up.

The Boomer Effect may have caused some to lie about their sexual escapades or to enhance them and others to compare their reality unfavorably to the myths. But it has also had a positive impact on younger and older Boomers alike. This generation, more than previous ones, has a sense of sexual entitlement. We do believe in the right to sexual pleasure, even for fat girls alone in small rooms where the burdens of their lives press upon them. Sex toys and other aids are acceptable replacements for or adjuncts to fingers.

A vibrator is standard equipment in American bedrooms, particularly those inhabited by single women. The first vibrators were available by prescription only. A few enlighted urban doctors in the 1930s did prescribe them for inorgasmic women as part of a treatment for "female hysteria," which was probably code for "sexual frustration, resulting from stimulation without release." Imagining a woman using one nearly seventy years ago and bringing herself not only to sexual release but to the point of soul restoration is like imagining a painter who was not van Gogh looking out the asylum windows and seeing "Starry Night"—so rare would have been the woman who could make the leap.

The Survey Says

- 74 percent of Vietnam-generation Boomers and 77 percent of the Watergate-generation have used a sex toy either as a masturbation aide or during sex play.
- 90 percent of those who have used sex toys have used a vibrator, either on themselves or a partner.
- Single women in both age groups were the most likely to use vibrators as a regular practice.

BOOMER SEX TIPS

Good Vibration
  (Recorded by the Beach Boys for Capitol Records)

Vibrators are useful toys for both sexes, during masturbation and as part of love play. Basically, they accelerate arousal and induce orgasm. Available in many shapes, sizes, and styles, vibrators can create a wide range of stimulation and sensations. (See appendix for suggested mail order sources.)

The basic techniques:

Hers. Most women reach orgasm with the vibrator by pressing against the clitoris, not through vaginal insertion. Experiment by varying the pressure and speed as you move the vibrator around your genitals. Tease yourself by alternating the stimuli when you feel close to orgasm.

His. Start on low speed. Run the vibrator along the shaft of the penis, then press it against the base, the scrotum, and the perineum. Experiment with higher speeds and firmer pressures. Have patience. It takes most men longer to reach orgasm via vibrator than through other forms of stimulation.

Theirs. Take turns massaging each other with the vibrator. Tease the genitals. Use the vibrator to vary stimulation while caressing your partner's genitals. A woman can hold a vibrator against the back of her hand cupping her partner's scrotum or holding his penis. A man can hold the vibrator against the back of his hand as he strokes her labia and the sides of her clitoris. Try in-

serting a wand-shaped vibrator between your bodies during intercourse.

Experiment with the attachments—the G spot attachment, for
example.

I CAN SEE CLEARLY NOW

"I can see clearly now, the rain is gone . . ."
(Recorded by Johnny Nash for CBS Records)

The happiest Boomers have integrated the generation's myths and expectations with their own experiences. They aren't kidding themselves about a
life they could have, should have, but didn't lead. Neither are they tormented by comparing themselves negatively to the mythmakers. They've
put the Boomer Effect to the best possible use: It has given them permis-
sion to follow their own erotic paths.

"I had to clear my head of the Boomer mythology before I could see
that I was really *happy*," Catherine says. "I kept comparing my life to those
of the standard-bearers. For my age group, that was the woman who had it
all—marriage, children, career, good abs. She baked her own bread,
pumped her breast milk in the executive washroom, and had multiple orgasms at the drop of a silk camisole. The Wonder Woman was quoted in
women's magazines and in the business section of newspapers. She was on
the nightly news. I thought I saw her everywhere I went. She was completely in control of every area of her life—and I wasn't.

"What did I have? I had a mediocre job, was never married, had no
kids. I had a lot less than 'all.' "

Catherine, forty-three, grew up in the Boston area. Her early sexual
playmates were future frat boys, and she found them disappointing. In
1970 she lost her virginity at fifteen in a carefully planned event while her
parents were on vacation.

"They went to Paris without me," she says. "I had to do something."

At fifteen, already a devotee of "films," versus "movies," and serious literature over *Valley of the Dolls*, she went to see Glenda Jackson in *The
Women* before "doing it" with "a kid who looked like Lenny Bruce on a bad
day." His parents were, however, very rich, which lent him a certain cachet.

"He had a really small penis," she says. "In the following years I was re-
lieved to discover how exceptionally underendowed he was."

Meetings of women's consciousness-raising groups were more common than Tupperware parties in her quiet suburban neighborhood when she left home for Barnard College in 1973. Her favorite song was "You're So Vain," by Carly Simon, and she hummed it until her mother shrieked for silence. Her mother's parting words of advice were: "You'll need to learn how to do sex without love." And her father's parting words of advice? "You'll need an MBA."

"Their messages were so conflicted because my mother had never worked. She excelled at spending money. I know now that both of them had their affairs, but I didn't know it then. She was discontent, but she didn't know what I did want or how important sex would be to my happiness."

Catherine dropped out of Barnard after one year, entered her "hippie" phase, and lived briefly in a commune.

"We were vegetarians who raised goats for their milk. I thought I had a grand belief system, but I probably had nothing more than a desire to get under Mummy and Daddy's skin. They were worried about the 'free sex' aspect of communal living. That would have taken Mummy's 'do sex without love' dictum a squidge too far. She sent me a pamphlet on syphilis that had been written in 1952 and about a gross of condoms. I'm sure she felt very enlightened after posting it.

"The big secret about life in a hippie commune: not that much sex going on. It was a rather priggish environment. All lefties, like their opposite numbers on the right, are sexually repressed. I have never met a sensual ideologue. There were a lot of rules about sex. We were mostly couples and were expected to have sex within the coupledom unless other arrangements were made. Girl and girl sex was less regulated. Why? Because men get excited by the idea of it.

"A single couldn't have sex with a member of a couple unless the partner consented. Sometimes the partner felt consent was the politically correct choice, but was actually torn by jealous anger. He or she said yes, but wanted to say no. That energy manifested itself in the daily negotiations between the 'scorned' partner and the 'other' woman or man. We worked, ate, and slept together in dormlike rooms. There was no privacy, and trying to find some was frowned upon.

"The sex was largely perfunctory. Sex advice was seen as a bourgeois tool for distracting the masses, so the men didn't feel compelled to learn anything about the care and stroking of the clitoris. It was awful. I lasted a year and wouldn't have lasted that long if my parents weren't begging me to come home."

Catherine's commune experience was similar to that of other Boomers surveyed. Only 1 percent did spend time in communal-living arrangements, and, like Catherine, they didn't remain in them for long. While some found the leftist politics, the slow pace, and the intertwined personal relationships more palatable than others, none said the sex was wild, out of bounds, "free." One woman said, "Drugs were free and easy. Sex was not. It was as difficult to cross the pair bond lines for commune members as it was for their parents back home, maybe more so." And a man said, "The women spoke in the same tone of voice as the actresses playing the National Public Radio talk-show hosts on a *Saturday Night Live* skit. They projected smugness, false enthusiasm for the smallest things, like mung bean sprouts, and a cloying but very particular kind of goodness—the goodness of those who believe themselves to be morally superior to the rest of the world. The men were worse than the women. It was the birth of political correctness, not a manifestation of sexual freedom."

After the commune, Catherine went back to Barnard, then left again after a semester. She moved to Philadelphia, where she worked for a non-profit arts organization and had an affair with a married concert violinist.

"He couldn't have been further from the commune lover," she says, "but they had some key similarities in the bedroom. They were both from the wham, bam, slam you ma'am school of fucking."

After Philadelphia, she lived in San Francisco, St. Louis, Chicago, Baltimore, and finally Washington, D.C., working for a variety of nonprofit organizations, including public radio. In D.C., where she's lived for the past fifteen years, she found her "true home." Her Adams Morgan condo is filled with artwork done mostly by friends and acquaintances and with tribal masks and icons purchased in neighborhood shops. A large oil painting of a nude woman who strongly resembles her hangs in the bedroom. She is coy about the resemblance.

"Oh, really, you think she looks like me?"

Yet she does acknowledge having had an affair with the artist, a Moroccan she met while on vacation in Kathmandu. She stayed with him in Morocco for three months before returning to the United States. He was, she says, the love of her life.

"Communication was a problem. His English was minimal, as was my French, his language. The sex was incredible. He was truly the first man I'd known who really knew how to make love. He was passionate and technically gifted. The first time I had an orgasm from cunnilingus was with him. I can still conjure the feeling by closing my eyes tight until I see orange behind my eyelids as I masturbate. His room was filled with the setting sun and everything was orange that day.

"I left him because there was nothing we could do but leave each other. He could not marry someone his family wouldn't approve of. I couldn't stay with him without marriage, not given the restrictions placed on women there. He had too many obligations to leave his country and come home with me. I thought at the time it broke my heart to leave him, and perhaps it did. But it also made me stronger. I knew I was always going to be okay alone, though I didn't acknowledge that until years later."

Though she was basically happy with her life—single, working in non-profit jobs, surrounding herself with friends and lovers whose lifestyles and ambitions matched her own—she rated herself a "failure" in comparison to the Boomer prototypes who represented her ideal.

"My mother would send me clippings about cousins, sons and daughters of friends, my own sister and brother. There was always someone getting a promotion, lending their names to a big, splashy charitable event, winning a professional prize. She let me know in not-so-subtle ways that she thought I was having the wildest sex life in the world. My mother thought I'd traded everything for sex, which I had those three months in Morocco. That was my life to her. To me it was the experience that freed me and helped me set performance standards for lovers. It wasn't my life."

She might never have stopped comparing herself to the mythical queens of having it all were it not for a series of small revelations. Her sister stunned the family by telling them she was leaving an abusive husband. "Who knew the perfect husband hit his wife?" Catherine asks. "We were beyond shocked." An old friend confessed that she and her husband rarely had sex. Another friend admitted she'd never been truly happy in her marriage to a wealthy man.

"I kept going home to my cozy art-filled apartment after having these long teary conversations with women I'd envied. Finally I realized how happy I was. I suppose every generation has its own set of myths and expectations, but it seems to me the Boomers set the bar impossibly high and then believed, contrary to all evidence, that everyone else was able to leap it in a single bound. I was past forty before I understood that nobody has ever really had it all, not all at once, anyway."

When I shared it with them, her story resonated with other Boomer women and even with some men. One man said he thought men had been slower to accept the belief that they should excel in all areas of life, personal and professional, but they had accepted it—"just as women were outgrowing the idea of having it all." The Boomer Code, unlike previous generational codes, puts a high premium on pleasure and the accumulation of personal experiences in addition to attaining career and financial performance standards. "Enough is enough," a thirty-nine-year-old man said.

"What does 'happy' mean?" a forty-year-old woman asked. "I've always thought it was the name for the stage I hadn't yet reached. I blamed myself for not working hard enough on 'happy' to get there. Our generation extended the work ethic to sex and relationships and to the concept of general happiness. When people talk about 'simplifying,' they mean transferring their address lists from paper to the electronic medium."

The Boomer Facts

- Some Boomers are living in the past, maybe a past they never inhabited in real life. Each generation has a tendency to embellish memory. Your grandfather walked ten miles through five-foot snow drifts to get to school. You received your first blow job under the bleachers from the head cheerleader; and that was only the beginning. Boomer myths are rooted in sex, drugs, and rock 'n' roll.

- High and unrealistic expectations in all areas of life, including sexual, have kept some Boomers from acknowledging that their lives have been generally happy, their sex lives generally fulfilling. As men and women move through their forties, they begin to let go of ideas that don't work for them anymore. It becomes more possible to define personal happiness and measure individual satisfaction and stop comparing oneself to Superman and Wonder Woman.

- The beliefs that life can be controlled and planned and that hard work can make anything happen, from multiple, extended, whole-body orgasms to pregnancy after forty, were the building blocks of the myth of "having it all." Younger Boomer women particularly bought into the myth. They were committed to timing in the form of life plans that postponed marriage and childbearing until careers were established. For some women, the plan backfired, helping create the over $2 billion-a-year infertility business.

- But the generational emphasis on personal satisfaction also created more lifestyle choices for everyone. The Boomers made divorce an acceptable option and living single a viable life alternative, freeing women especially from the constrictions of a married life not actively chosen. A pre-Boomer who deserves some of the credit for that is Helen Gurley Brown, former and longtime editor-in-chief of *Cosmopolitan* magazine and the author of *Sex and the Single Girl*, the book that led to *Cosmo* and dared to say: You can be single and have sex, good sex. In their youth, Boomer women bought *Cosmo* and the message.

3

Early Married, Sex?

A long-married friend in her early forties told me a story that, she thinks, says it all about married sex among the Boomers.

"We went with two other couples to see *The English Patient*," she began. "I told them the reviews said it was a very sexy film. When we were walking into the theater after buying our tickets, one of the guys said, 'Everybody raise your hand when you think it's sexy.' We all laughed, but we agreed to raise a hand at the erotic places. No hands went up. After the movie we walked to a little French café for coffee and dessert. When the waitress put the plates of rich chocolate tortes and other goodies on the table, the guy who had suggested the signal raised his hand. Everyone else followed. We laughed so hard we had tears in our eyes."

Boomers who married late or not at all sometimes speak disparagingly of those who married young. In some urban circles marrying in the late teens or early twenties and producing a child before age twenty-five can mark one as a redneck, hillbilly, or member of some other underclass—unless one moved on from the early faux pas to a quick divorce, graduate school, a splashy entrepreneurial venture. The early-married Boomers, they say, are all like the couples who went to see *The English Patient* together. They would rather have a piece of chocolate cake than sex any day.

"People who get married young have less chance of staying together," a Virginia psychotherapist told me. Oh, really? Not coincidentally, she is an older bride herself and is struggling to conceive for the first time at age forty-three—facts that put her opinion in the category of self-justification. I did not find her assumption to be correct.

The Survey Says

- 70 percent of the Boomers of both generations who married before age twenty-five remain married.
- Over 80 percent of them say they are satisfied with their sex lives and their lives in general.
- 50 percent of Vietnam-generation Boomers and 57 percent of Watergate-generation Boomers who married after age twenty-five remain married.
- Approximately 75 percent of both groups report satisfaction with their sex lives and with their lives in general.

Many never-married and divorced Boomers expressed some variation of what I call the Early Bonding Theory, the antithesis of the Later Is Better attitude espoused by the late marrieds. In short, they believe—or wonder if—the most successful and enduring relationships are those forged by couples in their twenties. Plenty of happily married couples who found each other later in life would dispute this, but it has the ring of truth to many singles. Judging from the couples I've interviewed who married early, I no longer assume, as I once did, that an early marriage is more likely to fail. Among this group, it was more likely to succeed.

On the other hand, the highest number of sexless marriages was also in this group. That led me to speculate about the nature of marriage. Often these couples who weren't having sex told me they were "best friends." Could marriage be almost as dependent on friendship as desire? Is a sexless marriage by definition an unhappy one? Maybe not. Maybe for some couples, at some point in their lives, it works fine.

These couples who married early, whether still passionate about each other or devoted best friends, seem to have formed stronger emotional bonds than their contemporaries who married later.

The Survey Says

- 11 percent of married Vietnam-generation Boomers have not had sex in a year or more.
- 8 percent of married Watergate-generation Boomers have not had sex in a year or more.

> • More than 60 percent of couples who have a sexless marriage (in both groups) were married before the age of twenty-five.

WOULDN'T IT BE NICE

"Wouldn't it be nice to live together in the kind of world where we belong."
(Recorded by the Beach Boys for Capitol Records)

Some Boomers, especially older ones, married early because of the sex. They liked it and wanted more of it. Frustrated by the limitations put upon them, they wanted to graduate from coupling in the backseat to making love in the bedroom, and marriage was the primary way to get a double bed. Sometimes they got married because the sex had led to nature's expected conclusion: pregnancy. Vietnam-generation Boomers, especially, saw marriage as the solution to the problem of unplanned pregnancy. Abortion wasn't legal until 1973. Middle- and upper-middle-class girls did not become unwed mothers.

"I married at nineteen because I was pregnant," Jessica says. "It feels strange to say that out loud because I never have."

At the café inside the Metropolitan Museum of Art in Manhattan on a spring day, Jessica wore a black suit with a knee-length skirt, slit halfway up the thigh, and a white T-shirt. Her highlighted blond hair was cut short and beautifully styled. Her only jewelry, aside from the huge diamond engagement and wedding ring ensemble, was a pair of gold hoops in her ears. The effect: studied casual elegance.

The daughter of a prominent New York City CEO, Jessica, her sister, and brother had a life of privilege in a northern New Jersey town approximately an hour outside the city. A bedroom community of oversized houses and lush lawns and gardens, this town was not a comfortable place to be unwed and pregnant in 1967. A hasty wedding was arranged between Jessica and Harris, the high school sweetheart she'd followed to the University of Pennsylvania, who was the father of her child. Their son was born seven months later. At her mother's insistence, birth announcements omitting the date of birth were sent out after a "decent interval," which Jessica remembers as being approximately six months later.

"I was popular. I had a lot of dates, but Harris was the one I set my sights on. I liked the way he looked the first time I saw him and I think I must have known even then he would be very successful. Would I have gone after him if I'd thought we'd end up in a trailer park or even a middle-class suburb? No. Oh, maybe. It's hard to say. Maybe I would have stayed with him until I got him out of my system and moved on.

"We didn't have a lot of money in the early years. We were both going to college, living in married-student housing, and working part-time jobs. Our families helped a little but not much. That was our punishment for getting pregnant. His family thought I did it on purpose to trap him, but I didn't. It just happened. The surprise is that it didn't happen sooner. We began having sex when we were seventeen. Our method of contraception was withdrawal. Harris was too embarrassed to buy condoms in a drug-store. Neither of us realized they could be purchased in the men's restrooms of the filling stations along the turnpike. God, we were innocent.

"We really didn't mind having to get married. Marriage was the only way a horny couple could get enough of each other in those days. I think we had sex almost to the point of delivery. I didn't ask my doctor when we had to stop, and he didn't say. We were relatively poor newlyweds, considering where we'd come from and where we were going, but we were happy. The sex was very good.

"By the time he'd gotten his first good job in Manhattan, our son was in school and the families had forgiven us. Coming home to the New York area was such a triumph, we were giddy. We lived in the city for four years in a rel-atively modest two-bedroom apartment before we moved to North Jersey, where we had always meant to end up. Those were good years in every way.

"I've heard a lot of women complain about men who have small penises or can't get an erection or can't keep one going. My single friends are more apt to talk about those things than married women. One friend told me a hilarious story about a man who wanted to have intercourse with a semi-erect penis and got very annoyed with her because she wouldn't, or couldn't, 'stuff' it in.

"Harris is well endowed, and I'm sorry, but I do think that matters. I've never had to 'stuff' him. He still gets good erections. In our youth, he was an iron man.

"I've always had orgasms, even when I was seventeen. Our sex life did suffer when our son was a teenager. He went through a difficult stage, ex-perimenting with drugs, skipping school, hanging out with girls we didn't consider very desirable. There was always a problem or crisis. Tension filled our house like smog. In those days Harris worked long hours and traveled a lot. When he wasn't traveling, we entertained.

"I felt a lot of pressure to play the role of the corporate wife and at the same time I was the primary parent. Harris seemed to make the decisions, while I was expected to implement them. It wasn't a sexy time. Senior year our son straightened up, and everything got better, including the sex.

"We had a four-year second honeymoon while our son was in college. Last year Harris retired early, and, frankly, he is getting on my nerves. I have my own little business going now, a pottery shop in Greenwich Village. He wants me to stay home with him, and I want to go to the shop or stay home and throw pots on the wheel in my workshop.

"He is more interested in sex than I am. Last week I told him I didn't think retired men were sexy. Is he going to sit around for the next thirty years? I'm proud of him that he did so well he doesn't need to work anymore. But I don't understand why he doesn't want to work at something, even as a volunteer. There is more to life than golf, travel, and pestering your wife for blow jobs.

"My friends who've also been married a long time feel the same way about sex now. It isn't a big priority. We aren't thinking about it all the time. The working husbands seem to be in the same place as the wives. Only the prematurely retired men like Harris have sex on the brain. I enjoy the sex, I really do, but I am not compelled to have it the way he is.

"He was sexier to me when he traveled a lot. I looked forward to his homecomings. Now, well, it's not as thrilling. We have sex twice a week, and I'm happy with that. He'd like more. If he traveled two weeks out of the month, I'd probably be happy to have sex with him five days a week the two weeks he's home.

"I flirted with other men a lot in those days, too, men I met in art classes or at charity events or other functions. I had lunches or dinners with some of them and, frankly, led them on, but I never went past a passionate kiss or letting them cop a feel of a breast. Those flirtatious moments are seldom possible now that Harris is around so much, and I miss them. I have never been with another man sexually, and really I don't want to be. I just miss the stimulation of being around other men. They get me up for my husband. This is not a big problem. We have good sex twice a week. After all these years, that's good, isn't it?"

In fact, it is.

The Survey Says
- 52 percent of married Vietnam-generation Boomers have sex at least twice a week—and two-thirds of them were early marrieds.
- 55 percent of married Watergate-generation Boomers have sex at least twice a week—and 59 percent of them were early marrieds.
- Less than 10 percent of unmarried Boomers of both generations have sex that often.

Married people are having more—and more satisfying—sex than single people, even those with regular partners. If I had a slight bias when I began researching this book, it was that urban single Boomers had probably enjoyed, and were likely still enjoying, the most satisfactory sex lives. That's not what I found. Married Boomers—moreover, those who had married early and had few if any other partners—report the highest overall satisfaction levels and seem to be having the most sex now. They may, like Jessica, have their small gripes about their partners, but the irritations don't loom large enough to get in the way of frequent, enjoyable lovemaking. Geographical locale, educational level, and other socioeconomic factors have limited impact on the satisfaction scale. Couples like Jessica and Harris, who live in a twenty-room home, and Michael and Barbara, who share a more attainable dream house, and Ray and Donna, self-described "poor folks," have better sex lives than most other Boomers surveyed, married or single.

What do they have in common? Intense and mutual sexual attraction. Early marriage. Shared values and goals. Positive sexual attitudes coupled with a willingness to learn new sexual tricks. Minimal sexual exploration with other partners before marriage. Only the rare extramarital affair.

They also appear to be less neurotic and more psychologically well-balanced (to the astute nonprofessional observer) than the unhappily-marrieds or the unhappily-singles. Not one of the highly sexed couples surveyed had been to a sex therapist, though all had purchased a sex advice book or video or used information in magazine articles to improve their sex lives. "When we have a problem, sexual or otherwise, we know how to work it out," one woman said. "We have been able to ride out 'flat line' times, when one or both of us has little desire for one reason or another."

BOOMERS SEX TIP

Here I Am (Come and Take Me)
(Recorded by Al Green for Hi Records)

If you want sex more often than your partner does, you have three options:

1. Improve the quality of the lovemaking. Become a better lover. You need to change the focus from "Honey, will you do this for me?" to "Honey, I'd love to do that for you again." There are two main ingredients to good sex: passion and skill. Upgrade your techniques.

2. Remove the impediments to frequency. If quality is not the problem, then time and energy are the roadblocks to your sexual satisfaction. Reduce the clutter in your life together. Make time. Find ways of helping your partner save energy. And put some of your own energy into being more seductive.

3. Beg and bribe. These are viable alternatives to the therapeutically correct process of compromise. Many of us respond positively to supplications and unexpected gifts.

SOUND BITE

From a phone interview with a woman in her early forties: "I think we all secretly believe we could go back and find our high school sweethearts if things just don't work out in the real world. Every woman I know still harbors fantasies of her first love. The memories of him are all mixed up with good memories of ourselves and how young and pretty we were then with the whole world opening up before us. It's inconceivable that he could be fat, bald, and boring."

I CAN'T GET NEXT TO YOU, BABE

"My life is incomplete because I can't get next to you, babe . . ."
(Recorded by the Temptations for Motown Records)

Not every Boomer couple who met and fell in love at a tender age have remained sexually active. You might be shocked to discover that some couples who seem most likely to be sexually active aren't, at least not with each other. Physical attractiveness is no guarantee of sexual fulfillment.

Gina is beautiful, and not just ordinarily beautiful, but outstandingly so. At forty, she honestly can pass for eight to ten years younger than she is. Tall, shapely, with long legs, a thick mane of burnished gold hair, near-perfect features, huge blue eyes, and full sensuous lips, Gina attracts admiring glances from both sexes walking down the street in Manhattan, where the inhabitants are well accustomed to beauty walking by. Not surprisingly, she works in the fashion industry. She has been married for ten years to Carl, with whom she lived for nine years before a pregnancy motivated them to legalize their relationship. A personal trainer, Carl has the requisite hard body in addition to his clean-cut good looks. In family portraits with their daughter, they look like the ideal California family.

"Imagine how shocked our friends would be if I told them we haven't had sex in a year," Gina says. "In the last three years I'm guessing we did it half a dozen times. But we look like a sexy couple."

She was twenty-one and he was twenty-two when they met, in 1979, on the campus of Rutgers University in New Brunswick, New Jersey. *Kramer vs. Kramer* and *Norma Rae* were playing in the local theaters. She looked at him, and the words to the Rod Stewart hit "Do You Think I'm Sexy?" ran through her mind. Yes, she did think he was. Both were theater majors. She'd had two sexual partners before him; he'd been with "probably half dozen or so" women before her. It was sexual attraction at first sight.

"We were so hot for each other that whatever we lacked in technical expertise we more than made up for in passion. My previous lovers, all two of them, had been lame in comparison. I remember thinking what thin pale wands their penises had been in comparison to Carl's sturdy one. I loved his penis. I gave it a name, Mr. Man, which seems silly now, but it delighted us then. Everything we did together delighted us. I used to like watching him come on my breasts or in my hand. I was enamored of his cum, that's how bad I had it.

"I really never looked at another man after Carl and I connected. I knew he wasn't going to make a lot of money. Being very analytical about this, I knew that, with my looks, I could hook up with a man who would bring in the big bucks. I've always been able to detach from my physical self and see what I look like, how it affects people, what I might do with it. With Carl, our looks match. I wasn't selling myself for financial gain. I liked that aspect of our relationship, but there was certainly more to it than that. I fell in love with him. I knew he was falling in love with me, not just with my body, but with all of me."

Her mother thought that Gina, another daughter of the New Jersey upscale suburbs, could "do better," and her father thought moving in with a man was "a poor tactical maneuver" for any young woman. Following graduation, she moved into Carl's one-bedroom apartment in Hoboken, New Jersey, against their advice. Gina and Carl were "deliriously" happy. They made love almost daily and spent Sundays in bed, getting up only to cook meals together or go out to buy the Sunday *Times*.

"Looking back, I know that we were never playful sexually, and I wonder if things would be different now if we'd learned to play. We were serious, passionate about sex, enthralled with each other's bodies. We're both very visual people. Carl wanted to put mirrors behind the bed and on the ceiling, but I talked him out of it. I liked to watch us as much as he did, but I knew I'd be embarrassed by the mirrors when anyone came to visit us. We compromised by buying an antique standing mirror at an auction, our first antique and first auction. We moved it to the side of the bed when we made love. We also got the taste for antiques and auctions from that first experience, which has been an expensive outlet for both of us.

"We weren't making love as often as I liked by the time I got pregnant," Gina says. "But the pregnancy intensified our erotic feelings for each other. We made love more in the early months than we had in the previous year. And the wedding was romantic. I was overcome with feelings of tenderness for him, and I know he felt the same way. We couldn't get enough of each other. I was six months pregnant when we got married, but I wasn't showing that bad. We were very optimistic about the future, excited about the baby. It was a good time.

"We had the wedding at a friend's apartment in the West Village [Greenwich Village, Manhattan]. She had bouquets of white flowers everywhere. That night we had a room at the Boxtree Inn, a tiny, charming, impossibly expensive hotel just above midtown. I wore an ivory gown that had been made for me by a designer who now works at Vera Wang. It was cut low to emphasize my pregnancy cleavage and clung to my proud belly. We took a cab uptown and got out ten blocks before the hotel so we could walk holding hands. I was so in love with Carl, my unborn baby, the city at night. I wanted him to come all over me.

"I've read and heard that couples typically experience a sexual drop-off after the baby is born, but we didn't. We couldn't wait for the doctor to say it was okay. We cheated a bit. We began making love at four weeks rather than waiting for the six-week clearance. I had some abrasions, and the doctor had to cauterize me. I didn't care. It was worth a little sacrifice.

"Things changed slowly. About a year or so after our daughter was born, I noticed that Carl's libido wasn't keeping pace with mine. But he was very busy. He had a lot of clients, and being a trainer is hard physical work. At the time I was only working twenty hours a week to his eighty. It seemed normal to me that he would often be too tired for sex.

"Now I work full time, too. I would like to have sex, but he's tired. I've stopped asking. I don't want to feel pushy. There's really nothing wrong with our relationship. We are each other's best friend. The only problems we have are financial ones. We don't make money as fast as we spend it. Carl worries about that. I do, too, of course, but probably not as much as he does. I like spending money. He would like to have more to invest.

"I read an article about 'sexless marriages' in a women's magazine. The author quoted therapists who said repressed anger was often the problem. Maybe he's mad at me about money. He frequently jokes that I wear our retirement on my back. But we don't make enough money to be serious players in the stock market or anything like that. I'm not sure we'd qualify as dabblers on what we could afford to invest if I stopped buying clothes and having lunches with friends. Working in New York is expensive."

The magazine article she cited no doubt had a prescriptive section in which the first piece of advice was: communicate. Having written numerous "relationship" articles quoting therapists who inevitably tout the miracle curing power of communication—using techniques they must teach us because we're too dumb to know how to talk to each other—much as evangelists tout the miracle of prayer, I feel as comfortable in making that assumption as I do in questioning the validity of the advice. Doesn't Gina already know that Carl resents her free-spending ways? And doesn't Carl know that Gina knows he does? If her spending is inhibiting his sex drive, will anything less than her not spending revive it? Gina, too, is skeptical of the therapeutic approach to problem solving endemic to troubled Boomers.

"I suppose this is the point where I should consider therapy, but I don't trust therapists," she says. "I've known a few. They were nuts, totally nuts. How can you trust these people with your psyche? I noticed a few years ago that Oprah virtually stopped featuring therapists on her show. She used to sit at their feet and worship. What does that tell you?"

This particular sexless marriage story is not unlike others I've heard. When a healthy, sexually appealing man and woman stop having sex with each other, something is wrong. Generally the root causes, according to the experts, include: hidden anger, buried resentment, unacknowledged personal or relationship guilt or conflicts, frustration with the partner's lovemaking style, or repressed homosexuality, more common than you might think. Sexlessness can also be the culmination of years of bad, and increasingly sporadic, lovemaking. But it's really only a problem if one or both partners finds it so.

BOOMER SEX TIPS

Start Me Up
(Recorded by the Rolling Stones for ABKCO Music)

Can you put the "sex" back into a sexless marriage?

Yes, but it won't be as easy as filling the gas tank. Here are your basic options:

Fix what you can fix. Be brutally honest with yourself. Are you fat? Lazy? Have you stopped dying your roots, plucking your nose hairs, dressing for dinner? Improve your physical appearance, your seduction and lovemaking techniques, your attitude. If you know something really annoys your partner—like overspending or shirking your share of the household chores—fix it. Become a more interesting and appealing person.

Seek professional help. Therapists say you can't put the sex back into a sexless marriage unless you tackle the underlying issues of anger and so forth. You may want to try this approach. It will probably be lengthy and expensive, but so is divorce.

Accept the status quo. Masturbate. Have an affair. Meditate. Contemplate. Gaze into your navel and search for the good in celibacy. Of course, I can't recommend the last course of inaction.

STILL THE ONE

"After all these years, you're still the one."
(Recorded by Orleans for Asylum Records)

"Am I satisfied with our sex life? In general, yes," Michael says.

"Oh, yes," Barbara says.

Michael, fifty-two, and Barbara, fifty-one, have been married for thirty years. That they still have "it" must be evident to the most casual observer. Both attractive, fit, and well-dressed, they radiate energy, physical and sexual. Lively and intelligent people, they are, separately and together, entertaining—*fun*. It would be possible to talk to them about anything, to find companionship and acceptance in their home. If you think people who marry young, remain true to each other, have never even thought about living in New York City or Los Angeles, and base their social lives around family and community are by definition close-minded and judgmental, think, as the saying goes, again. Wrong. Their love is inclusive and encompassing, forgiving and understanding, warming like a fire on a winter night.

On the evening I interview them, they sit side by side on a plaid sofa in the family room, touching each other frequently. Their comfortable house in a small southern Illinois community is decorated in a warm and engaging "country" style in shades of green, beige, burgundy. Beyond the deck, a backyard slopes into a pond where ducks and geese live. He has a senior management position for a major corporation in St. Louis; she has a job she enjoys but doesn't need at an art galley in town. They still do most things together. Neither has ever had another sex partner. After all these years, they *want* each other. And they believe this is "normal."

"We have a really good time together," he says. "We still have the pull toward each other, much like we had in our twenties. The attraction is strong. The longing, the hunger are still there. We call each other and say suggestive things. The need isn't as urgent as it was at twenty, but it's still there. Sex is a requirement. Four days without sex and it becomes a matter of urgency again."

They make love two to three times a week. For her fiftieth birthday, he took her to a resort. Flowers and champagne were waiting in the suite when they arrived. He had diamond earrings in his pocket. They had sex the minute they got there, then dinner, then sex again in the Jacuzzi. In fact, when I called to confirm a time for our dinner / interview, they put me off for an additional hour so they could make love. ("It had been three days," he explained.) They would make love more often, they say, if their younger son didn't live at home and their older son, his wife, and their adored grandchild didn't live two blocks away. The "pop-in" is a fact of life.

"Sex has actually gotten better for us," he says, and she nods in agreement. "When the kids were little, we had so many distractions. Life is simpler now. So far physical aging has only improved us as lovers. She has more orgasms, and I last longer."

"About seven years ago I had a minilaproscopy tubal ligation," she says. "Sex got better for me afterward. I didn't have to worry about contraception. Sometimes in previous years I'd had to push to have an orgasm, for the reasons Michael mentioned, and because I didn't always trust contraception one hundred percent. I feel like I'm reaching my full erotic potential now. The tubal was liberating. I should have done it sooner. Residual Catholic guilt stopped me."

"We finally got rid of the guilt," he says, laughing. He has a most mischievous laugh, accompanied by a boyish gleam in the eyes. "We reasoned that sterilization wasn't that much different from birth control."

Both reared in large Catholic families, they came from a similar working-class background in the same neighborhood. Her family lived on the better side of the highway than his did, but they attended the same schools, knew the same people, sang in the same church choir. She stopped singing in the choir, however, in junior year of high school, after he told her he loved her and was going to marry her someday.

"I said, 'Oh, Michael, you don't know what you're saying. You're seventeen years old, you don't know what love is.' He scared me. I started dating other guys."

"I knew it before she did," he says. "To me it was the most natural and obvious thing in the world. You look for someone like you. When you find that person, you know you've found your soul mate."

"I had to learn that others weren't right first," she says. "He gave me an ultimatum about dating others guys. We didn't speak for a year. Then I was seventeen. I was dating a guy named Jim. The closer I got to Jim, the more I knew he was not my kind of person. It was the holiday season. I knew the choir would be going Christmas caroling. I called Michael and told him I missed caroling and wanted to know the time and place. I could have called the choir director, of course. Michael gave me the information and said, 'Have a good time. I won't be there. I have to work.' I had to go Christmas caroling then or look silly."

But her ploy to let him know she was interested again worked. He invited her to a small New Year's Eve party at the apartment of the choir director and his new wife. That night Barbara knew what Michael had known: They were meant for each other. Within a few months, they were engaged. A good Catholic girl much under her mother's influence at the time, she was determined to remain a virgin until her wedding night.

"That was a difficult time," she says. "I wanted to go all the way, but I was afraid. In the days leading up to the wedding, we finally did everything short of ejaculation. He penetrated me but pulled out before ejaculating. We didn't use condoms. He had excellent control."

"I always had good control over my ejaculation," he adds, "and it kept getting better and better."

No religious prohibitions prevented them from fully embracing their sexuality after the wedding.

"We both have high libidos," he says. "And we felt that whatever we wanted to do together was perfectly all right. We are adventurous and creative in our lovemaking. We've read each other well and have been good at responding to the unexpressed wish as well as the direct request."

"Communication has never been a problem for us," she adds. "I read those articles telling couples to communicate, and I can't understand why a man and a woman need to be told to talk to each other about sex. We like sex. We like each other. We like being with each other. Sometimes we can't be together without sex."

"We still chase each other around the bedroom," he says, laughing. "We expected to stay married when we got married, and we knew that the sexual part of the relationship would go a long way toward smoothing over the rough spots."

Barbara adds: "All I ever wanted was to be with him. We bought our bedroom furniture months before the wedding and put it in my room in my parents' house. Every night I went to bed longing to be with him. I still want to be with him. I think our son and his wife must have something like this together. They are respectful of each other's wants and needs. He's not always an easy person to be with, and she is patient with him. When I watch them together, I think they must have what we do."

"I've not always been an easy person to live with either, have I?" he asks, and she laughs a huge laugh before touching his face.

The Boomer Facts

- Couples who married young and have had few or no other partners aren't necessarily missing out on some larger sexual experience. If their attraction is strong, their attitudes open and playful, and they are willing to grow and change sexually as they do in other areas of life, they probably possess the secrets of eternal happiness the rest of us seek. Attitude is key.

- Most couples will probably experience some adjustment problems, with an impact on their sex life, when one partner retires early. Starting a new career, developing a new interest or hobby, or volunteering can take the edge off sustained togetherness. If the sex was good before, it will be again. Space, not sex tips, is needed here.

- "Sexless" marriages are probably more common than most people realize. Who admits to being in one? If a couple aren't having sex, they may have other compelling reasons for being together, like a strong friendship. It is possible to put the "sex" back into the marriage, though it probably will require addressing painful issues.

- Couples who share an ongoing sexual passion also share important traits: high libido, commitment to mutual goals, shared interests, compatible personalities, the ability to work out their differences rather than letting resentments smolder. Individually, they are passionate people.

PART 2

At Long Last Sex

Not every Boomer was on the front lines of the sexual revolution. For various reasons, some remained virgins longer than the statistical average age while others lost their virginity but didn't find sexual pleasure until much later. Late bloomers include, but are not limited to:

- Some men and women who were unable to recognize or acknowledge their homosexuality, bisexuality, or "kinkiness" when young.
- Some who married the wrong person because they equated sexual awakening with true love, then followed the rigid guidelines for marriage their parents laid down, only to find the union stultifying. When they broke free of the marriage, they experienced their true sexual awakening.
- A few Boomers who grew up in sexually repressive environments. Coming into their own sexually didn't happen on the same timetable as it did for their contemporaries.
- Other Boomers, often labeled "commitment-phobes," who, rather than actively choosing to remain single did so by default because they can never find "true love," "the right person," the "soul mate," or the consuming passion of their lives. They have an excessively romantic view of love relationships, a perspective that precludes them finding a partner easily or, in some cases, at all.

- And still others who have unresolved issues with the opposite sex. Hidden anger and buried resentment keep them from forming the intimate relationships they claim they want. They can mask their neuroses and emotional problems by citing the dearth of available and acceptable partners. Late bloomers all, they discovered true pleasure in sex later than many, if not most, of their contemporaries—or they've yet to discover it.

4

The Virgins—and the Re-Virginized

The first time I interviewed a man who had remained a virgin throughout his twenties, I was somewhat taken aback. A woman, maybe . . . but, a man?

I didn't know there were Boomers like the lean, intelligent, and attractive forty-year-old man who said, "I didn't have sex with a woman until I was thirty-five. This sounds unbelievable, I know, but it's true. I was painfully shy until I was past thirty. 'Painfully shy' really doesn't begin to describe it. I couldn't look a woman in the eye. In college, I went from dorm to class to track practice or track meet and back again, full circle, without raising my eyes from the ground. I ran year round, in all kinds of weather. But I never had a date, much less sex. I remember running ten miles in sleet and snow one fearsome winter day. When I got back to the gym, there was ice in my hair and on my eyelashes."

I was wrong in another assumption, that Boomers all had some level of partner sex by their twenty-first birthday. Maybe they had stopped short of penetration. Maybe they had limited their sexual expression to petting, dry humping, and almost there, but they had surely been to the edge of the precipice.

Some Baby Boom men and women were late bloomers, and many hadn't come anywhere near the precipice until they were well past the age of "What do you mean you're still a virgin?" People older than we are were admired for restraining their sexual impulses in their youth. That has generally not been true for Boomers, even the Vietnam generation and certainly the Watergate generation. A girl might remain a virgin in high school, but her contemporaries looked askance if she finished college with hymen intact. Religion made a limited comeback among post-Boomer youth, but it wasn't popular on mainstream campuses until the last Boomers had matriculated. A fundamentalist Christian woman in her early forties told me that she was the only girl in her freshman dorm to choose celibacy out of religious principle. The other girls thought she was a secret lesbian and shunned her.

"Late bloomers were losers," says a thirty-eight-year-old woman who didn't lose her viginity until she was twenty-five. "Something was wrong. You were too fat or too thin, neurotic, sociopathic, psychotic. There was no good reason not to have had a serious relationship by your twenty-first birthday except that nobody had picked you because you were a loser."

This woman had a weight problem in high school and college. She came from an abusive family situation. After weight loss and therapy, she had her first date at age twenty-three. Not all late bloomers have such dramatic stories to tell. Many often had sex without the satisfaction, and their blooming occurred later when they were able to put the satisfaction into the sex. Some of them became sexually active the way they adopted the slang, fashions, and music tastes of their day. They wanted to assimilate. Years later, they would realize that, for one reason or another, the early sex was disappointing. For these late bloomers, true passion—and for the women, that often meant orgasms—weren't part of their early sexual experiences.

The Survey Says

- Fewer than 15 percent of women in both generations were still virgins at age twenty-one.
- Slightly more than 9 percent of men in both generations were still virgins at age twenty-one.
- But 25 percent of Vietnam-generation women and 22 percent of Watergate-generation women experienced their first orgasm with a partner after age twenty-one.
- And nearly 20 percent of the women in both groups say they didn't reach their full sexual potential until their thirties.
- Less than 8 percent of men in both groups say that was true for them.

I CAN'T GIVE BACK THE LOVE I FEEL FOR YOU

"Here's a tear for a souvenir . . . and a dream torn at the seams."
(Recorded by Rita Wright for Stone Agate Music)

Straight women were in relationships with gay and bisexual men long before the first Boomer was born. Such unions, like that of the writer John Cheever and his wife, flourished in the arts communities, but they also existed in small towns among the middle class. They were accommodations made necessary when women rarely could earn enough money to support themselves comfortably and men could not publicly love other men. Though living an openly homosexual life is possible now, particularly in urban areas, many gay Boomers, especially in the Vietnam generation, did marry and father children. Some of them have remained married and continue to see their male lovers discreetly on the side, while others have "come out"—out of the marriage as well as the closet. The most prominent example is Jann Wenner, the publisher of *Rolling Stone*, who left his wife, Jane, for a younger male lover, the model Matt Nye, after many years of marriage and three children.

"My first husband left me for a man," says Alice, forty-eight. "I wasn't expecting it, but I wasn't shocked either. "We got married in 1969 when we were both nineteen. Both lonely misfits, we connected in an intensely emotional way. I remember our courtship at the University of Illinois as the highpoint of our romantic life together. We started dating freshman year. I came from an alcoholic family, and he was from a hyper-religious family. No one understood us the way we understood each other. We took long walks across campus and into town. I can still recall the smell of burning leaves, the sensation of kissing someone when your nose is red and tingly and his mouth is soft and warm.

"If we'd been more sophisticated, we would have known we were each other's best friend. But we thought we were in love. We decided to get married without ever being intimate with each other. He 'respected' me too much. Not long ago I came across a bunch of photos taken when we were preparing for the wedding. In one, he is wearing my wedding dress. Because we were roughly the same height and size, I'd asked him to put it on, stand on a stool, and let me pin up the hem. He'd obliged. Now I look at that photo and I see clearly who he was, what was really going on. Then I thought the idea of my virgin groom modeling my wedding gown was funny."

Alice and John got married in the spring. They spent their honeymoon at Lake of the Ozarks. On the second day—"We were too tired and hung over the first day"—they consummated their union. The sex was hurried, furtive, unsatisfying. It was, however, effective. Nine months later their only child, a son, was born.

"We quickly settled into a sexual pattern of avoidance and excuses," she says. "They were good excuses. We were both going to school and working. I had a lot of morning sickness, a hard delivery, and complications afterward. We didn't make love much after we found out I was pregnant, and our son was six months old before we tried it again. If we had sex once a month after that, it was a good month. Why didn't it occur to us that something was wrong when two healthy young people don't have sex any more often that?

"For one reason, the sex wasn't any good when we did have it. I read an article about premature ejaculation and realized John suffered from it. Or he did with me anyway. I never thought he might be with someone else. I tried to talk about the issue with him once. He turned bright red and stormed out of the room. The next day he brought me flowers. End of discussion.

"We were busy and happy. There was just not much sex. About six or seven years into the marriage, I made friends with an older woman at the high school where I was teaching. I identified with her without knowing why. John and I went to their house for dinner. Her husband was, I now see, clearly gay. I was blind to the obvious then. He and John became friends—not, I'm sure, physical friends, just friends. She must have assumed I knew more than I did. In retrospect, I realize that her conversation was peppered with little hints.

"Shortly after our tenth anniversary, John told me he wanted a divorce. Before he said he was gay, I knew he was going to say it. Our friendship with the older couple had helped him realize he wanted a more honest and open life for himself and me, too. I had been living in total denial, but on some level I had always known my husband was secretly gay. What hurt was hearing that he'd had been having sex with men while I was leading a nearly celibate existence as his wife."

Alice and John had a truly civilized divorce. They kept the truth about his sexuality from their son until he was "old enough," at fifteen, to handle it. She eventually married again and reports that the sex in her second marriage is "frequent and satisfying." John now lives contentedly with a male companion in a neighboring Indiana town.

"I don't think our marriage was that unusual," she says. "I've met other women who were or are married to gay men. Maybe women who have sexual fears or issues gravitate to that kind of relationship. I was in therapy for two years after John left, and I learned a lot about myself. I was afraid of sex. John couldn't have fooled me if I hadn't wanted to be fooled."

I shared Alice's story with some Boomer husbands I met in an upscale private gay nightclub in suburban New Jersey. They all believed their wives did not know about their "other" lives. A few claimed they were able to perform "adequately" in their marriage beds. Most said their wives did not care about sex. Another group of gay husbands from the Beltway suburbs surrounding Washington, D.C., had the same responses.

"My wife married my salary and benefits," a corporate executive said. "I was able to give her the two kids before I lost the ability to perform with a woman at all. She's happy."

Does she have affairs?

"I don't know. I don't care." Then he added softly, "I hope so."

In some gay / straight marriages or otherwise committed relationships, the partners know what they're getting into and freely choose to be there. They want the companionship, social and professional acceptance, and other benefits of marriage. "I married my best friend," one woman explained. "We are a family. Sex, I can always get. Love and nurturing are harder to come by."

The Survey Says

- Approximately 7 percent of the Vietnam-generation men and 6 percent of the women identify themselves as gay or lesbian. All of the women had sexual experiences with men prior to coming out as lesbians. Ninety percent of the men had sexual experiences with women.

- Slightly more than 7 percent of the Watergate-generation men and less than 5 percent of the women identify themselves as gay or lesbian. All but two of the women had sexual experiences with men prior to coming out as lesbians. Eighty percent of the men had sexual experiences with women.

- Approximately one-third of the gay men and half of the lesbians in both groups are or have been married.

While lack of interest in sex can be an indicator that a husband is gay, not every sexually repressed man in a heterosexual relationship is. Some are angry at women—not a woman, but *women*—for whatever complicated and unrecognized reasons. Repressed anger doesn't hang only in the male half of the psychic gender closet. Some women are angry at men, for whatever complicated and unrecognized reasons. They may not open up sexually until midlife, when their anger begins to dissipate.

Some Boomer men and women are late bloomers because they had their sexuality stifled in childhood by parents who, for religious or other reasons, were overzealous in suppressing their child's natural curiosity about genitals. Little boys who are taught that sex is dirty and are punished for their interest in their bodies and their erotic feelings may become asexual men. Or they may develop fetishes or obsessions. If the anti-sex messages a boy hears while growing up have religious overtones, he may begin to associate sexual urges with his religious feelings—such as guilt or punishment. His sexuality takes a predictable path of indulging in the desired behavior followed by intense guilt. The pattern manifests itself in a variety of ways, from sadomasochistic behavior to exaggerated disease fears to hyper-religiosity.

John Money, Ph.D., professor emeritus of medical psychology at Johns Hopkins University and the author of several books on sexuality, is generally regarded as the first authority on paraphilias, or sexual perversions. His book *Lovemaps* explains how our patterns of loving are developed in childhood and set in adolescence. In many cases, the adult may not remember, or accurately remember, the incidents or experiences that formed his core sexuality. For example, tracing the influences that led a man to become a foot fetishist, someone who is aroused primarily by feet, or to exhibit some other form of fetishistic behavior, is something less than an exact science. He may remember playing at his mother's feet and feeling a tiny erection grow. Or he may not.

Money studied numerous men with paraphilias who came from repressive religious backgrounds to determine that there is a connection between privately perverse male sexual behavior and outwardly devout and self-righteous personalities. Because of their backgrounds, these men feel guilt over their "sins" and act out their "repentance" in public ways.

"When I see somebody who carries self-righteousness to excess, I automatically say if I scratch the surface on this one, I'll find the sin," Money has often said.

Until recently, expert opinion held that women who came from similarly repressed backgrounds were likely to respond in one of two ways: by developing a strong disinterest in, even aversion to, sex, or by having difficulty in achieving orgasm in their sexual encounters. When women indulged in "kinky" behavior, they were supposedly only doing so to please their men. The one true female fetish was masochism, the desire for pain or humiliation in sexual relationships. Like Freud's theory of the vaginal orgasm, this one is no longer regarded as sacrosanct by the "experts," a growing number of whom now believe women can be genuinely kinky too.

A little dose of kink in either gender is not deemed a serious problem by the majority of doctors and therapists. Many Boomers view kinky sex practices in the same way they do spicy ethnic cuisines like Indian or Szechuan Chinese. They add interest to the diet of routine sex and wake up the erotic palette. Kinky sexplay may be a safe way of acting out some of the general repressed anger men and women feel toward each other—as long as it is mild and mutually pleasurable behavior.

The Survey Says

- Of the Vietnam generation, 54 percent have indulged at least once in some form of kinky behavior, with light bondage and spanking being the most common.
- Slightly more than 50 percent of the Watergate generation have indulged at lest once in some form of kinky behavior, with light bondage and spanking again being the most common.
- Older Boomers were somewhat more likely to have explored the darker side of S&M, with 10 percent of the men and 6 percent of the women claiming to have used a whip or some kind of torture equipment.
- In both groups, 5 percent of men have paid a professional dominatrix at least once to "discipline" and humiliate them.
- Another 5 percent of the men have paid a phone sex service for verbal abuse.
- And 12 percent of Vietnam-generation men, 7 percent of the women, 17 percent of Watergate-generation men and 8 percent of the women have slipped into an S&M chat room on line.

WHIP IT

"It's not too late to whip it into shape. Whip it good."
(Recorded by Devo for Warner Brothers Records)

What happens if a woman with aberrant desires marries a man who likes sex to be the equivalent of a steak and potatoes—pass the salt and pepper lightly—diet?

"I rarely remember being sexually aroused during my marriage," Jenna says. "Looking back, I know that when I was aroused, my husband Greg wasn't the source of the excitement. I had been fantasizing or reading something erotic, and he happened to initiate sex at the right time."

She dated several boys in high school in Shaker Heights, Ohio, an up-

scale Cleveland suburb, but never had a steady boyfriend. Though she acknowledges she's probably exaggerating, she says she was one of "only a
handful of virgins" in her 1972 graduating class. Kenneth Tynan's play *Oh,
Calcutta*, was off Broadway, but *Bonanza* and *My Three Sons* were still television hits. Virgins in the Midwest were not an endangered species. "I was also
the only one who didn't weep over Ali MacGraw dying in *Love Story*," she
laughs. She skipped her high school graduation party to go to the movies
with her parents. They saw *The Godfather*. In her first year at Webster College, a small liberal arts college in St. Louis, she had two dates with the same
young man, who never called again. The next year she had her first real relationship. It lasted for six months. She didn't lose her virginity. Her boyfriend
assumed religious principles were holding her back because she was one of
the few students who attended church services regularly. She didn't try to
correct him. When he told her he needed to be with someone whose code of
behavior was more like his own—"sex mad"—she said she understood.

"I wanted something I wasn't getting from the few boys I'd known,"
Jenna says. "I couldn't articulate my desires, but now I know I was always a
little bit S&M. I remember being spanked by my mother when I was thirteen. She'd rarely spanked me as a child, and my father never had. But I
was a very difficult prepubescent child, moody, secretive, untruthful. I
pushed too many of her buttons that day; she pulled me down onto her lap
and delivered a hard set of blows. She hurt her hand. We both cried. She
never touched me in a violent way again, and I'm not saying I blame that
incident for making me kinky. I remember it so strongly because the
spanking was an awakening of sorts.

"I had a game I played in bed for months afterward. I rolled the bot-
toms of my shortie pajamas into the shape of a bikini and pulled the top
up to expose my breasts. I pretended I was being tortured and kneaded my
breasts hard, sometimes striking them softly with my fists, and twisting my
nipples until they smarted. I didn't touch my crotch. I knew that area
should be covered. In my fantasy, a man was torturing my breasts, but he
didn't want to see my ugly pubic hair. I imagined hanging by my wrists and
being whipped. I'd seen that in a movie.

"But I didn't touch my genitals. It wasn't masturbation. I remember
breathing very hard, so I was excited, but I didn't come. I didn't know what
masturbation was then. One of my girlfriends told me about it later that year.
I wasn't motivated to try it. The idea of touching my genitals did not excite
me. My secret shameful fantasies of being beaten and whipped did turn me
on."

When Jenna started dating, she suppressed her fantasies. She knew they were "wrong" and forced herself to replace them with romantic fantasies in which Mr. Right won her over after many tearful misunderstandings.

"I patterned my fantasies after the old romantic comedies of the thirties and forties that I watched on late-night television with my mother in the summertime," she says. "The lovers were kept apart for two hours by a series of miscommunications and misperceptions. The heroine, proud and willful, frequently stormed away from the caresses of the man she loved. Sometimes she got spanked. There was an amazing amount of spanking in those movies by today's standards. Spencer Tracy spanked Katharine Hepburn. Clark Gable spanked her, too. On television Ricky spanked Lucy. The spitfire women were most likely to get spanked. Only at the end did the movie romances come out right. Ricky and Lucy always hugged. Those were my fantasies. When I got to the end and all was well, I hurriedly shut down my mental movie theater. Hug, kiss. It wasn't interesting anymore."

At the end of her sophomore year at Webster she met Greg, a junior at St. Louis University majoring in philosophy. Athletic and graceful, he was a competitive swimmer. She admired his mind and his body. Unlike other boys she'd known, Greg was courtly. He treated her like the romantic heroine she imagined herself being. He was the perfect movie hero, and she expected him, someday, to throw her over his knee and make her his own.

"He arrived for our first date carrying a nosegay of violets," she says, "which was the most romantic gesture I'd ever known. When he handed me the violets, I thought I would swoon. We went to the movies to see *The Way We Were*, and afterward he bought me the Streisand recording of the title song. I played it over and over again. We dated for three months before we had sex. He didn't push me. It was important to him that everything be right for me once he realized I was a virgin.

"I doubt the virgin of a fairy tale lost her maidenhead in such a carefully planned scenario. Greg rented a room at the Cheshire Inn. He had champagne and flowers waiting in the room when we checked in. In his bag he'd packed silk robes for each of us, scented creams, oils, and candles—and his tape recorder and tapes of my favorite music.

"The sex was very disappointing. I didn't let him know how much. He knew I didn't get aroused and certainly didn't come, but I let him think my nervousness and fear had prevented me from fully responding to his touch. From that, it wasn't hard for him to extrapolate the story we both accepted as the gospel of our special love: I would need the security of commitment before my passion could be unleashed."

For Christmas he gave her an engagement ring. Her passion wasn't unleashed, but her acting skills were. Patterning her "responses" on the sex scenes in movies and books, she writhed, gasped, groaned, emoted. They were married in June 1976, following her graduation from Webster College. Having abandoned philosophy when he hung up his competition Speedo, he got a good job with one of the city's major employers. Tucking her virtually useless English degree into the drawer, she found employment as an administrative assistant in a small public relations firm. They rented a two-bedroom apartment with a deck in the Moorlands, a comfortable, leafy neighborhood in Clayton.

"We had everything," she says. "Promotions came rapidly. We bought an older house that we loved in Clayton, had a son and a daughter eighteen months apart. He was doing so well I was able to take an extended maternity leave with the second baby and stay home with them for three years.

"Oh, there was one little thing I didn't have: an orgasm."

One day, while reading a magazine article on multiple orgasms, Jenna started to cry. That was the first time she'd admitted to herself she'd never had an orgasm. Not one.

"I wanted to share this information with Greg, but I didn't know how," she says. "How do you tell a man you've been faking for ten years? The more I thought about the orgasms, I wasn't having, the more I threw myself into acting my way through the sex we were having. One night he actually said to me, 'Wow, sex is really getting better for us, isn't it?' I was disconnected from reality. I told him, 'Yes.'

"I found the erotica section in a local bookstore and began reading the kinds of stories that excited me. Inevitably they were full blown romances with light doses of corporal punishment inflicted upon the panting heroine by her masterful lover. I discovered *Stand Corrected*, the magazine for spanking devotees. For the first time in my life, I knew that my desires were not only shared by others, they even had names. There were categories of men and women interested in various types of sadomasochistic activity. I wasn't alone in the world, but I was very alone in my marriage. I knew there was no way that Greg could relate to this stuff, but I contrived to expose him to a small amount of it through videos I rented in the adult section of the video store. Maybe my prince was hiding under his pinstriped suit waiting for the signal from me to emerge.

"I asked him what he thought of a spanking video I'd brought home. He said, 'I thought it was dumb, didn't you?' He teased me about being in such a hurry to get out of the X-rated section without being seen by any of the neighbors that I'd grabbed the first naughty box I saw. End of discussion."

Then Jenna made the boldest move of her sex life: She rented a post office box, took out an ad in the "special" personals section in *The Riverfront Times*, the weekly alternative newspaper, and waited for Prince Charming, hairbrush in his pocket, to find her. There were twenty-eight responses, more than she'd expected.

She rejected most of them on the quality of the writing alone. Some men were further into kink than she wanted to venture. Others couldn't spell or write in grammatically correct sentences. A few sent photos that turned her off, like the man dressed head to toe in leather, including hooded mask, and brandishing a whip. Steven, the master / boyfriend who would take her to dizzying heights of passion, was one of two men she deemed interesting enough to meet in person.

"A personal meeting was a big risk, given the type of ad I'd run—'married would-be novice looking for masterful but discreet man'—and the fact that I was married and had lived in the area long enough to run into someone no matter how carefully I picked a rendezvous site. Steven and the other man were both married—safer than single men, I reasoned—didn't list extensive S-M bios, and seemed intelligent. The first guy was nice, but we didn't have the chemistry I was hoping to find. Then I met Steven at Blueberry Hill."

Yes, Blueberry Hill, my personal Boomer shrine. That gave me pause. An otherwise unlikely setting for the initial meeting between a woman who wants to be spanked and a would-be spanker, Blueberry Hill is *dark*. Amid the Howdy Doody memorabilia, 33⅓ record jackets from rockers like Buddy Holly, the Ronnettes, and the Fifth Dimension, several Wurlitzer jukeboxes from the Golden Age of rock 'n' roll, framed movie posters from films such as *Rock Around the Clock*, and other artifacts of Boomer youth, in a high-backed, hard wooden booth, Jenna met Steven. Their eyes locked, their hands met midway across the Monopoly board built into the table. He was, she knew immediately, the passion of her life.

"We arranged a liaison at a motel way outside the city," she says. "I wore a black garter belt and stockings and a silk teddy under my matronly dark slacks and sweater," she says. "He got there first. After kissing me passionately as soon as the door closed behind me, he ordered me to take off my shoes, slacks, and sweater and lie across his lap on the bed. I had never been so excited in my life. My nipples were hard, my heart was pounding, my pussy was lubricating. When I lay across his lap, I was trembling with desire and fear. I wanted him to slap me, hard, but I didn't know how I would handle it. He was the perfect master. The slaps were light at first, stinging and thrilling. Then they got harder until I was squirming in his lap. Periodically he stopped spanking me and stroked my clitoris with his thumb. At one point I was sure I was going to have the first orgasm of my life. Then he took his thumb away and smacked me hard square in the middle of my bottom. He kept up the smacks until I came. All the things

I'd read came true. I felt the 'explosive' orgasm of my fantasies. Afterward, he tenderly rubbed lotion into my buttocks and gave me a dozen roses he'd been hiding in the bathroom. When we parted that day, my ass was red and sore. I could hardly sit down on it when I got into my car to drive home. But I was happy. I had never been happier in my life."

Jenna's affair with Steven soon outgrew the space she—and he—thought it would take up in their orderly lives. They couldn't get enough of each other. In the beginning, they'd said they would not have "vanilla sex"—an S&M term for nonkinky sexual relations—with each other. They would limit their contact to spanking sessions and exploring other forms of light S&M. That way, they reasoned, they weren't "cheating" on their spouses. Gradually, their resolve weakened.

"I realized one day that I was having these incredible life-affirming orgasms with Steven, and I'd never seen his penis. I'd never made him come. I wanted more. I got greedy. I wanted the game playing, the pain and the punishment, the romance of what we had—and I wanted to be fucked."

When she told Steven what she wanted, he admitted he did too. That day they made love and discovered they enjoyed having vanilla sex together too. More surprising, Jenna had an orgasm the old-fashioned way, during intercourse, by stimulating her clitoris with her own hand as he was thrusting. Neither of them could live a compartmentalized life anymore. First Jenna told Greg about Steven, and then Steven told his wife about Jenna. Within six months, they were both divorced and remarried to each other.

"My one regret is that I told Greg too much," she says. "He was horrified by the S&M stuff. In his eyes I was a pervert, and he insisted on getting custody of the kids because of my perversion. I agreed because I didn't know what else to do. I did get very generous visitation and have remained an active part of their lives, but I'm sorry I lost my children because of my sexuality."

BOOMER SEX TIPS

Hurts So Good
(Recorded by Millie Jackson for Rhino Records)

If you want to put a little kink in your love life, heed the following advice:

Less is more. In your fantasies, you imagine thrilling to the sting of a whip. In real life, a gentle flick of a velvet covered leather strip will produce the desired affect. A hard blow will feel like punishment, because it is. Very few people are serious sadomasochists. If you were one, you'd know it by now.

Research the subject. Hidden on the bottom shelves of the sexuality sections in most major bookstores are how-to guides to various forms of kinky behavior. If you're intrigued by bondage, for example, you can buy a book on how to tie knots safely. Can't anyone knot a silk scarf? Yes, but wouldn't you rather do it with some finesse?

Lead your partner gently to the water you may not be able to make him or her drink. Don't issue ultimatums, like "If you won't try this, I won't perform oral sex anymore."

Be patient. The older we get, the more likely we are to indulge in kink—up to a point, of course.

Some Boomers married first and then discovered they hadn't yet met the love/sex of their lives. There were in those days a lot of reasons for marrying young that have nothing to do with passion or pregnancy. Marriage could seem like the ticket to adulthood, the route to escape from a controlling parent, or the thing to do because a friend or sibling had recently done it. A man, or more likely a woman, may have confused feelings stirred by developing sexuality with love for the person who happened to be nearby at the time. A couple may have forged an emotional bond during a traumatic phase of one or both of their lives and confuse the strength of the bond with everlasting love. I interviewed people who married suddenly after a parent died, a best friend had been killed in an automobile accident, or a young man had been drafted to serve in the Army during the Vietnam War.

"In the beginning, we seemed to have passion," said a man who married his high school sweetheart before going off to Vietnam. "Our passion was a manifestation of the times. There was so much energy, so much anger and anguish. When you're young, everything can be translated into a sexual equation. When I came back from 'Nam, we were strangers, but we were too embarrassed to acknowledge we'd made a mistake. We slept in the same bed for a year without making love before we talked about divorce."

Other couples confused need with love. A woman told me she married the first man she dated after college because she was terrified of ending up alone. It was 1969, a year after the My Lai massacre and the assassinations of Robert Kennedy and Martin Luther King, Jr. She'd worked in the Kennedy campaign and felt, she said, that the political was dead and there was only the personal. "I wanted, needed meaning in my life," she says. "I thought marriage would give me a purpose, a larger goal."

Choosing the wrong partner at an early age can stifle sexuality. "I was married for seven years to a man who didn't excite me," a woman wrote. "I shut down."

A man said, "I married a woman who was rather prudish about sex because I wasn't sophisticated enough to know she was. I was young and horny; and I thought she would grow into my lust."

BUILD ME UP, BUTTERCUP

> *"Why do you build me up, Buttercup, just to let me down?"*
> (Recorded by the Foundations for Rhino Records)

David married his college sweetheart because he had become dependent on her. She'd guided his academic development, taught him how to dress, improved his manners, and helped him prepare for his first job interviews. Coming from a higher socioeconomic bracket than he did, she persuaded him that the music he liked, mostly John Denver, wasn't "suitable" soundtrack music for the man he wanted to become. In its place, she taught him to appreciate classical and jazz. He didn't think he could be who he wanted to be without her. Gratitude, need, dependency—not passion—inspired his proposal of marriage. The sex was never, he acknowledges, "very good." He thought it wouldn't matter.

"My wife and I hadn't had sexual relations in eight years before we divorced," David says. "We gave each other and ourselves a lot of excuses for why that was true, but we both knew we were bullshitting. Secretly she thought I was gay. Less secretly, I thought she was incapable of sexual pleasure, the modern equivalent of 'frigid.' "

David, forty-six, is a well-known public figure on the West Coast. His wife, less recognizable, has a high-paying, high-prestige job in the entertainment industry. Both are physically attractive, though he is more so. During the eight years they were not having sex, they frequently appeared together at business and social functions, holding hands, touching each other lightly and frequently, and generally conveying through body language that theirs was a sexy union.

A friend of the couple recalls: "I thought they were so happy. I went with them once to a Los Angeles Dodgers game. It was a beautiful afternoon. During the seventh inning stretch, a Motown song was played. David and his wife danced in the aisle. It was a beautiful, spontaneous moment. I watched them and thought, 'Wow, they must be great together in bed.' Everyone around us applauded because they seemed so happy together."

"When we announced our plans to divorce, our friends and professional associates were stunned," he says. "We were the 'ideal' couple. Some of our friends were actually angry at us for splitting up. They kept looking for the other woman, the other man. There was none."

That's not to say there hadn't been, on David's part, at least, and he suspects, on hers, "little dalliances." With marriage as his excuse, he limited his contacts with other women to the practices of high school or college boys. There was flirting, kissing, heavy petting, dry humping. But his favorite activity was phone sex, ending in mutual masturbation.

"I really got into phone sex for a while," he says. "I was having phone relationships with women I'd met professionally, which wasn't really smart. I liked talking dirty and masturbating while I talked and listened to a woman talk dirty back. It sounds incredibly juvenile, but it was a consuming passion for a few years.

"I got into trouble when the inevitable happened. A young woman blackmailed me with tapes she'd made of our conversations. Unless I helped her get a local news job, she was going to make trouble for me. I called in some favors and got her the job. After that I was careful. I only had phone sex with women I knew well. But my wife caught me in the act one day. I thought she was asleep, and I went downstairs to use the phone in my den. Unbeknownst to me, she'd picked up the bedroom extension and was listening in.

"It led to a big, painful blow-up which cleared the air in our marriage. I can still see her standing in the doorway of my den, this stricken and disgusted look on her face. My heart was in my shoe. We both realized that something was terribly wrong when a man would leave his beautiful wife in the bedroom and go downstairs to talk dirty on the phone to a woman with whom he'd never been intimate. We went to marriage counseling. It didn't take. So we agreed on a divorce.

"I don't know if she still thinks I'm gay or a pervert. I don't think so, but I don't know. For a while, I wondered if she might be right. Then I began seeing Lilly, my second wife. Lilly is everything I always wanted in a woman but didn't believe existed. She is carnal. This sounds like a cliché, but we are soul mates. I believe she is the love of my life, the person I was meant to be with. She likes everything to do with sex, including giving me blow jobs, not that we don't do many other things as well. We have a full sex life. After three years together, I am still incredibly horny for her; and she for me. These days I only have phone sex with Lilly, when one of us is out of town.

"I really don't know what happened between me and my first wife or why we lived together for as long as we did without sex. We had a lot invested in the appearance of a good marriage. It meant so much to us to give other people the impression that we had it together, that we had it all. Maybe that need to project perfection bound us tightly to each other. My best friend believes that we were just two cowards who'd found a safe place together, a place we hated to leave for the scary world. That may be true. We were more like siblings than spouses. She played the role of 'big sister,' though I was older. She mothered me in many ways, personally and professionally. I wouldn't have achieved as much success without her coaching.

"Our marriage counselor kept looking for the hidden anger. I don't believe it was there. We have nothing but good feelings for each other. She was happy for me when I found Lilly. I was happy for her when she began dating again and called to tell me she was having sex with a man she really liked.

"What motivated us to live the way we did? Maybe we'll never figure it out."

Some people do find the strong emotional and sexual connection they crave in a second or later marriage. The first marriage was a union of convenience, duty, gratitude, guilt, or what seemed like necessity at the time. A significant percentage of marriages, whether between Boomers or not, probably fall into these categories, and many people will live in them faithfully for the rest of their lives, accepting a low level of sexual desire and gratification as "life." Others cannot.

They wake up one day, realize they've been missing something, and go out to find it. For women, the awakening may coincide with hormonal shifts occurring in their thirties; and for both sexes, it may be triggered by a confidence at last achieved. Whether they rhapsodize over the discovery

---

SOUND BITE

From a conversation with a forty-eight-year-old woman, in her second marriage: "I was thirty-four when I met the real love of my life. I'd been married and divorced, had lived with another man, and had at least a dozen sex partners. Yet I felt like singing the Madonna song, 'Like a virgin, kissed for the very first time.' I lost my true virginity with him. Making love to him was incredible. I finally understood that there is more to sex than a meeting of two bodies, however energetic. Our souls touched."

of a "soul mate" or "the love of a lifetime"—or analyze the attraction in more prosaic terms, these late bloomers are describing the same phenomenon. For them love truly is lovelier the second time around.

"After a false start that lasted nearly twenty years," one man wrote, "I found the love and the sex of my life."

I COULD NEVER LOVE ANOTHER (AFTER LOVING YOU)

"Are you really walking out on me?"
(Recorded by the Temptations for Motown Records)

"I did everything by the book. Coming of age in the sixties, I wasn't supposed to follow the rules, but I did. I was a 'Rules girl' before those daffy women made their fortune from the concept of following your grandmother's sex advice," says Sharon. "I followed the rules handed down by my mother—a former debutante who didn't follow the rules, married beneath her for passion, and lived poor and lost in regret. Playing the game, I got a husband, somebody else's husband. I was twenty-three, young but old enough to know better. My parents weren't pleased with his age—thirty-nine—or his marital status when I told them I was engaged, but they certainly admired his fiscal bottom line."

At forty-six, Sharon is near the top of her profession, earning a solid six figures per year, commanding the respect of her peers and a staff of hundreds. Her first husband had been her mentor, nearly twenty years her senior. He'd left his wife for her. And when she left him for a younger man, she did not do so lightly.

Sharon and A, her first husband, met at a professional conference in San Francisco in 1975. In the hotel bar where they shared a nightcap, someone kept playing Elton John's version of "Lucy in the Sky with Diamonds." A told her she had diamonds in her eyes. He was so taken by her sparkling eyes and her presentation that morning—made in a power suit with a miniskirt—that he offered her a job with his San Diego firm in his department. She looked, he said, like Farrah Fawcett with an MBA. Soon he was micromanaging her career, insisting she trim several inches off her layered "big" hair. She was enormously flattered by the attention he paid her, but she didn't pretend his interest was purely professional.

"I could have been another intern-in-the-Oval-Office story," she says, "if I'd gone down on my knees and sucked cock. I had too much pride, I thought. Now I know I was never that hot for him. If I had been, I would have gone down on my knees, my back, my forearms. When you're really hot for someone, you don't control the situation. It controls both of you. I would have sucked and fucked on the floor behind the desk. I didn't because I was never so carried away by desire for him.

"After we'd been working together a long time, I let him kiss me, but I pulled away when he tried to put his tongue in my mouth. A few weeks later, I let him thrust the tongue and caress my breasts. Finally, I didn't refuse to listen when he said he loved me. Almost six months after the first kiss, I let him put my hand on his penis. I had some sweaty makeout sessions with him. But I never could not say no. I kept on saying it. He pleaded, raged, and finally proposed. I didn't think he'd leave his wife when I accepted his proposal. Everything happened so quickly after that. There was never an opportunity to stop and examine what I was doing. He showered me with gifts. My career, under his tutelage, was taking off. He'd made such an enormous sacrifice to be with me, I had to believe I loved him. How else could I justify what we'd done to his wife and teenage children?"

Sharon was satisfied with the marriage for several years. The sex was adequate and sometimes good. Together they earned more money than she, from a blue-collar background, had ever anticipated seeing in bank accounts with her name on them. Her stepchildren accepted her presence in their father's life rather quickly, motivated, she suspected, by their desire to remain on his financial good side. But her career occupied center stage of her life.

"For years, I thought I owed A my success," she says. "The marriage was connected to the success in my mind. I felt guilty if my thoughts strayed to another man. Somewhere around our eighth anniversary, I developed a serious itch, not attached to any particular man. He was fifty and going through some personal and professional crises. That affected his libido. I didn't miss the sex we weren't having, but I resented the fact that we wouldn't be having it no matter what I wanted.

"He accused me of being 'distant' with him and blamed my reaction to his problems with erections. I stormed out the door. We were living in Manhattan by this time in a spacious duplex apartment on the Upper West Side. When I got off the elevator in the lobby, I realized I hadn't brought anything with me. I stood there debating whether to go back and apologize for storming off, or say nothing, grab my wallet and keys and leave again. While I was arguing with myself, an attractive young man asked if he could help.

" 'You could buy me a drink,' I said. To this day, I can't believe I said it. I'd never in my whole life come on to a man like that. He said, 'I'd be delighted.'

"We went to a little neighborhood Mexican restaurant and bar. The chips were greasy, the salsa was bland, the margaritas were watered down. Over the first drink, he had me questioning the basic assumption of my life, that I owed A everything. We fell in love that night."

B, the attractive young man, had an entry-level position in publishing, making less than $20,000 a year. He'd been in her apartment building lobby the evening they met because he was applying for a part-time job as night doorman, a job he didn't get. The difference between her income and his, between his level of achievement and hers or A's was considerable. She was thirty-two; he was twenty-two. She lived with her husband in an eight-room apartment; he shared a one-bedroom with two roommates, a not-unusual situation in Manhattan in 1984. Money, power, and work mattered more than anything to seemingly everyone, yet the majority of the people who lived there paid exorbitant rents for tiny spaces, worked long hours, and had little of the money and less of the power. Sharon shrugged off the trappings of her life as easily as she shed her suit jackets with the big padded shoulders.

"I didn't stop to ask questions of myself until months later," she says. "I went back to my apartment where my angry husband was waiting for me that night with one thought in mind. I had to get out of there, out of the marriage, get out to a place of my own so I could invite B over to spend the night. In one evening I went from a blasé woman who spent her spare time in exclusive shops looking for the right clothes, accessories, and home furnishings to a starry-eyed woman who wanted the most basic thing in the world: a private space with bed, air conditioning, shower, and fridge."

Two days later Sharon moved out of the duplex—"big mistake," her lawyer warned—into a modest two-bedroom off Central Park West. She knew she would have to look for a job because A would make working in his company untenable, and she was right. He did. She knew the divorce would be "messy," and she was right. It was.

"The worst moment I had occurred in my lawyer's office. A and his lawyer were there. We had nearly worked everything out to no one's particular satisfaction. At least it was almost over. Suddenly A let down his guard.

"He said, 'I hope this happens to you. I hope you wake up one day and find your younger lover, this person you've turned your whole life upside down for, is on his way out the door to meet someone younger than he is.'

"That gave me cold chills. But by then B and I had been lovers for months. I had *discovered* sex in bed with him. It wasn't like having sex with A. I couldn't say no to B. I wanted him so much, I turned to warm jelly thinking about him. There was no going back."

And, almost fifteen years later, there are no regrets for either Sharon or B.

"We have a nine-year-old son whom we both adore," she says. "He was born when I was thirty-seven. We tried to get pregnant again and couldn't. We considered and rejected fertility treatments. They would have played havoc with our sex life, and that part of our life has always meant too much to us to risk. Then one day I just got pregnant."

As his stature in publishing increased, her career took a down turn. Now they earn comparable salaries. Both insist that money, specifically who earned more, was never an issue with them.

"It's not important to us," B says. "We would rather have more money than less, but we don't put money ahead of our love for each other, our love for our son, our time."

And has the age difference between Sharon and B mattered to either of them?

"No," she says, "not after I got over the initial embarrassment of being the older partner."

"No," he says. "I'm the more mature partner, always have been." They both laugh. He continues, "We have a lot of fun together. From that first evening over bad margaritas and cheap salsa, we've enjoyed each other enormously. What we have transcends age differences. Besides, it's only ten years. Big deal."

The Boomer Facts

- A significant number of Boomer women have dated or married men they know, suspect, or find out to be gay. The straight woman/gay man alliance is not unusual in urban areas. A woman may be drawn to a gay partner for many reasons, including conflicts about her own sexuality or the desire to have a strong, loving partner who allows her to be free to pursue other sexual interests.

- For some Boomers, early marriage was a safe place to hide from sexual feelings they didn't understand or were afraid to express—feelings not limited to homosexuality. They suppressed aberrant or "kinky" desires, chose a suitable mate, and hoped for erotic peace. As they aged, their desires became more urgent, their confidence in themselves greater. Finding sex on their own terms represents a sexual rebirth for them.

- Boomers have mainstreamed light kink. Some men and women didn't have to leave their marriages to get their needs met. They were able to grow within the relationship.

- Some Boomers made early marriages for the same "wrong" reasons their parents or grandparents did. They confused emotional need with love or married for convenience or out of duty, gratitude, guilt, or necessity—even to get out of Mummy and Daddy's house. Sexually stifled in those first marriages, they describe second marriages or love affairs in almost spiritual terms.

5
The Perpetual Seekers

The Boomers made being "terminally single" socially acceptable, especially for women. Men had already been free to choose not to marry without cutting themselves off from their social support systems. Families would not only accept but also respect them. Married friends would invite them to dinner. Women arranged dates for them. Other men might envy them or pretend to do so. "Carefree bachelors," they were not "tied down." Single women in pre-Boomer days were "spinsters" or "old maids," terms seriously lacking in panache or cachet. It was assumed that the single men were getting all the sex they wanted and the single women were frigid, sexless virgins—or worse, lesbian. Nobody seemed to wonder with whom the single men were getting it on. If not the single women, then wives?

Now, thanks to the Boomers, the single by choice or the commitment-phobe may be female as well as male. There is even growing evidence to indicate women are more often than men choosing to live the untethered life. Numerous studies report they are happier than their male counterparts. Among the outdated gender stereotypes: the abandoned midlife spouse is always the wife. Today, more midlife women leave their husbands than vice versa.

The Survey Says

- 73 percent of Vietnam-generation women who are divorced (and not remarried) or never married say they are satisfied with their lives in general. Less than a third are satisfied with their sex lives. The overwhelming source of discontent: not enough sex, particularly for women who don't have regular partners.
- 67 percent of Watergate-generation women who are divorced (and not remarried) or never married say they are satisfied with their lives in general. Less than half are satisfied with their sex lives. Again, the overwhelming source of discontent: not enough sex, particularly for women who don't have regular partners.
- 68 percent of Vietnam-generation women and 63 percent of Watergate-generation women who are divorced initiated the divorces.
- Less than 50 percent of the never-married men in both groups are satisfied with their lives in general, but interestingly the percentage holds for satisfaction with their sex lives. Like women, they complain about not getting enough sex, but they don't complain as much as the women do.
- Only 24 percent of divorced (but not remarried) men in the Vietnam generation and 30 percent in the Watergate generation are satisfied with their lives in general—and their sex lives in particular.

Other Surveys Say

A *New York* magazine survey of a thousand single New Yorkers reported that single women who weren't in relationships were happier than either single straight or gay men who weren't in relationships. Seventeen percent of straight men, 20 percent of gay men, and 27 percent of singles who weren't dating rated themselves "happy." Who claimed to be seeking a relationship? More men, straight and gay, than women, straight and gay.

If numerous attitude and behavior surveys have reported that women are now more happy being single, why do we assume more women than men want to marry? Unhappy single women make more noise than their male counterparts. A segment of the publishing industry caters to their doubts, fears, and perceived needs. Men's magazines don't run features on where the girls can be found or how to get a woman to commit. Single men don't buy books on how to get married and how to keep their wives happy after they do. They aren't the gender who came up with the Rules. The women who do want to marry, and believe they have to trap, lure, hook, or somehow bamboozle a man into marriage, are the extremely vocal minority—rather like the Christian right faction of the Republican party.

Men who want relationships are more inclined to keep their feelings to themselves. They don't sit around with the guys bemoaning their single state. In fact, they may, in public displays of bravado, pretend they don't want what they do want most of all: a wife, or, at least, a monogamous relationship.

Ironically, the men and women who plaintively profess to be seeking the love and commitment they've been unable to find in twenty or thirty years of dating probably don't want to find it. If they did, they would have. One theme running through their stories: the best sex that never will be again or never has been at all. They have either had and lost the best lover they'll ever know or they've had incredibly good sex by anyone else's standards, *but* the deep connection, true love, total intimacy, or whatever, was missing. I met a forty-year-old man who personified the incurable romantic in Belleville, Illinois. His neighborhood florist wraps a single red rose every time he walks through the door.

"I've been buying single roses from him for almost twenty years," he explains. "I always take them on first dates."

SOUND BITE

From a conversation with a forty-three-year-old, never-married woman: "I had opportunities to marry but didn't want to take them. I am happy with my life the way it is. Ironically, the men I meet are more interested in commitment than I am. I've learned to recognize the guys who will be dropping the white picket fence hints. They tell me how satisfied they are with their lives on the first date. The men who swear they are in search of true love and want nothing more than the wife and kiddies in the house in the 'burbs—those guys are lying. When I want to get rid of one of them, I tell them I want the same thing they do. Otherwise they'll stick around and try to change my mind. It's the thrill of the hunt, not the capture, that drives their libido."

YOU CAN'T CATCH ME

"If you get too close, I'm gone like a cool breeze."
(Recorded by Chuck Berry for Chess Records)

I interviewed on separate occasions a man and his former lover, each in his or her own way terminally single. Tony, forty-eight and never married, says he is searching for the "perfect" love, a "beautiful, inside and out, soul mate," with whom he can have the children he desperately wants. Elaine, forty-one, and long divorced, was involved with him off and on for over a year. He says Elaine could have been the love of his life but she was too old to have children, and so he drifted away from her. She says he probably was the sexual passion of her life, but he was the "most dishonest man" she'd ever met, and so she left him.

"Elaine basically doesn't trust men," he says. In a Thai restaurant on Seventh Avenue in the Chelsea district on the west side of Manhattan, above Greenwich Village, women at other tables occasionally cast covetous glances in our direction. Tony stands over six feet tall and has a lean, lithe build. His shaved bald head gleams in the dim light. A very black man, he is striking in appearance and looks ten years younger than his age. His long hands end in improbably long, slender, elegant fingers. He is sexy, yet refined.

"She was sure I was seeing other women when I wasn't with her," he says. "Her antennae went up everytime I had a phone conversation in front of her. She wouldn't believe how much I cared about her. I felt like she was waiting for me to leave her." He smiles engagingly. "Do you think she left me before I could leave her?

"I had put space between us, and she said she knew what I was doing. She said she understood, but it was tearing her apart, and she wouldn't be able to see me anymore. Elaine couldn't give me babies. That's what really came between us." His big dark eyes turn into pools of sorrow. They might be enough to jolt flagging ovaries into production. I can imagine women wanting to dive right into them and rescue him. "I want children. I'm going to be fifty soon. Who's going to look after me in my old age? I'm terrified of being alone. It goes deeper than that, my need for a child. I don't want to die alone, without having a son of my own.

"I think in terms of a 'son,' but I'm sure I would be happy with a daughter. I want it all, the wife with whom I share a passionate love, the children, the house in the country, a four-wheel drive."

He already has the house in the "country," if you count the Hamptons, on Long Island, as country. There is a four-wheel drive vehicle in the garage. He keeps the Porsche garaged in Manhattan near his condo and the Mercedes in the garage connected to the building where his office is located. His combined auto-space rentals would make the mortgage payment on a nice upper-middle-class home in a small Midwestern city. A successful entrepreneur, Tony is the sole owner of his company.

"I came from the ghetto in Washington, D.C.," he says. "I never knew my father. My mother was fourteen when I was born. She had two other kids by two other men before she got her act together. I'm lucky she wasn't into drugs or alcohol. She earned her GED, got a job, and slowly worked her way through school to become a nurse. I'm proud of my mother. My half brothers are both dead, one in a drive-by shooting when he was fifteen and another from AIDS. He was a crack addict. I do business every day with people who couldn't imagine where I came from. They assume I grew up black middle class or better.

"I met Elaine doing business with her. I like women who are strong, who are out there humping and bumping in the business world. I'm not attracted to twenty year olds with vapid faces and no résumés. That's too bad, because I keep falling for women who can't give me what I want most, a child."

Like many post-forty Boomer males, Tony has suddenly realized he wants children. Unlike his contemporaries, he doesn't "fall for" the twenty-something and fertile. Unfortunately, he likes women his own age.

"I had one relationship in my twenties which could have led to marriage and kids, but it didn't," he says. "We lived together for seven years. Things went bad between us, but we stayed together. We didn't have sex for years. Yes, I was seeing other women while we weren't having sex. I have a powerful libido."

After they broke up, his business took off. He dated, but had no time for "relationships." When he decided to make time, he began meeting women who either weren't interested in commitment or "had a lot of emotional or psychological problems. For a few years, I met a lot of women on Prozac."

Then he met Elaine. She had encountered her own share of lovers with emotional problems. Elaine, who is white, says she had the best sex of her life with Tony, who says he hasn't yet had the best sex of his live. That will only happen when he knows he could be conceiving his child as he makes love. Elaine thinks Tony is "another middle-aged guy kidding himself

about how much he wants kids because he really just can't settle down."
But did she want to "settle down" with him? No.

"Finally, I couldn't deal with his lies," she says. We are having lunch at
Molly's, an Irish pub on Twenty-third Street above Gramercy Park. There are
peanut shells on the floor. The light is barely sufficient for reading the menu,
but in it, she looks thirtyish. Wispy blond curls fly back from her face. She
has high cheekbones, full lips, startling aquamarine eyes. The cheekbones
are implants; the aquamarine tint comes from contact lenses. Our burgers
are outstanding. Licking juice from her fingertips, she says, "He had several
relationships going while we were together. That would have been okay if
he'd told me. I was seeing someone else too. I just wanted truth, not fidelity.

"I overheard phone conversations, messages left on his answering machine. Other women's panties were sometimes in his bed, tossed in the corner
of a closet, the bathroom. He was unavailable often. Do I have to continue?

"His behavior turned me into a jealous snoop. I didn't like myself. One
night while he was in the shower, I went through his pants' pockets. I don't
know what I was looking for, just signs of other women, like I needed
more signs. I hated myself. I told him I had to stop seeing him.

"I wish I could have been more pragmatic. Why didn't I continue to see
him for the sex and ignore his lies? Tony needs to keep women off balance.
He needs to stay in control. If everybody knows what's really going on, he
loses control. By being the only one who knows, he keeps the upper hand,
something I like to keep myself.

"But I'll never forget the last time we made love. It was perfect. I met
him at a hotel in Washington, D.C. We were both in the city on business. It
was during the height of the O.J. frenzy. We joked about daring to be seen
having dinner together when we might remind everyone of O.J. and
Nicole. I spent the night with him. The sex was incredible. In the morning,
I knew we were truly going our separate ways. I had the earlier appointment, so I was showered, dressed, ready to leave. I paused at the bathroom
door to say good-bye to him. He was preparing to take a bath, not a shower.
He was crouched in this huge marble tub as it filled, lazily running his hand
through the water. His penis grazed the water. I have never wanted a man so
viscerally in my life. It took everything I had to walk out of there."

BOOMER SEX TIPS

Night Moves
(Recorded by Bob Seger and the Silver Bullet Band for Capitol
Records)

Tony developed his signature intercourse position, the seated missionary, to take the pressure off his knees. Years of athletic endeavors
from college football to midlife jogging had weakened them. He
says, "There's a great deal of latitude in this position. A man of lesser
endowment could use it to advantage, because he can thrust deeply
simply by scooting closer to his partner. Women like this position so
much because you can look into their eyes, fondle their breasts, and
fuck them at the same time. They feel more comfortable in this than
the female superior position because they don't have to take
charge—or worry about their breasts hanging down."

It's hard to understand why a woman would walk away from her best
lover when she could have him again or why it be should be difficult for a
successful, attractive, intelligent, and sexy man to find a woman with
whom to have a child unless both want something more than what they
say they want. Some Boomers have surely used the changing social con-
ventions of our times to prolong their period of seeking the perfect and un-
attainable mate. Once only the young dated, and dating was expected to
lead to marriage. Now dating into midlife and beyond is acceptable. Lifelong daters blame fate for keeping them from their true loves, out there
somewhere, lost in the land of Saturday night when it is really the possibilities of Saturday night that intrigue them more than the probabilities of
commitment do.

Living with someone who clearly isn't "the one" kills time even more ef-
ficiently. After the couple break up, each can lament the years wasted on a
living-together arrangement that didn't lead to a commitment. Time
passes. The love of one's life is never found because the wrong toothbrush
took up space in the holder.

The sex may have been good, even great, but never "the best." There is
comfort in knowing that.

MIDNIGHT LADY

"Sexy dancer, hot and hardy, love to party."
(Recorded by Marvin Gaye for Columbia Records)

"A gay male friend says the best sex is the sex you haven't had yet," Marie says. She laughs. "I suppose that's right. If you're not in a relationship with someone you expect to remain with forever, then how can you say you've had the best sex of your life yet? It still has to be out there. If it isn't, you were a damned fool to walk away from it. I've never thought about this before, but what if I didn't know the best sex while I was having it? What if my expectations are so high I'll never be satisfied?"

Marie, forty-three and never married, was recently downsized out of a high-paying corporate job. Now she's struggling to establish her own consulting firm in San Francisco, where she's lived for the past decade. After losing her job, she considered moving back to Philadelphia, her hometown, but decided against it. She didn't want to lean on family connections in her job search.

"At the same time that my career was going bust, I was getting out of a three-year relationship," she says. "It was a traumatic time. I almost did go back to Philadelphia, but I couldn't compromise my independence now. I've always felt like my brothers were waiting for me to fail and to need them to help me out. Then my sisters-in-law could let me know I wouldn't have such problems if I had a husband to pick up the slack. Everyone would have enjoyed it too much.

"I have never wanted kids. I think I'm probably too selfish to be someone's mother. My mother has seven grandchildren from my three brothers. I don't feel any compulsion to give her another. I don't want kids, but I would like to have a husband. My life is a series of romantic disasters. Every time I think I have found the man, I haven't. Either he's married to someone else or he has a drinking, drugs, or money problem or he can't commit or he can't commit to me because I'm not his ideal woman. There's always something wrong."

Marie has had more sex partners than most women of her generation. "At least a hundred," she admits. "I didn't keep an accurate count. I was pretty wild in college and in my twenties. I picked up men in bars, at parties, on vacations. When other women were agonizing over whether you should ever, ever have sex on the first date, I was having sex without a date, an hour after meeting. There was always alcohol involved. I drank way too much. It would be appropriate to say that I deeply regret that phase of my life, but I don't. I had fun. I was wild. Luckily, I didn't get a disease or worse. I know I took some crazy chances, and I was fortunate things didn't go bad.

"To be honest, I did go through a period in my thirties feeling guilty about my behavior. I had a good job in Philadelphia with some community visibility by the time I was thirty-two and had to be more careful about my image. It was '87, a solid Reagan year. Michael Douglas starred as Gordon Gecko in *Wall Street*. 'Greed is good' was the mantra of my generation, not 'Do it till it feels good.' I couldn't go to a party where I might run into someone who knew someone who knew me at work and get shit-faced and have sex with the bartender in the bathroom anymore.

"I had a split life. I worked long hours, rarely dated, and lived a nunlike existence in my overpriced and underdecorated apartment in Center City. Philadelphia is a city of great affordable apartments, but I managed not to find one. Most nights, I came home from the office late and alone. It was me, a spoon, and a carton of Haagen-Dazs. Three or four times a year I took a vacation, a long weekend or a week, to someplace warm and sexy— the Caribbean, Key West, Cabo San Lucas. Immediately following check-in, I found the most decadent tropical bar, began drinking, and made my first connection. I called those my 'bad girl' interludes. A Portuguese sailor I met in Cabo actually followed me back to Philadelphia, but I was able to get rid of him fast.

"After two years of this schizophrenic sexual lifestyle, I met George at a business dinner. He had his own company. He was handsome, unmarried, charismatic. And he was obviously and strongly attracted to me. He sent flowers to my office the next day. When I called to thank him, he invited me out to dinner that night. I know I should have lied and said I was busy and made him wait until the next week, but I didn't. I was never very good at making men wait."

A strikingly attractive woman, Marie is typically beautifully dressed, most often in exuberant colors, not the black, white, cream combinations favored by many business women. Clothes are important to her, she concedes, and one of the reasons she has a hefty credit-card debt. Appearances aside, she says she lacked "self-esteem" until she was almost forty. She credits the Forum, Werner Erhard's post-Est self-actualization therapy for Yuppies, with helping her discover her inner confidence. For almost two years, she attended meetings, seminars, and workshops where she encountered herself in the presence of other "strivers"—for large fees. She dropped out because she found it increasingly hard to recruit people for meetings, one of the requirements for achieving actualization.

"I went on a week long Outward Bound–style trip where you had to let everyone critique you in a bathing suit," she says. "It changed my life. If you can survive that, you can survive anything."

She does not think herself "pretty," pointing to small breasts, "heavy" thighs, and fine lines around her eyes—damage from the sun.

"I was sun-baking long after I knew better," she says. "Sun, water, and alcohol just seem to go together."

It was summer when she began dating George, and he had a house on the Jersey shore in addition to his Center City town house. She liked the fact that he had money. A lover with his own wallet full of gold cards was a welcome change from beach bums, straying husbands, men with more lines than a fishing trawler.

"We were at the beach house when he told me he was having a little cash-flow problem," she says. "We'd just made love in the Jacuzzi. I could hear the waves lapping against the shore outside. Who could think analytically? I understood cash-flow problems. I was always running up enormous credit-card bills that I paid off with bonuses. He explained the details of his problem, but I wasn't really listening. I didn't pay much attention to money in those days. I made it and spent it. He said he had a temporary problem. I asked if I could help. Later that day I wrote him a sizable check, expecting to have the 'loan' repaid within two weeks. We made love again that night.

"George wasn't a great lover, not as good as the beach bums I'd known. He was a little rough, a little too fast, reluctant to go down on me though I enthusiastically gave him head. The night of the first loan he spent more time on cunnilingus than he'd done before. I should have been suspicious.

"The loan wasn't repaid. The cash-flow problems continued. I wrote more checks. Gradually it occurred to me that he couldn't afford the town house, the beach house, the cars. Then I learned he didn't own any of them. Everything was rented or leased, except the furnishings in the town house. And most of those belonged to his ex-wife, who wanted them back. The sex got worse. He was rougher, faster, less attentive. We fought, and I cried.

"Yet I clung to the 'relationship' until he broke up with me. He was seeing another woman, a younger woman with thin thighs. I met her when I dropped by the town house unexpectedly. It was an ugly scene.

"P.S., I never got my money back from George."

As that relationship was ending badly, Marie was offered a job in San Francisco with a sizable pay increase and greater prestige. She considered "for a nanosecond" before accepting. Enthusiastically, she embraced the idea of a new life. But she spent her first year in California repeating the familiar pattern, going from office "nun" to vacation "whore." Then she had a series of short-term relationships with "unsuitable" men. Sometimes the sex was "adequate," sometimes not.

"I saw several therapists, including one who almost had me convinced I'd been sexually abused by my father and had simply forgotten about it. Recovered memory of sex abuse was a hot concept in the late eighties. I had given up on therapy by the early nineties and decided there was no hope for me having a real relationship when I met Kevin."

Marie thought Kevin was her "equal" when she met him. A handsome man only a few years older than she, he was well known within her business circle. Unlike George, he was provably solvent. And he was obviously attracted to her.

"I should have known when he sent flowers so quickly," she says. "Every time I get instant flowers from a man, the card should be signed 'Warning, warning, danger ahead.'"

Kevin's financial statement was above reproach, but he had a significant problem with women. Like Marie, he'd made foolish and reckless romantic choices in the past.

"We'd been dating a few months when I discovered that he had two vindictive ex-wives. As nasty as they proved to be, they were pussycats compared to the angry ex-girlfriend. She was a stalker. And she had a gun. One night after we'd been to a charity function together, she shot at us. Fortunately, she missed. When she was arrested, she was carrying a 're-venge plan' against Kevin and me. When she sent me a dead cat in the mail, I knew it was time to cut my losses."

After Kevin, another spate of "bad girl" quickies, and then she met Rudolfo.

"Eurotrash," she says, "but I was too stupid to figure that out. He was good in bed, which was more than could be said of his recent predecessors. I didn't see that he was George with an accent. My checkbook came out again. He was a consummate eater of pussy—until I got downsized. I wrote him a check that bounced. He told me how disappointed he was in me. I wish I could say I found my pride and told him I never wanted to see him again, but I didn't. He stopped taking my calls."

Marie is currently "taking a break" from men.

BOOMER SEX TIPS

Ticket to Ride
(Recorded by the Beatles for Apple Records)

Marie's advice for getting the best sex from the worst guy: "You have to believe while you're naked with him that he's better than he is. When you get to the point where you can't believe, and can't project belief, he will be his true worst self in bed. As long as you believe, he'll give you the best he has to give in sexual currency."

Is the craving for "more" expressed by many of the terminally single Boomers an attainable goal? An affirmation of faith in love? Or a symptom of the neuroses afflicting the commitment-phobe?

When the young say they are waiting for true love or overwhelming passion, we listen and nod in sympathy. A man or woman at twenty, twenty-five, even thirty has reason to believe the best is yet to come. How realistic is that assumption after thirty-five, forty, forty-five, fifty?

"One day I realized I was holding out for something nobody ever had outside romance novels and old movies," a thirty-eight-year-old recent bride told me. "I was waiting to be swept off my feet by the love of my life while the man who truly loved me was waiting for me to grow up. I grew up and married him."

And a forty-four-year-old recent groom said, "I was Peter Pan for long enough. Our parents knew something we've resisted knowing: Sometimes you have to make a commitment before you have the best sex, the deep love, the truly intimate connection. We, as my grandmother often said, insisted upon putting our carts before our horses."

Some Boomers would have it no other way.

WHAT A FOOL BELIEVES

"The wise man has the power . . . to reason away what he sees."
(Recorded by the Doobie Brothers for Polygram Records)

"Typically it takes me six months to get a woman out of my system after it's over," Ron says. "This time it's been almost a year, and I still miss Angela, think about her sometimes. I started dating again after eight months, because I knew it was time to move on."

Ron recently celebrated his fortieth birthday at a party he threw for himself in the Ventura, California, condo with ocean view he'd shared briefly shared with Angela. The condo is his, purchased almost a decade ago. When she moved in, she put her bedroom furniture in the second bedroom and hung her clothes in his closet. When she moved out, she had little else to add to the van load of possessions.

"She bought some big plants," he says. "She took those. I liked the plants. Eventually I'll probably buy some. They lend a certain ambiance, don't they?"

Angela decided to leave him, he says, because she was turning thirty and he wouldn't marry her.

"She freaked out about being thirty. Her biological clock was ticking. I understand. I sympathize. But I don't want kids. You can't raise kids to please someone else. It's not like compromising on a movie, a restaurant, a vacation."

Angela was only his fifth "serious" relationship. Each lasted at least two years and one five years. A serial monogamist, he doesn't "cheat" until the relationship is "winding down." He met Angela while he was living with Belinda.

"That relationship was winding down," he explains. "Living with Belinda was a mistake. She moved in when she lost her own apartment. I didn't plan on her staying. She just did. After she moved in, she gained about thirty pounds. My friends called her 'cow' behind my back. Speaking of friends, she didn't get along with mine. Belinda wanted to change my life, everything about it, but especially my job and my friends."

Though he has a college degree, Ron has worked as a waiter for twenty years. Employed at a high-quality restaurant in the nearby Ojai Valley, he earns a comfortable income. He likes the freedom the job affords him to pursue athletic interests during the day. An avid golfer, Ron also enjoys running, swimming, tennis, and boating. His friends are sports enthusiasts too.

"Our watering hole is a local sports bar," he says. "She hated the place, even before I met Angela there."

When Ron met Angela, she had just been hired as a waitress in the bar. The outfit of snug red T-shirt and white short shorts flattered her curves. It was instant flirtation.

"We had immediate banter," he says. "I heard through the grapevine that she really liked me. It started as a friendship. We talked a lot. I told her about Belinda. She was getting out of a relationship too. One thing led to another. The first time we had sex was in my car in the bar parking lot after closing. It was steamy, intense. When she pulled up her T-shirt, her breasts popped out of her little white cotton bra. I took them in my hands, and I was in heaven."

For two months Ron and Angela had sex in his car, on the floor behind the bar on nights he stayed to "help her close," and occasionally in his apartment when Belinda was traveling on business. Angela had moved out of her boyfriend's apartment into her parent's house in Santa Barbara.

"She needed to get out of her parents' house. We needed a place to fuck. And I needed to get Belinda out of my life. The week before Memorial Day I told Belinda I'd found someone else and was moving her in. It was tense. She cried, yelled, threw things, broke some glassware. But the bottom line is: I own this place. She was out; Angela was in.

"Everything was great between us for about six months. The sex was really good. She was as horny as I was. Unlike Belinda, she was uninhibited. She liked doing it in the chaise longue on the deck. We went to topless beaches. Angela knew she could get me hot as a firecracker by flashing her breasts at me. She let me titty fuck her and come on her breasts. Everything was great—until she started wanting more.

"I blame her sisters and her parents for some of it. They put the idea in her head that I could be 'doing better' working at a 'better' job. With their prodding, she began looking for ways to turn me into husband material. We had fights. At first, the fights ended in great make-up sex. After you've had the same fight for several months, you stop falling into each other's arms and start bolting the slammed doors."

Angela told him she was moving out the week before the Fourth of July holiday, almost two years after she'd moved in. She was seeing another man. Tearfully, she told him she loved him but she had to move on. She wanted marriage and children.

"I was caught with my pants up," Ron says. "I wasn't seeing another woman. I wish I had been. I wish I'd had someone on the string, for sex if nothing else. Once she said she was leaving, I couldn't get interested in anyone else. I was afraid I couldn't get it up.

"Angela wasn't the love of my life, but breaking up with her was the hardest breakup I've gone through."

And who was the love of Ron's life?

Brandy. She was sixteen, and he was twenty-seven. They met at a cocktail party given by her aunt. Ron was the bartender.

"I thought she was eighteen or nineteen," he says. "She was wearing a skimpy blue halter dress and wandering around with a glass of champagne. It never occurred to me she was still in high school. I learned later that her aunt was an artist and very progressive. After the party, Brandy French-kissed me. She knew how to kiss. It blew me away. I asked if I could see her again. She gave me her phone number."

She insisted on driving her own car and meeting him in a public place on their first date. Their second date was dinner at his place—and sex.

"I've never had sex like the sex I had with Brandy before or since," he says. "It was beautiful, perfect, emotional and physical at the same time. I was head over heels for her. I didn't find out she was sixteen until she went back to school in the fall. It was a huge shock, but it didn't stop me from being with her. She was more woman at sixteen than most women ever are."

When Brandy's parents found out about the relationship, they insisted on meeting Ron. They thought he was twenty-one. They weren't happy about that, but they accepted it. A few months later Brandy broke up with him. She'd met another "boy."

Ron says, "He was eighteen, the most annoying snot nose. I followed them one night after he'd picked her up at her parents' house. He took her to the movies to see *Out of Africa*. I waited outside the theater for them to come out. When they did, she was hanging on his arm, her eyes misty, looking up at him in the dreamy way she'd looked up at me. I went over to them. He was cool, reasonable, in the way only a rich kid who thought he was better than any waiter could be.

"I should have punched him, but I walked away. She was the love of my life, and I walked away."

The Boomer Facts

- Single is not a transient premarital state for many Boomers. They will live all or most of their lives unmarried. Whether happily single, terminally single, or single by commitment-phobia, they have developed coping mechanisms for living in a world where being paired is still the norm. One group of singles, the perpetual seekers, appear to be striving for the coupled state. In reality, they have romanticized and mythologized the quest for the true or perfect love/sex.
- The perpetual seekers are more often men than women. Perhaps men, as they age, simply have more opportunities for continued dating and get more support for their mythmaking from friends and as-

sociates. How many women would let a female friend get away with self deception on a major scale for twenty or thirty years?

- Holding onto the memory of a lost love—or lost "best sex"—can be a way for women and men alike to remain comfortably single. Why try to make a relationship work when you've had and lost the best?

- Women as well as men have used casual sex to avoid developing intimate relationships. Both men and women sometimes form doomed relationships with inappropriate partners to avoid connecting with someone who might give them the love and respect they say they want. Therapists and others might say they lack self-esteem, have self-destructive dating habits, or don't believe they deserve love. In some cases, maybe. It's also possible they just don't want to be married and have children, but aren't comfortable with not wanting what everyone is supposed to want.

- The older they get, the fewer sexual options perpetual seekers—especially the women—have left, the less satisfied they are with their lives in general, and their sex lives in particular.

6

Late Married, Sex?

A woman who married for the first time at age thirty-seven said the most striking change in her life following marriage was regular sex. She'd had droughts between relationships that lasted as long as two years. "People think you don't have to get married anymore to get sex—and you don't," she said, "but getting regular sex is easier if you have a partner in the bed beside you each night."

She hit upon the central truth of the single life: A lot of very attractive men and women go to bed alone night after night after night.

Boomers started the trend toward marrying later. The average age of a woman at marriage was twenty in the 1950s, twenty-two by the seventies and twenty-six in the nineties. The reasons are fairly obvious to any armchair sociologist. Reliable contraception in the form of the birth control pill, relaxed attitudes about sexual experimentation before marriage, and the increasing role of women in the workplace reduced the need for early marriage. In the fifties, marriage was the primary means to a sex life, the safest place to be if pregnancy occurred, and the sole means of comfortable support for most women. Young people were expected to marry when they finished their educations, whether high school or college.

Almost fifty years later, marriage or cohabitation is still the primary means to an active sex life. Two incomes are almost as necessary for a reasonably comfortable life as one man's salary was then. And a great social debate rages on whether or not children raised by single mothers or divorced parents are disadvantaged. Marriage is attractive to men and women today for a variety of reasons, not the least of which is regular sex. Now they are free to choose not to marry—and encouraged by parents, peers, and experts to marry later when they do.

Most people, and Boomers are no exception, still get married, at least once.

The Survey Says

- 50 percent of Vietnam-generation women and 46 percent of Watergate-generation women were married by their twenty-second birthday.
- 32 percent of Vietnam-generation men and 21 percent of Watergate-generation men were married by their twenty-second birthday.
- But 18 percent of Vietnam-generation women and 23 percent of Watergate-generation women married after age thirty.
- And 31 percent of Vietnam-generation men and 39 percent of Watergate-generation men married after age thirty.
- The average marrying age for Vietnam-generation women was twenty-three, for men, twenty-six.
- The average marrying age for Watergate-generation women was twenty-five, for men, twenty-nine.

Surprisingly, the couples who married after thirty in both generations reported less overall satisfaction with their lives and less satisfaction with their sex lives in particular than their early-married counterparts.

The Survey Says

- Late-marrieds among the Vietnam generation have sex less often, an average of 1.6 times a week to the early-marrieds' 2.1.
- Among the Watergate generation, late-marrieds have sex an average of 1.7 times a week to the early-marrieds' 2.2.

That is not what I expected to find, given the general enthusiasm for later marriage within the culture. Late-marrieds are having less sex at the same ages than early-marrieds are. Why?

Perhaps sex is more important to those who married early. Some early-marrieds floated to the altar on clouds of desire. In contrast, some people who marry late list their criteria for a marital partner in the most pragmatic terms. The young lovers either made, or had, more time for lovemaking than late-marrieds, who more often say they are "too busy" for sex now. "If you start out making love five to seven days a week," an early-married man explained, "your drop-off over the years isn't as precipitous as some couples' who were only getting it on two or three times a week the first year."

Possibly, late-marrieds have more advanced degrees and work in more demanding jobs that leave them less time for sex. A recent study did find that people with advanced college degrees made love on average less often than college graduates and high school graduates. And maybe it's babies, the late ones created in many late marriages. Couples who had their children in their twenties have very different private lives from those who started families in their late thirties or early forties.

"I'm postpartum and perimenopausal," a forty-one-year-old woman said. "I'm not very interested in sex."

Men and women who postponed marriage often had specific ideas about what they wanted to achieve in their own lives before they married. The longer they remained single, the longer the list of their ideal mates' qualifications grew. A lot of people told me they eliminated prospective partners for superficial reasons, like the way they dressed, their food and drink choices, their taste in movies, music, and other forms of popular culture. A Los Angeles single woman in her forties said, "Five years ago I broke up with a man because he combed that long piece of hair over his bald spot. Today I would take him to my hairdresser and get it clipped."

Now she is looking for a "fixer-upper" because she'd like to have a family before it's too late. How sexy is that?

YOU'RE HAVING MY BABY

"What a wonderful way of saying how much you love me."
(Recorded by Paul Anka for United Artists)

"I did get married young, at twenty-one, but I got divorced two months later," Ian says. "In my senior year of college I married my girlfriend because we thought she was pregnant. It was 1974. My kid brother gave me a Steve Miller album as a wedding present—the one with the single 'The Joker.' Little did I know how appropriate that was. This was before home pregnancy tests. When a girl said she was pregnant, you thought she knew. You didn't know how, but you thought she knew. A month after the wedding, she got her period. Apparently the medication she was taking for schizophrenia caused her to miss an occasional period.

"I found out she was schizophrenic when she explained why she'd missed her period without being pregnant. I knew she wasn't like anyone else I'd ever dated, but I thought she was refreshingly and wonderfully wacky. I was a kid. In those days I thought people who'd considered suicide were more interesting than those who hadn't. I was just the person to find a schizophrenic glamorous. Without telling anyone, my glamorously wacky little wife decided to stop taking her medication altogether so she could get pregnant.

"In her delusional phase, she became convinced that I was trying to kill her. That turned out to be a stroke of luck, because she wouldn't have sex with me. I couldn't get her pregnant if I wasn't having sex with her, could I? You'd think I would have been smart enough to put an end to the sex myself and get the hell out, but I wasn't. At that age, I'd do just about anything to get laid. She divorced me. I didn't fight her. Periodically, over the next several years, she would come back into my life for some reason or another, make me miserable, as well as frightened for my life, and scare off the woman I was dating at the time.

"I finally lost her by moving from New York City, where we'd lived together, to Columbus, Ohio, and leaving no forwarding address. I had a new job, new apartment, new life. I don't know what ever happened to her. By the time I was clear of her altogether, I was twenty-six and less inclined to marry on impulse. It was almost the eighties. I thought I was going to be a master of the universe."

I met Ian for breakfast at a Pennsylvania Dutch café on the outskirts of Columbus. I got there first and eavesdropped on a conversation between the heavyset waitress and the (apparently) aging Boomer couple in the booth next to mine. Before her arrival, they had been verbally ripping apart a single mother who was perhaps a neighbor "and no better than she needs to be" and another couple of indeterminate age and marital status caught kissing in the Wal-Mart parking lot.

"Are you going to be open on Sundays?" the man asked. "No," the waitress replied, "we have no plans for that. I wouldn't work on Sundays. I go to church and she [the owner, presumably] does, too."

"Church is the place to be," the woman said. "We love our church."

The waitress left. They went back to the verbal evisceration of their neighbors. I read the local paper. An ugly murder topped the front page.

"Welcome to the heartland!" Ian boomed. "Isn't it good to be here? Away from the crime and nastiness of the East Coast! People are decent folk here!"

The Boomer couple looked around at us and smiled smugly.

"This is the kind of community that grows the McCaugheys"—parents of the septuplets—he says. "I laughed at places like this when I lived in Manhattan, both times."

At forty-five, Ian has rediscovered the "heartland" and married for the second, or as he sees it, the "true first" time. After moving to Columbus the first time in 1979, he switched careers and began a geographical odyssey of the country as he climbed up, across, down, and up again the corporate ladder. It was, in his case, he says, a corporate "game of chutes and ladders."

"I moved seventeen times between '79 and '93," he says. "That averages out to more than one move per year. I was career-building, but I also made a lot of mistakes. I could and should have done things differently. As it is, I have ended up back in Columbus again, with a good job.

"While I was bouncing around the country like some kind of demented ball, I was also dodging commitment. When I got involved with a woman, I was on the verge of being transferred or quitting my job and taking another in a different setting. A shrink would probably tell me that I lived my life this way to avoid commitment, and that may be true. It wasn't a conscious decision by any means."

His return to Columbus coincided with his fortieth birthday, a watershed event for most Boomers. It was 1995. His hair was rapidly thinning. He was painfully aware that the President wasn't much older than he was. Mel Gibson was starring in *Braveheart*, and Ian, because of his Scottish heritage, couldn't help comparing his personal history in a negative way to another, great man's story. He was mildly depressed. It was beginning to feel like a permanent condition.

"I spent my fortieth birthday alone in a rented condo. My belongings hadn't been shipped yet from my previous home, in Baton Rouge. I'd ordered a mattress and box spring from the 1-800-dial-a-bed people. So I had a place to sleep, but no sheets. I'd bought a pillow, two towels, a face cloth, and a floor lamp from a discount store. That and the contents of three pieces of luggage were all I had. I bought a bottle of champagne to celebrate my birthday and realized belatedly that I had no glass to pour it into. Imagine spending your fortieth birthday swigging champagne from a bottle on your brand-new mattress, no sheets. I was ready for a change.

"Two weeks later I met Claire, a career counselor. The irony. We met at a hotel bar during happy hour. I was immediately attracted to her. She has beautiful short red hair, big green eyes, and a wonderful smile. She'll tell you she needs to lose weight, but she doesn't. She's perfect the way she is.

"I asked her out that night, and she accepted. We made love on the third date. I knew right away that this was going to be a different relationship for me. The lovemaking was more tender. I felt vulnerable with her, really vulnerable in a way I hadn't felt since I was twenty-one and saying 'I do' to a paranoid schizophrenic. This time, however, I had a solid person in my arms.

"Claire's thirty-eighth birthday fell a few weeks after that. We drove to a quiet spot in the Allegheny Mountains that I love. She fell in love with it, too. We had good sex that weekend, the best we'd had so far. She was passionate and emotional, alternately gentle and fierce in her desire for me. I was humbled by the experience.

"Driving back to Columbus, we talked a lot. The car radio reception in the mountains isn't good, and I'd forgotten to pack CDs or tapes. We kept driving from one N.P.R. station's receiving area into another's. We'd heard *Fresh Air* for the second time that day when she said to me, 'I have stopped using birth control.'

"We were driving through the tunnel in Kittatinny Mountain when she told me she had stopped using birth control. I had this excruciating moment of déjà vu. The witchy presence of my first wife was hovering over the car. We got through the mountain, the dulcet tones of N.P.R. flooded the car. I knew I would be okay.

" 'Do you want to have my baby?' I asked her.

" 'Yes,' she said. She was crying without making a sound. I glanced over and saw the tears running down her cheeks.

"I reached across the space between us, took her hand, and squeezed it. 'I want that, too,' I said. Until I said it, I had no idea it was true. Once I'd said I wanted a baby with Claire, I wanted it more all the time.

"For the next six months, we made love like bunnies or teenagers. We couldn't get enough of each other. I look back on that time as the best sex of my life. We were so open to each other. Every time we made love, we thought, 'This could be the night we make a baby.'

"She didn't get pregnant. We can both do the math. She was coming up onto her thirty-ninth birthday. We had little time left. Either we committed to each other and to starting a family together—which meant seeing a fertility doctor—or we lost the chance. It was one thing to make love without using birth control and see what happened, but another to say, 'It's not happening. What do we have to do together to make it happen?'

"I asked her to marry me. She said, 'But what if we get married and I can't give you a child?' I told her I didn't care, I wanted to marry her. It was the most romantic moment I'd ever shared with a woman. For the first time, I made a wholehearted commitment. It felt good. Ironically, I felt freer than I ever had."

Ian and Claire were married on his forty-first birthday. After they returned from their honeymoon in Paris, they saw a fertility specialist, who quickly ruled out Ian as the problem.

"After the temporary elation upon hearing my boys could swim, I realized it didn't matter which one of us was technically in need of support. Infertility was 'our' problem, not hers or mine. We were lucky. After a few months on fertility drugs, she conceived one healthy beautiful child, our son Niles.

"I was with her the entire way. We went to Lamaze classes together. Her labor was long and difficult. As much as she wanted to have a vaginal delivery, she couldn't. Niles was too big for her to deliver naturally. The doctor explained to me that first-time mothers in their early twenties will dilate sufficiently to allow delivery of a large baby, but older mothers often won't. I was with her in the delivery room when she had a C-section. I saw the incision being made. When they pulled Niles out, his color was ice blue, and my heart stopped. Then he cried. The nurse wiped some of the gunk off him and handed him to me. My eyes met Claire's as I took our son into my arms. I will never forget that moment.

"The rush of love I experienced for her and our son was like nothing I could previously have imagined. I was transformed by it. I couldn't have experienced this emotion in quite the same way as a younger man. I thought when I married Claire that I was doing it for a multitude of pragmatic reasons: to begin a family, honor a woman whose love and courage honored me, give myself an anchor and put an end to a rootless existence. When Niles was born, everything changed. Our love for each other, our motives for being together, all were transformed into something much larger. It was a transcendent moment."

For the most part, the late-married Boomers I interviewed seemed to fall into one of two groups: They had at last found "true love" or "the one," or they had settled for something less than the kind of love that makes the earth move (or stand still) because they wanted commitment, security, a stable emotional and sexual life, a family. Men want these things as often as, if not more than women. Ian very much did not want to spend another birthday alone on a bare mattress swigging champagne from a bottle. Claire was the answer to the prayer he hadn't thought to utter. Then a funny thing happened on the way to the pragmatic solution: He fell in love with her, with their son. Ian is a lucky man.

Many men and women who've led less enchanted love lives also count their late marriages in the success column. A pragmatic choice can be a largely satisfying one, especially if the timing is right when the choice is made. Couples who marry in their late thirties or forties benefit from the hormonal and psychological changes associated with aging. Sex becomes more intimate at this point in life. Men, no longer driven by hormones alone, seek intimacy. Women more comfortable with their sexuality and secure in their responsiveness, don't push as hard for intimate connection as they did in their youth. The psychotherapist Carl Jung described the point in midlife where men and women cross sexual and psychological paths as "the contrasexual transition."

Yet the survey respondents who married late are less likely than the early-marrieds to describe themselves as "satisfied." One reason must surely be children—the very children they avidly desired when they married. Boomers who married young and started their families early now have grown children. Making the contrasexual transition is easier for couples who aren't changing diapers, chasing after toddlers, helping with home-work, and driving in car pools.

"I would die for my babies," says a forty-year-old first-time mother of twins conceived on fertility drugs, "if they don't kill me first. We knew having twins would be a lot of work, but we didn't anticipate how much it would tire us out. Sex is a luxury we can seldom afford."

Another reason for the satisfaction gap? Perhaps people do bond more intensely in their youth and, once strongly bonded, continue to crave each other's touch. Each stage of love has its own chemistry. Helen Fisher, Ph.D., the Rutgers University psychology professor and author of *Anatomy of Love*, identifies three types of love and their chemistries: Lust, fueled by estrogen and testosterone; Romantic love, inspired by norepinephrine, dopamine, and serotonin; and Attachment, the bonding stage, fed by vasopressin and oxytocin. Oxytocin, a hormone secreted by the pituitary gland, has been called "the love hormone," "the touch hormone," and "the cuddle hormone." Fisher says it is "the star neurochemical in long-lasting love" because it creates "a chemical addiction" for the touch of the beloved; and the young, particularly women, produce it in greater quantities than the middle-aged.

"I fell in love fast and hard when I was younger," a forty-two-year-old woman says. "I didn't meet my husband until I was thirty-seven. When I fell in love with him, it was more subtle and diffuse. Sometimes I have to remind myself that I love him, I'm happy, I have what I always wanted to have. It didn't hit me like a ton of bricks falling on my head."

Late love can be, like late success, savored and appreciated without turning your world upside down.

"Maybe people just don't know when they're satisfied after a certain point," a male friend, one of the late-marrieds, mused. "They get used to feeling like something is missing. I was single for so long I developed a habit of resentment. I resented other people's happiness. And I found myself doing that for a while even after I had happiness of my own."

As we age, we evolve sexually. A man and a woman who were fortunate enough to find each other early and evolve together share a history and a passion that sets them apart from others. But theirs isn't the only path to satisfaction. There are other places on the evolutionary scale where a couple can connect.

I FOUND A TRUE LOVE

"I swear by the stars above, I know she's mine."
(Recorded by Wilson Pickett for BMI)

"Getting married late can be a real advantage for a couple," Keith says. "You've had your freedom long enough to be quite familiar with the downside of that ubiquitous phrase 'no strings.' I was almost forty and my wife, Nan, was two years younger when we got married, each for the first time. We were comfortable with our lives alone, but we didn't romanticize them. Nan tells people we got married in the year of *Forrest Gump*. She has a quirky sense of humor. Friends of ours who married in their early twenties and really never had a single adulthood do romanticize that life phase. There are benefits to being married and to being single. We say being married means you never have to accept a date to *Forrest Gump*.

"We have never had to ask one another for 'space,' because, having lived alone for as long as each of us did, we know how to give and take the space we need. It's not an issue. When we met, we were both established in our careers. We each owned a Center City [Philadelphia] apartment. With fewer worries than we'd had in our twenties and more time to devote to a relationship than either of us would have had when we were working seventy-hour weeks, we came together at exactly the right moment in time."

Unlike many late-marrieds, Keith and Nan, now forty-four and forty-two, did not want children. Each came from big Catholic families. Nieces and nephews abound. Nan admits that she would have had a family if she'd married in her twenties because, at the time, she thought it was something she "should" want. Keith was one of those men single women with biology on the brain love to hate. He knew he didn't want to be a father.

"I would tell women, 'I don't want children *yet*,' never fully comprehending how that was driving them up the wall. They're thinking, 'Oh, he can delay as long as he wants, while my time is running out.' I was saying '*yet*,' because I thought saying 'I don't want any kids *ever*' was tantamount to expressing a desire to boil babies. The women I dated for a long stretch were in baby lust. They wanted to be impregnated more than they wanted to be loved. I am not putting them down. I do understand. My sisters and brothers have the same need to reproduce, and I'm glad they do. I adore my nieces and nephews. I just don't want to be a father. When I passed my thirtieth birthday, I discovered that all relationships with women were doomed to crash on the rock of fertility.

"They held back sexually when they realized I was not going to morphe into a father figure. I don't mean they intentionally suppressed their sexual responses. They couldn't help themselves. It just happened."

I'd had several conversations and one meeting with Keith when I finally met Nan at Jim's Steaks on South Street. Like everyone who's spent enough time in Philadelphia to have an opinion on the great steak question—Who has the best steaks, Jim, Pat, or Gino?—she had one. Jim's. Over incredibly delicious steak, cheese, onions, and hot pepper sandwiches, we discussed the importance of sex in the life of a late-married Boomer. She had an opinion here too. Very important.

"I met Keith while shopping in Show of Hands, a little crafts gallery on Pine Street," she says. "We both love art pottery, and the shop has some good pieces. It was a Hallmark card commercial kind of moment. Our hands met across the same piece. We smiled at each other. There was an instant recognition of like-minded souls. I demurred. He purchased. 'May I buy you a drink?' he asked.

"I know, I know. When I told my friends about it, they said, 'I don't believe this. You're making it up. You picked him up in a bar, didn't you?' "

That late-Saturday-afternoon drink turned into a later dinner. They went from dinner to a jazz club in the neighborhood. At the end of the evening, he kissed her and gave her the pottery as an 'I want to get to know you' gift. After they were married, he told her he'd known the pottery wasn't going out of his life.

"He called the next day. We had a midweek date and a weekend date the first week we knew each other. There was never a time with Keith where I seriously wondered, 'Will he call again?' I knew he would. It was a comfortable progression from the beginning."

Both say the "turning point" in their relationship—the moment each knew this would end in marriage—came when the word "children" was brought up.

"We were at a party at a friend's condo on the Delaware River," she says. "We were standing together at a window admiring the view of the Ben Franklin Bridge lit up at night. He asked me what I wanted in life that I didn't already have. I said, 'More of the same.' He said, 'Does that mean more of me, too?' I said, 'Yes, it does.' He nuzzled my neck and asked, 'What about children?' Shivers went down my spine. Was he hinting that he wanted children?

"Was I going to lose him if I told the truth? I had to risk it because I was at the point in my life where I could no longer lie to please a man. I said, 'I like children, other people's children, but I don't want children of my own.' I could feel the sigh of relief running through his body and into mine like an electrical change. I turned to him, and we kissed, quietly, deeply, passionately."

Keith also said their relationship progressed rapidly, and happily, from that day forward.

"The sex," Nan says, "got better from that night on. It's as if we were both liberated by acknowledging the harsh truth: In a world where almost everyone wants to have a child, we do not. I felt the same kind of sexual freedom I've heard women say they experience after a tubal ligation or menopause. I let go for the first time in my life.

"Orgasm had never been easy for me, and suddenly it was. I felt these enormous orgasms starting in my clitoris and radiating throughout my genitals. Sometimes they seemed to spread into my entire body."

For his part, Keith too said he began experiencing sex in a new, more intense, way after he and Nan had their "meeting of the minds." He attributes this in part to the relief they shared and in part to the physiological facts of life. Keith was ready for intimacy and Nan for stronger orgasms.

"Keith is solidly grounded in reality," she laughs. "I like that about him. It doesn't prevent him from being romantic, thoughtful, caring, passionate. We both know we wouldn't be together if one of us had passionately wanted children. That's our relationship bottom line. Most couples don't recognize theirs. We do."

The "relationship bottom line" may be more easily identified by couples who are no longer very young and inclined to romanticize both their emotions and their sexual responses. That doesn't mean they're incapable of romance.

BOOMER SEX TIPS

Adult Education
(Recorded by Daryl Hall and John Oates for RCA Records)

A woman has to adapt her lovemaking style as her partner ages. Boomer males not only want, but *need* more foreplay. Women expect a man to get an erection without a lot of physical stimulation, but they don't anymore. Touch lavishly. When you're holding his penis, use a firm grip. The limp handshake won't do anymore.

WALK ON THE WILD SIDE

"Hey, babe, take a walk on the wild side."
(Recorded by Lou Reed for RCA Records)

Amy and John attended the Fifth International Conference on Bisexuality held in Cambridge, Massachusetts, in the spring of 1998. It coincided with their fifth wedding anniversary, an omen, she says laughingly. Amy is bisexual, John is heterosexual. She has affairs, and he doesn't. John is free to have affairs with men—which doesn't appeal to him—but not women. That would dishonor their marriage vows.

"I accept the full range of Amy's sexuality," he says, "and I understand her need to have occasional sexual relationships with women. I wouldn't accept or understand her having sex with another man."

"It may be confusing to other people," she adds, "but it makes sense to us."

Amy and John married on his forty-second birthday; she was four years younger. Both say they probably would not have married if they'd met ten, even five, years sooner, before he was able to understand and accept bisexuality, before she was willing to commit to a man.

Several late-marrying couples said they made partner choices at thirty-five-plus they couldn't have made at twenty-five. Professional women married blue-collar men. Women married poorer, shorter, much younger men. Couples crossed race, ethnic, socioeconomic, and religious barriers they wouldn't have crossed when their families, friends, or insecurities held sway over them. Amy and John are perhaps the most colorful examples of that group who define their late mate choices as "mature."

"You don't know who you are, what you really want, and what you can do until you're thirty-five," he says. "Before then, I would have had the knee-jerk male reaction to Amy's bisexuality: Ogle the lesbian, make jokes out of the corners of my mouth. Her bisexuality would have titillated but also scared me. I would have wanted to prove I could make her come, but ultimately I would have walked away because women can make her come. I would have been threatened by her sexuality because I wouldn't have been capable of understanding it.

"I would be jealous of another man," he says. "But I am not jealous of her being with women. I can give her what a woman can't. That's how I rationalize things in my mind. A woman isn't a threat to me at this point in my life, but a man would be."

The Survey Says
- 6 percent of Vietnam-generation men and 8 percent of the women describe themselves as "bisexual."
- 7 percent of Watergate-generation men and 8 percent of the women describe themselves as "bisexual."
- Slightly more than 75 percent of the Boomers describing themselves as "bisexual" are or have been married.

While millions of American have had sex with both men and women, relatively few define themselves as "bisexual." Statistics are scarce, but estimates put the number of women and men of all ages who practice bisexuality at less than 2 or 3 percent of the population—less than in the Boomer survey. In some circles, bisexuality is chic. Rumors about male rock legends, movie stars, and bisexual behavior have been around for years. Pop star and Boomer Madonna is probably the most visible bisexual. Frequently accompanied by "gal pal" Ingrid Casares, she has flaunted all aspects of her sexuality. She is, according to Amy, a patron saint of bisexuals, a group who often find themselves ostracized by both the straight and gay communities.

"The lesbian women I know tell me I'm selling out by having sex with a man. They see it as something I do to appease the gods. I am appalled that their vision is so narrow. Both straights and gays can be narrow-minded in their judgment of bisexuals."

Before he met Amy, John had a fairly typical dating résumé. He lost his virginity at sixteen to "a little blond girl," also sixteen, whom he'd worshipped since kindergarten. "She was the aggressor," he says. "I was petrified of making a fool of myself but eager and willing." They dated steadily until high school graduation. She stayed in Edwardsville, Illinois, where she enrolled in Southern Illinois University, while he went to Cornell University, in Ithaca, New York, on a full scholarship.

"We promised to stay true to each other, but, of course, by the time I was home for Christmas holidays, our lives had changed irrevocably. She was seriously dating a college senior. I'd had a few one-nighters with townies, girls from Ithaca, who were either using or being used by the college boys. She told me not to wait for her. I called another classmate, Jill, who'd also gone away to college but was home for the holiday. We had a passionate fling lasting the entire ten-day Christmas break. She was the first girl I'd been with who knew how to perform fellatio. If we hadn't both been going our separate ways, I probably would have been down on my knees proposing to her within another ten days. I tried to stay in touch with her, but she wasn't particularly interested."

In his second year at Cornell he became romantically involved with a girl who worked in the student cafeteria. She was an artist, who also posed nude for classes when she wasn't slinging scrambled eggs and bacon in the mornings.

"That was my most significant relationship for years before I met Amy," he says. "I was a science major, and she thought I was too uptight to be her life partner. But I loved her. She was hot in bed. She liked to talk dirty while we were doing it. And she introduced me to heterosexual anal sex. I didn't know what to do when she first presented her ass to me to be fucked.

" 'You want this?' I asked in astonishment. 'Use a lot of lubricant,' she said. It was an incredible experience. When I saw the head of my penis against her anus, I didn't think I could be forceful enough to push into her. I was afraid of hurting her. I was probably afraid of enjoying myself too. In those days we thought men who liked anal sex with women were only using the socially acceptable substitute for what they really wanted: to bugger a man.

"She pushed her ass back against me. That was all the signal I needed. Some primal instinct took over. I pushed past her sphincter muscle. She grunted. I pushed a little further, harder, then harder again. I pushed the length of my penis inside her. She was sweating and panting, rocking and moving with me. That was down and dirty sex, and I loved it."

The relationship ended when she moved to San Francisco to pursue her art and another artist. John, who now had a masters degree in science, was bereft. He also knew it was time to find a real job and a "real" relationship, with the kind of woman who wanted marriage and family. It was 1977; he was twenty-six. He wanted a real woman who looked like one of Charlie's Angels and had the charm of Annie Hall, especially in the scene where she wore a man's ribbed undershirt and smoked pot in bed with Woody Allen. He found the real job in Boston; the woman evaded him.

"I almost got married to the same woman twice. We met at a Democratic party fundraiser with Jimmy Carter in attendance, hit it off immediately, dated and lived together off and on for ten years. Once she backed away from the altar, and the other time I did. We called it quits after the second canceled wedding. Neither of us wholeheartedly wanted to end the relationship, but we were both getting a lot of pressure from family and friends to do so. Their influence on her was particularly strong then. She had a wedding dress hanging in her closet, and the unworn dress became the symbol of us—what was wrong with us, what had not materialized between us.

"I missed her a lot after we broke up. There was no one significant in my life until I met Amy five years later. I had some lovers, some celibate time, more of that than I wanted to have. Nobody clicked with me until Amy came along."

Before Amy met John, she'd had more female lovers than male. Her first sexual experience, however, had been with a boy. She was fifteen, and he was seventeen. They went to high school together in Sarasota, Florida. She fell in love with his eyes.

"He had the most beautiful big brown eyes," she says, "so brown, they were almost black. When he was happy, you could see flashes of gold in them, and when he was sad, they were truly black. He'd been with two other girls before me; and I felt a little cheated not to be getting his virginity as he was mine. He told me, 'Girls don't get boys' virginity anyway. It doesn't work that way.'

"I was lucky to escape getting pregnant because we didn't use birth control the first few times. One of the girls in my class did get pregnant and had to be whisked away somewhere for an abortion. That shook me up. I went to my mother, told her I was having sex, and asked her to take me to her doctor and get me on the pill. After crying and yelling for a few hours, she dried her eyes, calmed down, and made the appointment. It was 1971. Mary Tyler Moore was playing Mary Richards on television. Even TV sitcom single girls had implied sex lives."

They broke up a year later. But she stayed on the pill. Her mother made no comment.

"I knew I wanted to remain sexually active," she says. "I liked sex. I liked sex with boys. I didn't turn to women because men had disappointed me. In fact, I didn't realize I was attracted to women sexually until my first year of college, at Smith. My roommate seduced me. It was a long, slow and delicious seduction, lasting most of freshman year. At first I didn't know what was happening. I would see her sitting cross-legged on her bed wearing nothing but a big white shirt—I mean nothing, no panties—and wonder why I was experiencing butterflies in my groin.

"She had a charter subscription to *Ms.* magazine, and she talked a lot about sexual politics. One lovely spring evening when we were both lying on my bed sharing a joint, she told me she'd had sex with one of the graduate assistants. 'You had sex with a woman?' I asked. 'Yes,' she said, very matter-of-factly. 'So what?' My mind started spinning.

"A few days later she leaned over me to read something I was typing at my desk. I could feel her breasts inside her blouse against my back. She wasn't wearing a bra. I had trouble concentrating after she left the room.

"Sex was inevitable between us. It didn't happen in our dorm room. She'd invited me home to Dallas to spend a weekend with her family. Ostensibly I was being fixed up with her brother. We loathed each other on sight. She and I made love for the first time in her childhood bed with her parents sleeping in their bedroom on the floor below. It was different from having sex with men—all soft edges, no hard ones—but equally as thrilling. She taught me how to eat pussy, and she was a connoisseur."

Amy had love affairs with several other women over the next decade, but she always separated them in her mind from the "relationships" she had with men.

"With women, it was about sex. With men, it was about sex and love and all the mundane and domestic things that couples do together."

She has not lived with a woman after college. Nor has she ever considered herself in love with a woman. Her own gender, she says, "cannot complete me. I need the other."

For years, she didn't tell the men in her life about the women. When she accepted a marriage proposal, she "considered" telling her fiancé about her secret life, but decided against it. A conservative lawyer, he was, she felt, "not able" to deal with all her truths. He returned early from a business trip and caught her in bed with another woman.

"It was the classic scene jacked up a few emotional levels," she says. "He was furious, sickened, disgusted. My playmate couldn't get out of there fast enough. I kept telling him it had nothing to do with us, but he didn't see things that way. He felt I'd cheated on him, and the betrayal was worse because I'd cheated with a woman. 'You're sick,' he said. He asked for his ring back that night.

"I thought it was the worst discovery and breakup story until, several years later, a friend discovered her fiancé was a cross-dresser. She'd gone over to his apartment when he was supposed to be out to set up a surprise birthday party for him. He was wearing a red silk teddy, black garter belt, and spike heels. She ran screaming out of there. But she kept the ring. She had the diamond turned into a necklace."

Amy promised herself she wouldn't try to hide her bisexuality after the broken engagement. Before having sex with a new man, she told him. Some were titillated; a few were "sickened." Until she met John, none saw "bisexual" and "wife" in the same sentence.

"I wanted to get married, not for children necessarily, though I would have welcomed them if they'd come along, but for the sake of being married. I want to share my life with someone who understands and accepts me. John wants the same thing. We give each other the understanding and acceptance we've both craved."

John adds, "It doesn't matter to us if other people understand and accept or not. We have support from close friends and through a bisexual network of Amy's. What else do we need?"

Amy says she practices safe sex with her female lovers, though she believes having sex with other women is safer naturally than with men. Statistics do show that the incidence of woman-woman transmission of HIV is low. There are other STDs, however, that a woman can give a woman—for example, any STD that can be spread by contact with mucous membranes or bodily fluids. But, again, the infection rate of female-to-female transmission isn't as high as heterosexual statistics.

The Boomer Facts

- Boomers who marry late probably bring greater financial security and emotional stability to the relationship than couples who married early. Whether they marry out of pragmatism or the conviction that they have at last found true love, they don't have as much sex as the early-marrieds. They will not be amused to discover this.
- This group of Boomers frequently chose partners they wouldn't have chosen when younger. They are more able to cross racial, ethnic, religious, and socioeconomic lines in marriage now. Having lived independently for years, they are less influenced by the opinions of friends, family, or society.
- Late parenthood puts greater stress on individuals, women's bodies, and relationships than most late-marrying Boomers were led to believe. Infertility is also a problem for a great many couples. There are already indications that Generation X-ers have gotten the message. Some studies show the average marriage age declining again.
- On the plus side, couples who marry later aren't likely to romanticize the single life. Many of them are glad to be settled in a committed relationship—and are willing to make more concessions and adjustments than they might have made if they'd married sooner. In the coming years, statistics may show they were less likely to divorce and started having sex again in their old age, after the children left home.

PART 3
Sex, Again

Lucky are the Boomers of either generation who have never experienced a sexual drought. The men and women interviewed for this section have all known periods of undesired celibacy. They include:

- Men and women who married early and divorced early.
- Singles who had difficulty finding sex partners after their twenties or early thirties.
- Those who had to go through recovery for addiction to drugs or alcohol.
- Couples in "sexless" marriages who had stopped making love, often for years, because of hidden anger, buried resentments, or other emotional or psychological factors.

Unlike late bloomers, they had good sexual relationships established early in their adult lives followed by dry spells—and then, Sex Again.

7

Dating, Again

Becoming suddenly single after many years in a marriage or other committed relationship is like stepping from the warm Jacuzzi and diving into a chilly pool. Up is down, right may be wrong, and nothing works anymore the way it once did. Yet many Boomers will play the dating game over and over again throughout their adult lives as marriages and relationships end and they begin the search for new ones.

Boomer men will date longer than their fathers did. And Boomer women can expect to spend up to half their adult lives single and at least intermittently dating. Later marriages, the sustained 40 to 50 percent

SOUND BITE

From a forty-seven-year-old woman who worries about getting a date on Saturday night: "I have friends who have almost never stopped dating. They had dating relationships that ended before the dating phase was over, followed by another dating relationship, and another. Some Boomer women have never been with one man long enough for the dating to cease and the lying around together on weekends in sweat suits to begin. I married at nineteen, was happily married for twenty-five years, and now I am dating again. I didn't plan for my body to be seen by strangers at this age."

divorce rate, the 40 percent and falling remarriage rate, and longer life expectancies are all contributing factors. "As an adult, you need to reinvent dating," a forty-year-old divorced woman told me. She's right. The rule books were written for girls dating boys, not women sleeping with men. (It goes without saying: Men don't take relationship advice any better than they do road directions.)

Midlife dating—especially when one never meant to date again—is made more difficult by anxiety about aging bodies, sexual performance worries, and the interference of teen and adult children. The prospective lovers may approach each other from positions of extreme caution. The optimism and idealism about love they had when they were young has been replaced by caution, even suspicion. And, as if they needed another nagging worry, there is fear of STDs. Rather than deal with their anxieties, some people retreat into celibacy. Most do not, because their desire to be connected to another person is stronger than their fears.

The Survey Says
- 39 percent of Vietnam-generation men and 41 percent of women are divorced. Another 15 percent of men and 16 percent of women are (or have been) dating again after the breakup of a long relationship.
- 34 percent of Watergate-generation men and 37 percent of women are divorced. Another 17 percent of men and 20 percent of women are (or have been) dating again after the breakup of a long relationship.

Other Surveys Say

Studies continue to show that age is an impediment to marriage for women.

According to U.S. Census figures, 13.2 percent more women between twenty-five and twenty-nine are married than men. In the thirties, the numbers are nearly even. By age forty, 6.2 percent more men are married than women. At fifty-five, 14.9 percent more men than women are married.

Another study estimated that divorced women in their twenties have a 76 percent chance of remarriage; in their forties, a 32 percent chance, and in their fifties, less than a 12 percent chance.

What does that mean? More midlife single men than women are dating, and the men have a greater chance of getting off the merry-go-round again.

SLIP SLIDIN' AWAY

"She said a bad day's when I lie in bed and think of things that might have been."
(Recorded by Paul Simon for Warner Bros. Records)

"I was almost forty when my husband came home one day and said he wanted a divorce," Catherine says. "I didn't believe him. I thought I'd done something to upset him, but he'd get over it. I thought he was going through a midlife crisis, but he'd get over it. I thought he might be suffering from a mild depression, but he'd get over it."

He did not get over it. For four months, Robert told Catherine he wanted a divorce. She didn't, couldn't, listen. Consequently, she didn't do any of the things a lawyer would have advised her to do is she'd consulted one as soon as he had announced his intentions. Catherine's situation became commonplace among women as Boomer men reached their full mature power. An unknowable but very large numbers of trees have been felled to provide the paper to print the magazine articles and books telling women like her how to protect themselves in the clinches of divorce. As is often the case, she, who needed guidance most, did not seek it.

"When Robert moved out, I was in a fog, alternating between excruciating pain and a denial that was maddening to my family, friends, adult children. He had moved into a furnished condo, everything paid for with money I didn't know he had. Most of our funds had disappeared from our joint accounts. I thought he would come back.

"I crashed when I ran out of money. When I called him, he told me it was time for me to face reality, to meet with his lawyer, to consent to his terms. Blindly, I did that. He could have treated me worse than he did, but he certainly didn't give me what a quarter century of being his lifetime partner entitled me to, under the laws of the state of Illinois.

"There was another, much younger woman, of course. Everyone knew but me. I found out when she showed up with him at our first grandchild's christening, five weeks after the divorce was final. It was like a scene out of *The First Wives Club*, except I never got the revenge."

Three years after the divorce, Catherine is living in a small but charming Chicago apartment. She has a job she likes. And she's dating.

"Robert was my high school sweetheart," she says. "I dated two boys before I met him and none after. He told me he fell in love with me when he looked out the window of his chemistry lab and saw my girl's field hockey team practicing on the green below. 'Your hair was gleaming like burnished copper in the sun,' he said. 'Your thighs were slender and sexy. Your breasts were full and bouncy. You were exuberant. I said to my lab partner, "I'm going to meet that girl." '

"He graduated two years before me and went to the University of Illinois at Champaign-Urbana. Unlike all the other girls I knew who had older boyfriends, I held on to mine. He wrote and called and came home every other weekend. I couldn't have put it into words then, but I had power over Robert, and I held the power for a long time, until we were well into our thirties. When I graduated, we got married. I found a job in Champaign and he continued with school. We made careful plans, and they all worked out."

According to plan, Robert graduated with honors and found a good entry-level corporate job in Chicago. Catherine signed up with a temp agency to earn "extra money" and "keep busy" until she got pregnant, which she did the following year. Their son was born on the cusp of national change, in 1973, the year the military draft ended and the Supreme Court legalized abortion. In 1974, they moved into a beautiful big old house in Palatine, Illinois, a Chicago suburb. And in 1975, their daughter was born.

"The sex was great," Catherine says. "In the seventies the women's magazines began running sex advice articles in every issue. I read them and was surprised to learn that so many women apparently didn't have orgasms or weren't satisfied with their sex lives. I had orgasms. I was satisfied, very satisfied."

Catherine remembers fondly the intimacy of the cozily domestic married life. Making love midway through a head cold because she, or he, couldn't wait any longer. Eating fried egg sandwiches in the middle of the night, standing guiltily in the kitchen naked under their robes, hoping the smell of food wouldn't wake the children. Reaching across a toddler to take her husband's hand in silent grateful acknowledgment of how much he had given her. She was born for that life.

"Some of the most ordinary events stand out as deliriously happy ones," she says. "I remember coming back to our big home in Palatine after we'd been shopping with the children. They must have been three and five or thereabouts. We'd taken them to dinner at the mall, and they had been good. I don't remember exactly what we bought that night, but I recall the shopping bags dropped in the hallway when we came in. Robert herded the kids upstairs for bed preparations while I went into the living room to start a fire. I turned on the television. *The Tonight Show*, starring Johnny Carson, was on. I knew I was completely happy. It's rare to have a moment in life where you understand that you are completely happy, that you need nothing else. You have it all. I went upstairs and helped him put the children to bed, and later we made love in the living room by the lights of the fire and the television."

"We went through a bumpy time in 1986," she says. "Robert had an affair with a woman he'd met at a company conference in Houston. It had been going on a while when I found out. The clues had been there, but I'd been ignoring them. When I called him late at his hotel room, the phone would ring and ring before being picked up by the message center. He'd say he must have been sleeping so soundly he hadn't heard. He would change plans, always delaying flights until later in the day or the next morning.

"I couldn't avoid knowing when I found his personal American Express bill while looking for something in his desk at home. He'd charged flowers, jewelry, lingerie I hadn't received. There'd been dinners and lunches and hotel stays that had to be personal or he would have used the company card. I remember sitting in his chair and staring at the numbers for what seemed like hours. I was numb. I couldn't cry. He found me there when he came home. I started crying. All I could think was, 'Thank God, the kids are at camp. They don't have to know about this.' "

Robert told Catherine that he was sorry, that he didn't want to lose her. He cried, too. The lovemaking they shared that night was "the best it had been in a long time." Though trusting him again was difficult, Catherine willed herself to do so. She did not want to lose him.

"Looking back, I think the affair was a turning point. Maybe I forgave too easily. Maybe things would have been different if I had forced him, us, to deal with the underlying issues. Though he was the perfect husband outwardly, he seemed to value me less than he had before. At the time, I just wanted to get past it. I didn't want the children to know anything was wrong when they came back from camp. I wanted them to begin school secure in their home and their parents' love."

• • •

For the next nine years, Catherine thought "everything was fine." She de-lighted in her relationships with her maturing children, other family mem-bers, and friends. Many of those friends had restarted careers in midlife or gone back to college, but she was content with the life of an upper-middle-class wife. She served on committees, volunteered once a week at a home-less shelter, periodically took classes in drawing or pottery, and enjoyed leisurely afternoons at art exhibits in Chicago's many museums.

"I was a lady who lunched," she says, laughing. "Now I can see how Robert may have lost interest in me because I was happy being a 'consum-mate consumer,' as he put it in one of our more nasty pre-divorce phone exchanges. But I was happy. I thought as long as I didn't get fat, kept my hair and nails done, my look fashionable, and our home inviting, my hus-band wouldn't lose interest in me. I could not have been more wrong—or more naive."

Catherine's first "mature date" was arranged by a mutual friend, almost two years after her divorce. Everyone, including her son and daughter, thought she was ready. She wasn't, she says.

"He was awful. A little pudgy, bald, boring, bland man. I cut the evening short after dinner, came back to my apartment, and bawled my eyes out."

Her friends persisted. There were more arranged dates, invitations to parties where single men were shuttled to her side. She was luckier than many midlife single women who wish their friends would make the intro-ductions and find themselves shut out of "couples' parties."

"I had to begin dating in my own time," she says. "A few months after the first blind date, my daughter called to tell me her father and his new wife, twenty years his junior, were expecting their 'first' child. That did it for me. I spent one weekend in a last emotional orgy of grief and anger and hurt pride. Then I moved on. It was past time. The people in my life were understandably losing patience with me. Finally I lost pa-tience with myself. I looked in the mirror and said, 'Your marriage is over. If you ever want to have sex again, you'll have to go out on dates first.'"

Perhaps because she was at last "ready," she met a "datable" man within weeks. On a Saturday afternoon at an exhibit at the Chicago Art Institute, she literally backed up into the man who would become only the second lover of her life. Appropriately named Art, he was tall, slender, graying, and handsome.

"When he took my arm to help me regain my balance, I felt electricity. I look back on that as my 'spark of life' experience. He kicked the switch on my libido with the simple act of touching my arm. We walked through the exhibit together, shared coffee and cake at the café, and made a date for the following Wednesday. I was so excited, I went straight home and called my daughter."

Art and Catherine became lovers on their second date.

"I could have played games and extended the time," she says, "but why wait? I was nervous. I would have been nervous if we'd waited another week, month, or year. I wanted to make love to him. He was almost courtly in his approach. That helped me overcome my shyness about showing him my body. It's a good body for my age, but it isn't a young body. He seemed not to notice the sags and bags and was admiring of my breasts, my slender legs. I felt sexy, desirable.

"When he put his face between my thighs, I was lost in passion. All the body anxieties disappeared. He gave me an oral orgasm before he entered me. His penis was firm and steady. He had excellent control, and the love-making lasted and lasted. I was delighted with him."

Art and Catherine were lovers for six months. Abruptly, he ended the relationship. He said he wasn't ready for another serious involvement. "I was married for almost thirty years," he told her. "I don't want commitment again."

Catherine says, "I was devastated, but, unlike the way I was after Robert left, I knew I would survive. I hoped I would find a lover again."

She did. For the past year, Catherine has been seeing a man sixteen years younger than she is. They met at work. He "fell" for her immediately. She resisted him.

"I thought it was unseemly. He's only seven years older than my son. When I did agree to have dinner with him, I made it clear we were going out Dutch treat, as friends and colleagues. It wasn't a date. I had so much fun with him. I couldn't remember laughing that hard in years."

Shared lunches, dinners, shopping trips, museum outings became a regular pattern. Sometimes she allowed him to kiss her goodnight. Frequently they held hands, hugged, and embraced. She knew how much he had come to mean to her when she experienced a "heart smile" with him.

"I was waiting for him in a little bistro. I saw him come in, before he'd spotted me, and I felt a smile spreading throughout my chest, as if the edges of my heart were turning upward in happiness."

They went to a Pearl Harbor Day party, given by one of their colleagues, that night. He insisted on seeing her home. At the door of her apartment, he asked if he could come in for a few minutes. She acquiesced. Inside, he took off his jacket, then pulled his sweater over his head.

"Instinctively, I reached out to touch his chest hair. Neither Robert nor Art had much chest hair. Who knew how much I would be aroused by chest hair?"

He took her hand, led her to her bedroom, and they made love.

"I felt like someone had given me back my youth," she says. "I know it's on loan, not a permanent gift. Being with a younger man is exhilarating beyond belief. He's gets so hard so fast. His excitement level is high. He can get erect again in a shot time. I never thought I'd get to experience this again in my life.

"A young man is truly a gift from the goddess, whoever she is."

The Survey Says

• 27 percent of Vietnam-generation women and 24 percent of Watergate-generation women have dated a man at least five years younger than they are.

• 20 percent of Vietnam-generation women and 17 percent of Watergate-generation women have married a man at least five years younger than they are.

Catherine does not think her relationship will lead to marriage. Nor does she particularly want a commitment from him, but she does want one from another man, someday.

"Inevitably, the day will come when he'll want to be with someone closer to his age or younger," she says. "I'm not going through that again.

SOUND BITE

From a conversation with a fifty-year-old white woman: "It's easier to date black than date younger, but the hardest divide of all to cross is class. Unless you're going to throw them out of bed before morning, you have to have something to talk about, something in common. Otherwise, it's just sex, and the aftermath is lonely."

But I'd be lying if I said I never want to marry again. I do. Sometimes I worry that I'm wasting time now, time I should be spending looking for the man who could be my partner for the rest of my life. It's not easy to balance living for today and hoping for tomorrow."

BOOMER SEX TIPS

Sexual Healing
(Recorded by Marvin Gaye, courtesy of Columbia Records.)

A sexual drought can be demoralizing as well as frustrating. It's worse if you're celibate not by choice but because your spouse left. To survive the drought:
- Strengthen your emotional ties to family and friends. It's hard to get the occasional hugs you need from strangers.
- Consider adopting a pet. If that isn't feasible, buy several down pillows. They're expensive, but more huggable than the polyester-filled variety.
- Become more sensual. Indulge in bubble baths, silk lingerie, expensive body creams and lotions.
- Masturbate. Yes, it is true that if you don't "use it," you "lose it."
- When the sexual opportunity again presents itself, take it easy. Don't set up difficult performance standards for yourself or your new partner. Do whatever it takes to help you feel good about your body, from investing in new lighting to sexy lingerie that can be worn in bed.

SOUND BITE

"There's something my friends and I call the Condition," says actress Laura San Giacomo. "It happens when you're in your thirties, suddenly single, and there's no one to have sex with. What do you do? Meet some guy, call him up, and say, 'You wanna come over for some peach pie?' No. When you have the Condition, a lot of impulse buying goes on. Furniture and things with feathers."

Some Boomer women, thrust suddenly into the Condition in their thirties or forties, learn how to take charge of their sexuality in an assertive way. They exercise their bodies into better shape, research the most likely local sites for meeting single men within their age parameters, explore their options in creative ways. They may target younger men, or men of a different race, or men in different socioeconomic brackets. The operative word is "target."

"There are two kinds of abruptly single women at midlife," a forty-year-old, white recent divorcée said. "The ones who want to get married and the ones who want to get laid. If marriage is your goal, you approach the problem of dwindling partners differently than you do if you want to get laid. I can't bring a black steelworker home to the family, but I sure as hell can bring him home to my bed."

Both "kinds" of women can be surprisingly adept at taking charge of their lives.

EVERY MAN NEEDS A WOMAN

"Every man needs a hand to hold . . ."
(Recorded by Booker T. Jones for Stax Records)

"My friend Kelly and I got divorced at about the same time," Annette says. "She called me from Los Angeles one afternoon to tell me her husband was leaving her; and I had just returned from the session with my therapist in which I decided to leave my husband. It was spooky."

The two women celebrated their fortieth birthdays and their new divorce decrees on a trip together to Cuernavaca. They might seem to represent opposite ends of the "starting over" spectrum, but they had a lot in common. Neither wasted time mourning their loss, and both quickly took steps to get their needs met. Kelly, whose goal was to find another, richer, husband, spent afternoons poolside making lists. Annette, whose goal was "to get laid," spent evenings in the kind of clubs where something resembling disco was still being played in 1993.

"I think they were calling it 'house music,' " she says, "but it sounded like disco to me. I avoided the pool and hit the clubs for a strategic reason: I looked better in short flirty skirts and high heels than I did in a bikini. And I had the advantage of the cover of darkness. Kelly could afford to let her cellulite peek out because she wasn't interested in any of the 'pool boys' hanging around her. Her to-do lists included things like liposuction, facial peels, getting a membership in an exclusive L.A. exercise club. My to-do list was more like: buy large-size condoms and look for a guy to fill them that night."

Within a year, Kelly had found a second husband, a sixty-two-year-old Northern California industrialist, while Annette had found, in addition to several condom fillers, a more lasting solution to the problems created by the Condition: a Friend You Occasionally Fuck, or FYOF, pronounced *"fawn"* by West Coast women in the know.

"I met Lorenzo at Pike's Market in Seattle," Annette says. "We were each looking for fish for a dinner party. His parents were visiting from Spain. I was having a few friends over to celebrate a promotion."

Annette has lived in the Seattle area most of her life, but meeting Lorenzo at Pike's Market was her "first cute local meet." They fell easily into conversation. She wanted it to be a romance, and later, after they became "friends," he admitted that he did, too.

"Please," she says, laughing, "we wanted *Sleepless in Seattle*. Can you blame us? The sex was good—not great or deeply emotional, but solidly good. We made love in a healthy, almost athletic way. I remember the first orgasm I had with him. It shuddered down into my toes. I said, 'This is a man who knows how to do it, how to suck and fuck.' I did not say, 'I'm falling in love.' "

Annette's ability to separate sex from love, gauge accurately her sexual and emotional responses, and aggressively get her sexual needs met has shocked some of her friends.

"I'm a sexual pragmatist," she says. "I have a high libido. And I genuinely like men, to be with men, in bed and out. Why should I cut myself off from that part of life because true love is hard to find? I don't think I've ever had true love in my life. I probably never will."

Her early sexual profile isn't that different from the typical female Boomer in her age group. She began experimenting sexually at fourteen, lost her virginity to a steady boyfriend at sixteen, had four partners before she met her future husband at twenty-two. They lived together for a year and a half before the wedding. That they would marry was never in question.

"He was the appropriate choice," she says. "Catholic, middle class, college-educated, motivated, good-looking. The sex was good in the early days. He wasn't a creative lover, but he was solid in the meat-and-potatoes performance categories. I liked intercourse. We were healthy young animals. If I thought about it at all, I guess I thought our lovemaking would adapt over the years into something more technically diverse and emotionally varied. It didn't."

"The predictable happened. His erections grew a little less hard and frequent. I got bored. And, inevitably, I learned about the power of communication from Phil, Oprah, and Sally. I thought all I had to do to create sexual magic was get him to have a heart-to-genital talk about the state of our sex life.

"He said, 'I'm happy. I have no complaints.' End of discussion."

Dissatisfied, Annette sought help from a succession of counselors, therapists, and self-help books. She had two brief affairs, one with the husband of an acquaintance, that left her feeling "demoralized." Finally she went back into therapy with the goal of ending her marriage.

"Once I made the decision to get out and move on with my life, I quit therapy," she says. "My feelings about therapy and therapists are mixed. Like many Boomers, I embraced psychology in place of religion. In some ways, therapists helped me, mostly by helping me to identify the questions I needed to ask of myself and answer. There's a lot of bullshit in the process. I don't believe there are many good therapists. If we all had truly good friends or close ties to siblings, we wouldn't need therapists. We could hash this stuff out over tea or coffee at the kitchen table the way our mothers did. One of my therapists was arrested for stalking a coworker several months after I stopped seeing him. What does that tell you?"

Divorce "liberated" Annette sexually.

"I have a healthy sex drive, and I acknowledge that," she says. "Lorenzo was my first real relationship following the divorce. For a few months, both of us tried to turn what we had into something it wasn't: a great romance."

Lorenzo adds. "We were trying to live a movie script. I remember stopping at a flower stall to buy her a gardenia before meeting her for a drink. I was so conscious of myself carrying the flower into the restaurant where she was waiting at the bar, pinning it into her hair, brushing my lips across the nape of her neck."

The night he told her he loved her for the first time, she cried.

"At first I thought she was happy," he says. "Then I knew she wasn't. She said to me, 'I know you love me, Lorenzo, and I love you, too, but not that way, not that way.' If we hadn't cared for each other as much as we do, as friends, we probably would have parted after that. We talked a lot about our feelings and realized we did have something precious: a friendship with sex. How many people want that and can't find it?"

Someday, they both acknowledge, one or both may become involved in a serious love relationship and choose to end the sexual part of their friendship.

"If it's going to happen, I hope it happens for both of us at the same time," she says, laughing.

Both of them have had other involvements but not monogamous ones.

"The test for me with a new woman is this question: 'Would I be willing to give up sex with Annette for her?' So far, the answer has been no."

For Annette, the answer has been the same.

"There are advantages beyond the obvious to having a FYOF," she says. "For example, I can share my sexual fantasies with him without worrying I'll chase him away or threaten his ego. In a romantic relationship, you have to be more careful what you say. He is the creative lover my husband never was. I can try things with him I couldn't try with a casual or new lover, like anal sex, bondage, spanking. If one of my fantasies fails to arouse either of us in the acting out, we can laugh and open a bottle of wine and talk about something else.

"He isn't my soul mate. It's possible I will never have a soul mate. I'm not sure everyone does."

SEX TIPS FOR BOOMERS

Easy Lover
(Recorded by Phil Collins for Atlantic Records)

When to Have Sex with a New Partner:

Never mind the oft-quoted rule of three: not before the third date, third week, third month. The answer is: *when you're both ready.* People your age really should be able to figure this out for themselves.

SOUND BITE

From a conversation with a forty-nine-year-old man whose wife left him after their children were grown: "I'm glad there is Viagra. I have no confidence in my ability to start a sexual relationship without some help now. It's one thing to be in a relationship with a woman who can remember when your cock was a hard, throbbing love machine—and another to be with a woman who only knows you as Mr. Softy."

HIT THE ROAD, JACK

"Woman, oh, woman, don't you treat me so mean."
(Recorded by Ray Charles for Rhino Records)

The stereotype of the abandoned Boomer is a wife fast approaching fifty, abandoned for a younger version of herself. But as the statistics show, the Boomer who leaves now is more likely to be a woman than a man, and the man she leaves, though he may have an easier time finding a second spouse, may have more sexual problems than his female counterpart. Starting over not by choice isn't easy for either sex.

Jeremy's wife left him not for another man, not for a woman, but for herself. Completely unaware of her intentions, he was "blindsided" by her announcement that she was getting a divorce. No murmurs of discontent, as he recalls it, preceded her declaration. At thirty-nine, he thought he was living the life he was meant to live with his one true love. When she said she was leaving him because she'd never been her "true self" with him, he was more than hurt and confused. He was "demolished."

"We were each nineteen when we married," he says. "There hadn't really been anyone else for either of us. I don't know if she was technically a virgin. She'd dated. I'd dated. Virginity wasn't an issue with me. There had been no significant love relationship, only crushes.

"We went to the same high school but didn't really know each other. We traveled in different circles. She was part of a popular clique, and I was something of a studious nerd. In 1967, being a studious nerd was a sure way to limit your access to pretty girls. I was between the slide-rule generation and the computer generation. But we connected at a graduation party. With her, I felt myself becoming more than I'd been before. I believed then, and maybe still do now, that you know you've found your mate when you feel yourself metamorphosing into a better self.

"The line Jack Nicholson says to Helen Hunt in the film *As Good As It Gets* resonated with me. He says, 'You make me want to be a better man.' She did, and I was. I was immediately a better man with her, even at eighteen."

Jeremy and Janie dated steadily that summer. In the small southern Indiana town where they lived, early marriage was fairly common. They hadn't planned to marry "for years," because each had been accepted at Indiana University in Bloomington.

"We became lovers very soon after we got together," he says. "Unlike a lot of teens in those days, we were careful. We used protection. I bought condoms every time I had the chance and stashed them away in the glove compartment of my Mustang convertible. I took the Mustang to I.U. with me. Janie had to ride with her parents. My parents said good-bye to me at home. My dad was an alcoholic, and my mother worked a full-time job in a retail store and did part-time sewing for a local tailor to keep everything together. She was on my side, one hundred percent, but she never had the luxury of accompanying me or my brothers on our initial trek to college. Her life was too hard for that.

"At I.U., Janie and I settled into a happy routine, each of us busy with our class schedules and part time jobs, but still committed to being with each other. We had sex mostly in the Mustang, because we lived in dorms back in the days when girls and boys didn't live in the same building, much less the same room. To this day, I can't see a photo of a '67 Mustang without thinking about me and Janie doing it in the backseat, the front seat, on the hood, on the ground in a cornfield beside the car.

"Twenty years later she told me she was only able to have orgasms because I got immediately hard again after my first ejaculation and went again, and sometimes again. After I lose the ability to 'recover rapidly,' she said, I stopped satisfying her. She couldn't come because I didn't last long enough on one go around and could no longer do it twice or more.

"But then, in the glory days of innocence and sexual hubris, I thought I was a stud. I came and came; and she came. I knew she came because I felt her strong vaginal contractions, sometimes in time with my spasms of ejaculation."

Jeremy and Janie were solidly identified as a couple. He was satisfied with that. Twenty years later, when he learned he hadn't been satisfying her for a long time, he also learned that she'd resented the couple designation. In fact, she'd been practicing her "breakup speech" when she discovered she was pregnant. The speech went to the back of the mental file cabinet.

"Her pregnancy shocked the hell out of us. We were using condoms. In our naiveté, we thought Trojans were impenetrable. Well, they weren't. And she was pregnant.

"I will never forget how she looked when she told me she was pregnant. Her blue eyes were huge and radiant with recently shed tears. Her skin was luminous. She wore her hair long and wildly curly. I, like nearly every other college freshman in America, was taking an art appreciation course. How could I miss the Botticelli connection?

"We were sitting side by side in the Mustang parked on a country road beside a wheat field. She was more beautiful than she'd ever been, than I'd ever imagined a woman sitting beside me could be. And she said, 'I'm pregnant.' With my child. My heart swelled. My penis swelled. I took her into my arms, tenderly possessed her on the front seat, stick shift in my ribs and all, and asked her to marry me as the sweat streamed off both our faces. She said yes."

They were married on campus in the student union building with his newly acquired best friend/roommate and her sister, who'd driven down from Indianapolis, in attendance. The priest, a university chaplin, had heard everyone's confession, one by one, in his office cubicle minutes before the wedding—everyone's except Jeremy's. He wasn't Catholic.

"I think I swore to raise our children in the faith," he says. "I don't remember. It doesn't matter because she had stopped going to church before the wedding and went only sporadically afterward. The Catholic marriage was a sop to her absent parents. She thought it would make them feel better, and I think it probably did in the long run, especially after their grandson was born."

The early years of their marriage were a struggle. They were determined that neither of them would have to sacrifice a college degree. "I didn't want her to earn her P.H.T.—putting hubby through—while I got the real thing," he says. So they each worked and attended school, balancing their schedules to accommodate his and hers goals and priorities as well as the demands of child care.

"It took us six years to get our degrees," he says, "but it was worth it. We were so happy when we got those sheepskins. It meant so much to us. My mother and Janie's parents were there. It was a celebration for us in every sense of the word. We kept the graduation photo of the two of us, our son, and our parents framed and hanging in the living room of our home until we split up. She said I could have it then."

Their egalitarian approach to marriage extended to the job search. They agreed that they would move to the city where either of them had the best job offer. The other would then seek employment.

"As it turned out, I got the best offer, and we moved to Chicago," he says. "She was delighted for me. Shortly after we moved, she got a job she liked. Everything was going well for us. I thought we were having the best sex of our lives. As it turns out, I was but she wasn't. She told me she faked the majority of her orgasms in those days.

"The irony is that I recall hearing about, or possibly reading about, women who faked orgasms, and thinking what fools the men must be not to know. I couldn't imagine that a man who was a good lover, in tune with his partner, would not know. Well, I didn't know. When she told me, I was more hurt than I'd ever been about anything in my life. I felt my penis shrivel. I wanted to die."

Jeremy wanted another child, but Janie didn't. He accepted that. It was, he reasoned, his only unfulfilled desire. He had a good job, a beautiful home, a son he adored, and, most of all, his beloved wife. What more could a man want?

"More sex," he says, laughing. "Somewhere around our tenth anniversary, it occurred to me that I had as much trouble getting laid as the single guys in the office who were always complaining. I wanted more sex than Janie did, a lot more sex. I tried everything, from seducing her with romantic gifts, flowers, dinner reservations, to falling on my knees in front of her, pressing my face against her pubis, and begging. I tried to convince myself that it was natural for men to beg for sex and women to disdain their entreaties.

"In other areas of our life, we lived as equals. We had an equal marriage before the women's movement told us we must. Why didn't it occur to me that something was awry in the bedroom when she didn't want to and I did? I don't know. I wore blinders. I loved Janie so much that I couldn't ask the right questions of myself or her for fear of getting the wrong answers."

In 1988, when Jeremy and Janie were thirty-nine and their son was twenty, she told him she was getting a divorce. There was, she said, no room for negotiation. She wanted out. Now.

"It took me two years to accept that she was never coming back," he says. "For those two years, I lived a celibate life. I was angry at her for abandoning me. I thought badly of her. Surely it was her fault that our marriage had failed. Her failure to communicate. Her secret sexual repression. Her neuroses, psychoses, whatever.

"Then I lurched to the other side. It was my fault. My failure to arouse her. My inability to excite her. My obtuseness which had led me to ignore her distress signals. My neuroses and psychoses, whatever. I was afraid to be with another woman. I was afraid I would be impotent."

Sex didn't happen again for Jeremy until he'd been divorced for five years. He had a few "furtive couplings" with women who were "as sad, lonely, and distressed" as he was, followed by a brief liaison with a younger woman, a single mother to whom he was attracted "out of empathy for her plight." They remain friends.

"I was able to perform adequately with her, and that gave me some confidence," he says. "She was a generous lover. Being with her was part of my healing phase, and I think I have been part of hers."

He met Virginia after he'd lost hope that he would ever meet a woman who stirred his deepest passion again.

"She was, quite improbably, working in the neighborhood convenience store. I made small talk with her every time I shopped. One night I asked her what she was doing there. She was obviously smart, educated, and, at what appeared to be nearly my age, surely too old for a minimum-wage job. I made her angry by asking the question. She cut me off without answering. About a month later, when I'd stopped in there after midnight for some detergent because I wanted to do my laundry, she said, 'I'm here because I lost my job to downsizing, my husband to a younger man, and my only child to a motorcycle accident. This is all I can do right now. Okay?'

"I was speechless. I nodded affirmatively, paid for my detergent, forgot to pick up the change from the counter, and stumbled out the door. I knew if I asked her out, there'd be no turning back, and there wasn't."

Two weeks later he invited her to dinner. She accepted.

"We had sex on the first date," he says, "hot, steamy, stiff-cock sex. Both of us were hungry, angry, reaching out as much in pain and need as in loving desire. But the connection between us was strong enough to survive everything that had gone before in each of our lives. I felt the way I did in the beginning with Janie—powerful, potent.

"Because of the situation she was coming out of with a gay husband, she needed me to worship her pussy. I knew that. I could do it naturally. I love pussy. I love burying my face in a woman's sex and breathing her into my soul. With Virginia, I felt more strongly than I ever had.

"This may sound crazy, but I think I breathed life into her through her pussy. She grew stronger after we were together a while. We'd only been lovers for six weeks when she was able to put her résumé together and begin the search for a real job. After several months, she found one. She told me that our sexual relationship made it possible, and I do believe that is true."

When Virginia and Jeremy got married, Janie sent a congratulatory card to him.

She wrote: "I'm happy for you that you are starting over with someone new. Life is too precious to live in the past. Sometimes I am sorry I didn't appreciate what I had when I had it, but for the most part, I think the choice I made was the right one for me. And now for you. We will always have our memories. No one can take those away, not even new lovers, new spouses."

Six months later, Janie was diagnosed with colon cancer. Within the year, she was dead.

SEX TIPS FOR BOOMERS

Hot and Nasty
(Recorded by Humble Pie for A&M Records)

The New Position

Every couple, including the erotically innovative, have a favorite position, and it's usually one of two. Simply getting into that position with a new partner might evoke memories you'd rather not have. Change the position. Here are some easy ways to adapt the two basics:

Missionary. Try the more advanced version, knees to chest. Instead of her spreading her legs, she lifts knees to her chest and hooks ankles over his shoulders. Unexpected advantage: greater penetration and possible stimulation of anterior vaginal wall. A less athletic variation: the seated missionary. He sits between her widespread legs; she has her knees bent. Unexpected advantage: The limited thrusting power is offset by the direct angle of penetration.

Female superior. If she is accustomed to spreading her legs outside his, which are held close together, then she should draw her knees up until she's in a kneeling position, straddling him like a rider on a horse. (And if she straddled her former long-term partner, she should try it the other way.) Another possibility: woman astride, facing away. Unexpected advantage: The suddenly intimacy challenged can avoid looking into each other's eyes until they're ready.

The Boomer Facts

• Some have really never stopped dating, but most Boomers facing the prospect of dinner with a near stranger haven't done this in a long while. Many would rather have a root canal. But dating is the requisite initial step to forming a new sexual relationship.

- The man or woman who is left by a spouse of more than fifteen years has the greatest difficulty with dating again. The ex may have been dating secretly from within the safety of marriage. Knowing that doesn't help either.
- Boomers are more likely to have "sex friends" than their parents or grandparents were—or than their children are so far. Having such a friend helps men and women avoid the pitfalls associated with having sex with improper strangers. It can take the pressure off dating.
- Men are being left at midlife in increasing numbers. Women who have good jobs don't have to stay in a stagnant marriage for financial reasons. Those who stayed for the sake of the children don't have a reason to stay when the nest is empty.
- Becoming sexually active after a long dry spell often presents some difficulties. Performance anxieties, body-image concerns, and other issues can delay lovemaking or make it less enjoyable than it should be. A midlife lover needs to be more considerate and understanding than he or she was at twenty. Lust will prevail.

8

At Long Last, Monogamous

The maxim is: Once a cheater, always a cheater. But it's not necessarily true.

A forty-eight-year-old man who gets a faraway look in his eye when you whisper the phrase "the sixties" was explaining how his life had evolved. "We used to say that the personal was political and mean it," he said. The "we" of his past, as he remembers it, made personal choices based on politics. He, for example, married a woman who literally fell at his feet in a college protest against the Vietnam War. She'd been knocked down by a security guard. He picked her up, their eyes met. They were in bed together that night.

"I swore my undying love, we were married, I cheated on her at every opportunity," he said. "In the beginning, cheating was politically correct. By the end, I was a plain old jerk. My second wife is a Republican. The sex is good."

The moral of this story: Some of the least likely people are now married to Republicans and may even be Republicans themselves, and in these Republican marriages, the sex may be good enough to keep the partners at home in their own bed. Who of the "Make love, not war" generation would have guessed they could end up like this?

The song says that "love is lovelier the second time around." For many people, sex is sexier in the second or later marriage, especially if they don't have to contend with the demands of small children or stepchildren.

Maybe they know themselves better and have made more informed, if subconsciously so, choices. Or maybe they just got lucky. Some couples claim the sex is more "intimate" or "emotional" than it was with their previous spouses. Contrary to the popular belief that "cheaters" can't be reformed and will always stray, many men and women find they are at last capable of monogamy. Possibly their sex drives have diminished with age, and one partner is finally enough.

I interviewed many men and women who had found monogamy much the way others find God. Their reasons include:

Religious conversion. Some Boomers, like members of preceding generations, are finding religion at midlife. Organized religion is not generally considered the tent under which fornicators are free to cavort. And who follows the rules more closely than converts?

The renunciation of drugs, alcohol, "sex addiction." The twelve-step programs preach abstinence in its many forms, including abstinence from adultery. People new to the programs and not in sexual relationships are encouraged to remain celibate until they make headway into the steps. The married are counseled to be faithful.

The ultimatum. Sometimes a husband or wife who has ignored the obvious for years, decades even, suddenly says. "Enough."

The disastrous affair. Not all lovers go quietly into the afternoon once the delight is gone. Some make trouble that spills into the marriage. A cheating spouse who's survived a stalking scare, had to explain an STD, or merely had to deal with a broken heart may reach the "Enough" conclusion without an ultimatum.

Natural evolution of sexual desire and behavior. As desire becomes less urgent and, for men, performance less predictable, monogamy begins to sound like a good idea.

New mate. A new marriage may be the impetus for change. This marriage may be more intimate, creating less need for an affair, and more guilt about having one. The commitment may be deeper in the later marriage for a variety of reasons, including the greater emotional depth of the partners.

The Survey Says
- 74 percent of Vietnam-generation men and 79 percent of women who were not monogamous in the past and are now in a second (or a later) marriage say they are (and plan to remain) monogamous.

- 66 percent of Watergate-generation men and 53 percent of women who were not monogamous in the past and are now in a second (or a later) marriage say they are (and plan to remain) monogamous.

SOUND BITE

From a conversation with a forty-three-year-old man: "I wasn't faithful to my first wife. It cost me my marriage. I promised myself I wouldn't marry again until I was ready to become a one-woman man. I've been with my second wife five years and haven't cheated on her. I know she wouldn't tolerate it, and I don't want to lose her."

COCAINE

"If you got bad news, you wanna' kick the blues . . . cocaine."
(Recorded by Eric Clapton for Polygram Records)

"I was a wild man in the seventies," Ted says. "Last week I had lunch with a woman I'd known personally and professionally back in the those days. We'd worked together then, and the irony is we're working together now. But times have changed. I was her boss at one of Manhattan's hottest advertising agencies—two marriages, a cocaine problem, and a financial collapse or two ago. Now she has a top editorial job with a major publisher, and I am a one-man ad shop with an office in the boroughs.

"She's still an attractive woman. Reminding me of how I'd pursued her, she said, 'You were a randy fellow in those days.' I conceded I had been, but teased her about being an uptight little girl from the Midwest. 'Try me now,' she said. I laughed and passed off the comment as a joke. If she was serious, I'm flattered, but at forty-seven and happily married—for the third and final time—I stray for no woman. The road to where I am was a long, twisted, and arduous one."

Ted had more than one motive for becoming monogamous. He'd overcome an addiction at the same time he was shifting into a different psychosexual mode. And he was in a new relationship. True, some people might have continued to behave in the familiar way. Habit has a power all its own. Buoyed by the stronger power of these external forces, he chose monogamy, overthrowing the habit of an adult lifetime.

The only son of "East Coast Jewish-intellectual" parents, Ted went to Brown University, where he majored in philosophy, before dropping out in his sophomore year, in 1971. He turned twenty the following week. Living back home, in his parents' Upper West Side apartment, he failed to find a job paying better than minimum wage. They suggested he enroll in New York University, his father's alma mater.

"The suggestion was not made lightly," he says. "I switched my major to English literature and pulled out my book bag. I think my mother suspected I was boffing the super's daughter, a Puerto Rican beauty, while they were at work—which I was. Conchita has a special place in my erotic memory. She wasn't my first—more like the tenth or twelfth—but she was the most sensual woman I'd been with up to that point in my life.

"I have wonderful memories of lazy afternoons making love to her in my childhood room. It was like being Balthazar in *The Beastly Beatitudes of Balthazar B.*, and having your fantasy come true, sex with the nanny. She was actually a year younger than I was, but more experienced. I can still see her standing in my bedroom, dressed down to her panties and bra, slowly unhooking the bra while looking me in the eye. The fabric would fall away, those luscious brown globes would spring forth, and I had an erection I could have hammered nails with. She would cup her breasts in her hands and offer them to me. And her pussy hair was so thick and curly. What hair! I learned to twirl it with my tongue. I was forever finding a piece of it stuck between my teeth after she had dressed and gone.

"I have less wonderful memories of going with her to a shabby doctor's office in Queens where she had an abortion. She said it was my child. I took the money out of my savings account and paid. I convinced myself it was probably some other guy's child. Only in recent years have I wondered if it was mine, if it was a son or a daughter, what it would have been like now.

"After the abortion, I didn't see her very often. Things felt different for me. I got involved with Laurie, a nice Jewish girl, smart and pretty, exactly the girl my mother wanted me to marry. We had sex on the first date in her room at her parents' Upper West Side apartment. It was the Christmas holiday season, and her parents were gone. They always got out of town for the holidays, she said, because they felt 'left out.' Why any Jew would ever feel left out in Manhattan, on the Upper West Side, I can't imagine.

"She was tentative at first, a little nervous, not a virgin, but not much short of one. I was the older man taking charge of her erotic education—thanks to my little Puerto Rican honey. I felt guilty about Conchita and the abortion the first few times I was with Laurie. Between her shyness and my guilt, we didn't have the best sex. I could tell the potential was there.

She was eager to learn how to suck cock. What man wouldn't think that was a good sign?

"Then Laurie got pregnant. I knew I was smack dab in the middle of the one life situation I couldn't get out of. When she called me to say something awful had happened, I knew. She hadn't confided about her period being late, but in the back of my mind I'd been doing the math. Hadn't I all too recently been down this path? Walking to the Szechuan Palace to meet her, I knew. She would have the baby. We would marry. My life would be irrevocably changed. It was a beautiful October day, clear and crisp, and I gulped the air into my lungs, my last gasps of freedom. I was panting by the time I got there. I could see the future in my mind's eye. And that's pretty much what happened. I didn't need the fortune from the fortune cookie to predict it. My dad pulled some strings and got me a job at an ad agency run by a friend of his. I wasn't quite twenty-one, had more than two years of college to go, but none of that mattered. Laurie was carrying their grandchild. My parents agreed to pay my tuition so I could continue going to school—nights, weekends, whatever I could manage. They believe strongly in education.

"The wedding was hers from the start, hers and her mother's and my mother's. I remember standing under the wedding canopy wearing my yarmulke and feeling like the biggest fraud on the planet. A friend of mine had just been to his brother's wedding on a farm in Connecticut. I had dutifully looked at the pictures. Suddenly, as my bride turned her hopeful face up to me, I couldn't see anything but the hippie bride in her long shapeless beige dress, the circle of flowers in her hair, a goat by her side. I do not know why, but the hippie wedding images followed me all day. When I got to the part of the day where the groom is at last alone with the bride in the hotel room, I could still see the hippie girl and her goat.

"Her parents gave us a nice little starter home in Scarsdale for a wedding gift. Why Scarsdale? I don't know. We had the best sex of our relationship in those early months of marriage. Laurie was happy to be married, thrilled with the house. And she took to pregnancy like an earth mother. She glowed. Her breasts were picture perfect, and so was her hair. The only weight she gained was right in the middle of her belly. She looked like this adorable tiny girl carrying a basketball under her clothes.

"My parents adored her. I adored her. We fucked in every conceivable way possible. In the final weeks, I jerked off between her breasts every day. She loved it. I remember the morning she woke up flushed and moaning. She'd had her first ever sleep orgasm. Eight and a half months pregnant and she was coming in her sleep. I couldn't wait for the basketball to be taken away from the space between us.

"I wasn't prepared for fatherhood. Aaron was a colicky baby. He cried when I held him. Laurie was immersed in her role as his mother. I was jealous of the baby, and being jealous of a baby made me feel like a jerk. Her breasts belonged to him now. They were frequently engaged and sometimes also engorged and painful. I wanted her to give him the bottle, but she persisted in breast-feeding even when her nipples became red and angry and ugly.

"I threw myself into work. To everyone's surprise, including my own, I had a real talent for advertising. I spearheaded the creatives on a small account that turned into a big one, thanks to the successful advertising campaign. In 1974, I got a bonus that was twice my previous year's salary. I was on my way up. My ego swelled and took my penis with it.

"I had the little wife in Scarsdale, the little kid who cried when I picked him up, and the high life in Manhattan. The money I was making justified the long hours I was spending away from home. Laurie was having such a good time charging on her new plastic, she didn't miss me. We never recovered sexually from childbirth.

"But I was part of the swinging seventies in the big city. I fucked secretaries, clients, ad reps, women I met at Studio 54. A big-name woman writer—before she was famous and was still freelancing ad copy—once bounced on my lap and told me her anal sex fantasies before sucking my cock under my desk. I was hitting on women, but women were also hitting on me. In those days a woman had two Bloody Marys and said, 'When do you want to fuck me?' I was king of the world—until I blew a big account, got fired, and lost my wife, just like that, one, two, three.

"By then we were living in a bigger house in Scarsdale, having traded up from the wedding gift starter home. I'd been out all day and well into the night, ostensibly job hunting, but really drinking. My key didn't turn the lock. I called her from a pay phone, and she said I should only talk to her through her lawyer from then on."

Ted's first divorce was far from amicable. From the perspective of twenty years after, he can understand her position. At the time, he didn't.

"After the agreement had been signed, I lucked into another advertising job, a better one than I'd had. That encouraged me to keep doing what I had done before. I was a sex machine. To the mix of sex and alcohol, I added drugs. Under the influence, I married again. The two of us crashed together in 1982. She went into rehab before I recognized I had a problem. It would take another firing, another divorce, a bankruptcy before I caught on.

"I got sober. I got off drugs. I discovered meditation and meditated myself into a state of celibacy. In that state, I realized I hadn't had good sex since the early days of my marriage with my pregnant wife. Everything after that was 'just sex.'

"I met the woman who would become my third wife in this state of mental, emotional, and physical purity. At the time, I was studying Buddhism, too. In the seventies and the eighties when sex and then sex and coke were the driving forces in my life, I laughed at people who talked about spirituality or spiritual values.

"With Chloe, I knew I was going to make a strong spiritual as well as sexual connection from the start. When we met I'd just started up my own agency and was doing freelance copywriting on the side. I'd moved to a small community in the Peekskill mountains because I knew I couldn't sustain a spiritual life in Manhattan. Some people can, but I'm not one of them. Chloe had also recently moved to the area from Manhattan. I might as well say it: We met at a Narcotics Anonymous meeting.

"Because of our histories, we moved slowly. I'd had sex with the other women in my life almost immediately. Chloe and I dated for two months before we made love. We talked about it first. When we came together, we did so in spirit as well as body. It was an intensely emotional experience."

Though Ted doesn't acknowledge it, his new ability to experience "intensely emotional" sex, a kind of lovemaking other men describe as "more intimate," is surely due in part to aging, both physiologically and psychologically. Most people, regardless of age, probably never get a good sense of perspective on their own lives. They see themselves as unique and fail to recognize how they fit into patterns of behavior shared with others. The Boomers are, if anything, more inclined to romanticize their individuality.

Ted's "very personal journey" led him to a crowded place.

SEX TIPS FOR BOOMERS

Baby, I Need Your Loving
(Recorded by the Four Tops for Motown Records)

Recovery Sex
Making love sober for the first time is an experience one man compared to that of the near-deaf suddenly getting a hearing aide that works. His senses were under assault. Some suggestions for making the adjustment:

- *Accept anxiety as a natural state.* It won't last forever, but it won't go away with initial arousal either.
- *Suspend performance standards.* You are not going to be the greatest lover on the planet the first time you make love without an alcohol buzz in a decade. Decide what's important—probably satisfying her for a man and arousing him for a woman. Ask your partner for help in meeting your minimal erotic goals. Review the directions for oral sex. Anyone can learn to perform fellatio and cunnilingus well.
- *Develop new romantic rituals to replace the seductive glass(es) of wine.* Try slow dancing in a candlelit room.
- *Expect to be very emotional during and after lovemaking.* You need not be ashamed of these feelings, but don't let them overwhelm you. Accustomed to feeling the emotions you've dulled with alcohol or drugs, your partner may not share your euphoria.

(YOU MAKE ME FEEL LIKE) A NATURAL WOMAN

"You're the key to my peace of mind . . ."
  (Recorded by Aretha Franklin, for Motown Records)

"The sex in my second marriage is better than the sex in my first," Jackie says. "For one thing, there's more of it. My first husband lost interest in sex, at least with me, shortly after I learned how to have an orgasm. I was a slow learner, or the marriage wouldn't have lasted as long as it did."

Like many older Boomer women, Jackie didn't become confident enough about her sexuality to invoke her right to pleasure until well after marriage. She was nineteen and was three years younger than her first husband when they married, in 1968. Both were the youngest children in close-knit families of three children. Their fathers had gone to high school together in a small Iowa town, the same high school where Jackie and her husband met in her freshman, his senior, year. "The next thing to a virgin," she'd had several boyfriends in high school, but none who "rounded the bases." She lost her virginity midway through senior year. Though she was "going steady" with her future husband at the time, he was not the one.

"I'd gone with my cousin to visit my brother at the University of Iowa," she says. "He was enrolled in the creative writing program, and my cousin and I, who had literary pretensions of our own, were eager to breathe in the rarefied air—and perhaps flirt with a few potential famous writers. I met X while I was standing outside the hall where relatives and other guests were put up, our suitcases at my feet. My cousin was off parking the car.

"X, who did go on to become a writer of some significance, looked the part of the suffering artist, circa '68. His hair was long and scruffy, his clothes didn't work together. Most of all, his attitude was nothing like that of the boys back home. They had big puppy eyes, full of longing, hope, and eagerness to love. He had this sardonic look in his eyes.

" 'One of the little lost girls who haunt the fringes of our hallowed halls?' he asked. I'll never forget that opening line. I thought it was so deep. My blushing, gape-mouthed response must have given him all the information he needed about me. That night, after we got rid of my brother and cousin, we did it. He smuggled me into his dorm room, a not too difficult feat since his roommate was away for the weekend. And who would have ratted him out? The students thought they were Iowa's last hope at having any kind of intellectual identity.

"He hadn't brushed his teeth or sprayed his mouth with Binaca. I was used to boys who surreptitiously freshened their breath before kissing me. I was almost pre-engaged to a boy like that. When X kissed me, he shoved his tongue into my mouth, and he tasted like garlic and onions, maybe pepperoni, too—leftover pizza. I wasn't really turned on by his kissing or the way he touched me. Looking back, I know he didn't know what he was doing. Then, it seemed rough, abrupt.

"If I'd been on a date with X, I would have brushed him off at the door. I was in his dorm room. I'd wanted to be in his dorm room because I had this fantasy of him as a future famous writer who would write innumerable versions of the story of our night together. He would never get over me, of course.

"So we did it. He was surprised and embarrassed when I bled. 'We must have started your period,' he said, in a swaggering way to indicate he wasn't as uncomfortable at the thought of menstruation as he appeared. 'No,' I said, 'I was a virgin.' I wish I hadn't said it, but I did. He looked at me in the oddest way. I think he wondered why I had given myself away so lightly to an undeserving stranger. For the next two months I worried that I might be pregnant.

"I turned up the heat on my relationship with my steady, Joe. I'd read that it was possible to get pregnant from fooling around, no penetration, if several drops of pre-ejaculate made their way up the vaginal path. I told him I wanted to hold his penis, rub it against me, and jerk him off with my hand. He was overjoyed. I told him I liked it so much I wanted to do it again and again.

"By the time I got my period, I had him so used to rubbing against me and coming in my hand, there was no going back. He proposed, and getting married sounded like a better idea than anything else that had been suggested. We got married the summer after I graduated, the summer before his senior year in college. Our first year of married life was spent on the University of Kansas campus. I took some classes and worked full time in the bursar's office.

"The original plan had been for me to get pregnant when he graduated and got a job, but I liked school. I wanted to continue. That created some problems for us. Fortunately for me, he got a job in Philadelphia, and I was able to work and go to school at Temple University. He agreed to delay pregnancy for a year or two, to give me time to 'get some more classes.' Finishing a degree wasn't something he imagined for his wife. 'Anyway,' he told me, 'it's probably better for me to have a career solidly established before becoming a father.' "

It was 1970, and the women's magazines had discovered sex. Jackie bought a copy of *Cosmopolitan* to read at her part-time job as a receptionist in a law office in Center City. An article on orgasms caught her attention. She began to read and, to her surprise, discovered she'd never had an orgasm.

"I never knew 'orgasm' existed. I didn't know the word. I was in college, married to a college graduate. I'd had my first sexual experience with a man whose short stories were now showing up in important places. And I discovered 'orgasm' in the pages of *Cosmopolitan*.

"My emotions were all over the map. I was excited, angry, confused. I felt betrayed by my husband, my mother, who might have told me about this, my girlfriends, everyone. Who had known and hadn't told me? Now I know that men were supposed to ask, 'Did you come, dear?' Nobody had ever asked me. My husband routinely asked, 'Are you hot?' before penetrating me. I knew I was supposed to moan and move around a lot; and I had been doing that. I'd heard the word 'climax' and dimly assumed it meant feeling at the zenith of a sexual-emotional connection. I didn't know it was something you could measure, something that was definable as a series of contractions.

"One of the lawyers walked through the office, saw the stricken look on my face, and asked me what was wrong. I burst into tears. He got one of the secretaries to cover my desk, took me into the conference room, and said, 'Tell me what's wrong.' I told.

" 'Oh, you poor baby,' he said, stroking my hair. Before I knew what

147 • STILL *Sexy*

was happening, he was kissing me, slowly, tenderly kissing me, sucking and nibbling at my lips. It was delightful. He put his hand on my breast, and my nipple hardened. 'I want to give you an orgasm,' he whispered in my ear. I should have stopped him, I suppose, but I didn't. I wanted that orgasm if he could give it to me.

"As it turned out, he could, without even taking my panties off. He kissed me, licked and sucked my breasts, and nuzzled my neck, then kissed me again, the whole time massaging my clitoris—another word I had just read—with his thumb. I came. Oh, God, did I come. It was astonishing. I felt my whole life had changed. Certainly my outlook on my marriage had."

Jackie went home that night and told her husband she'd read a magazine article about sex. He raised his eyebrows. "About sex?" he asked. "What kind of magazines are you reading?" She showed him the cover, opening the magazine to the right page, and began to read. Before she was finished, he took it out of her hands and said, "That's enough, Jackie. If I'd wanted to hear my wife talk like that, wouldn't I have married a different kind of woman altogether?"

Her marriage, she thought, was all but over. She'd discovered sex, and she liked it. Her husband, on the other hand, liked the status quo. Divorce, however, wasn't in the cards yet. Jackie was pregnant. Her doctor, as a precaution typical in those times, had insisted she stop taking birth control pills for six months after having been on them for two years. She and Joe had been relying on a diaphragm for contraception. She was pregnant.

"Joe pretended the 'orgasm talk' had never happened," she says, "in his delight at learning of my pregnancy."

Jackie had her first extramarital affair when she was six months pregnant. Her lover was a Greek soccer player who was studying at Temple on a one-year student visa. He taught her the joys of oral sex, both giving and receiving. She had orgasms. Her dissatisfaction with her marriage increased.

"Sex with Joe was always the same," she says. "After minimal foreplay, which never involved my clitoris, he mounted me, took a brief ride, and ejaculated. He didn't sweat. He didn't make noise. My Greek lover, with whom I never experienced penetration, sweated, moaned, writhed, cried out. He, like the lawyer before him, was an erotic revelation.

"How could I stay in this marriage with this man after I'd seen what sex could be like with other men?"

Jackie filed for divorce from Joe when their son was two years old. After Joe, there was a series of men, discreet liaisons fitted into the available time of a working mother. She had a rule: No men stayed over when her son was home. Since Joe had him two weekends a month and occasional weeknights, she could live comfortably within the rule. Not until her son was in high school did she meet a man with whom she was ready to have a "serious" relationship.

"Dick and I were a perfect match," she says. "He had joint custody of his kids and therefore understood the restrictions of my life. We shared a lot of common interests. I was working in public television and not making a lot of money; he was a public defender and not making a lot of money. Our politics, our goals, everything meshed. But the sex never rose above the ordinary.

"It took me a long time to figure out that, with Dick, I had found someone much like my first husband sexually. His libido wasn't high. His political activism was like my first husband's political conservatism in an important way. Both found excessive pleasure irrelevant. And the female orgasm was excessive pleasure. Dick tried harder in bed than Joe had, but he did not make love with joyous abandon. I knew how to make sure I had an orgasm by then. I touched myself freely during intercourse. And I asked for what I needed.

"But I cheated on Dick, numerous times. The friendship we had was worth preserving. The comfortable easy relationship made it possible for me to deal with the trauma of raising a teenager and other things. The sex was not enough. I thought sex with one man never would be enough for me."

Dick threw a big party for her on her fortieth birthday. Her son, now twenty, came home from college. Several old friends traveled considerable distances to be with her. She remembers looking around at the assembled group and thinking, "How lucky I am. Why isn't this enough? Why do I think I have to have great sex and an emotional connection too?"

Five months later she met Brad. He was a reporter for a Philadelphia paper assigned to interview her for an article about public television. She had allowed forty-five minutes in her schedule for the interview. They spent five hours together, including a long lunch, which she put on her expense account.

"Once Brad and I started talking, we really never stopped," she says.

It was love at first sight. Or she would have acknowledged that it was love at first sight if he hadn't been twenty-five.

"Twenty-five," she says. "Can you imagine? I was careening toward forty-one on the downhill slalom, and he was a dewy-cheeked twenty-five. He had just turned twenty-five. I remember thinking how significant that was. He was only just twenty-five, not almost twenty-six—like ten or eleven months would have made a difference."

He'd had two "serious" relationships. She'd lost track of her body count. He was barely five years older than her son. She was about five years younger than his mother. The numbers alone made her crazy. After his article had appeared, he called to invite her out to dinner.

"Not as a date," she blurted out.

"Yes, as a date," he said.

"I'm a lot older than you," she said.

"I guessed that when I saw your résumé," he countered.

She said, "Okay."

They went to bed together on the third date, a milestone a younger colleague told her was once deemed the appropriate time for initiating sexual contact. That was news to her. She was reminded of the 1970 article in *Cosmopolitan,* the one about orgasms.

"I am not a cutting-edge woman," she laughs. "What is news to me is commonplace to everyone else. I might have decided never to see him again because I felt silly about having sex on the third date—if it hadn't been the best sex of my life.

"What he lacked in expertise, he more than made up for in passion. But more than passion, he had something I'd lost a long time ago, a quality of erotic innocence and hopefulness. He believed in love, in truly making love. When he touched me, I felt younger than springtime. I could almost hear Frank Sinatra crooning it in my ear.

"Of course, his stiff young cock didn't hurt anything, either."

A month after they'd become lovers, she gave Brad the key to her apartment to feed the cat while she was away at a professional conference. When she returned, he'd moved in. "I took a chance," he told her. She was a little angry, but she didn't ask him to leave.

"I did call the newspaper the next day to be sure he still had a job," she says. "I couldn't one hundred percent believe it was just me he wanted until I did, and he hadn't been fired. It didn't occur to me that living with him would make it harder to cheat on him. That would have been my first thought if he'd been any of the men I'd previously known."

They settled into a monogamous routine together. The lovemaking "got better and better." He proved adept at performing cunnilingus. Playful as well as passionate, he taught her the joys of "playful sex," painting each other's bodies with edible colors, making love in the hot tub, standing up in the shower, in the parking garage at the mall. When he mentioned marriage, she changed the subject. Then the unexpected occurred. She discovered she was pregnant at age forty-two. Her twenty-six-year-old lover was delighted.

"He wanted the baby, really wanted marriage. I didn't know what to do. Hormones were boiling my brain. On the one hand, I wanted to marry Brad, have the baby, and believe in happily ever after. On the other hand, I was terrified. Would the baby be okay? Would I survive childbirth? Would I ever be able to afford liposuction and a face-lift and could I hold on to my husband in another few years without them?

"I told him I couldn't think about marriage until my pregnancy had progressed far enough for amniocentesis. If the baby was okay, I was going to have it—and maybe I'd marry him. He agreed to wait."

"But," Brad says, "I made it clear I wanted to marry her, no matter what, baby or no baby. I knew the first day I spent with Jackie that she was the love of my life. The age difference doesn't mean anything to me. Sometimes I am aware of it, most of the time I'm not. When I notice the difference in our ages, it's because she's said something that sounds very sixties to me. I might chuckle inside."

In Jackie's eyes, the age difference loomed bigger as her belly grew. When tests showed she was carrying a healthy boy, she wept for an hour, in relief, joy, and fear. Brad had the first sonogram framed and put it on his desk at work.

"He came home one day when I was in my seventh month, told me he'd been promoted to an editorial position, and wanted to get married that weekend. I said, 'Okay.' He said he had an errand to run, returned an hour later with a diamond ring and a dozen roses. Then he got down on one knee. I burst into tears and sobbed my acceptance. We were married that weekend with my son and his girlfriend, Brad's parents and brother, and a few friends in attendance."

They continued to make love up until a few days before Jackie delivered their seven-pound son. Fortunately, she had few problems during pregnancy, delivery, or afterward. Within six weeks, she was back into her pre-pregnancy wardrobe.

"Brad and I had intercourse as soon as the doctor said it was okay. We were so horny for each other, I don't think we could have waited another day. I never lost desire for him. Less than a week after I delivered, we were petting like teenagers. We'd done everything short of penetration when the waiting period was over. This was a big shock to me. I'd expected to be too tired, too stressed, too caught up in the role of new mother, especially at my age, to want sex."

Jackie has found being a mother easier the second time around. With her second son, she has worried less and had more help from his father. How has the marriage worked out?

"Very well," she says and he agrees. "There have been times, especially early in our marriage, when I felt impatient with him because he hadn't as much experience in living as I'd had. I thought I was right or knew the right way to do things. Often he surprised me. His way was better. There is a difference in our levels of maturity, less noticeable now than then. It's not as important as I feared it might be. The benefits of the age difference outweigh any negative aspects. I love his energy. Men seem to lose their energy earlier than women do, so we are well matched. I love his enthusiasm for life, for lovemaking, for our family life together.

"Brad and my older son are good friends. Not long ago he told Brad that he thought it was better for the wife to be significantly older than for the husband to be. Joe married a much younger woman, and my son says that doesn't appear to work nearly as well as our marriage does. I'm sorry for Joe, but not surprised. He was too old for me."

Recently Jackie's younger son turned seven and her first grandchild, a girl, was born.

"When I found out I was going to be a grandmother, I considered a face-lift," she says. "I still might do it, but I've gotten over the shock of dealing with my age. I'm just delighted with the baby."

Jackie has not been with another man since she met Brad. That, she says, is the "most significant thing I can say about our relationship."

How rare is Jackie's happiness?

According to U.S. Census Bureau figures, among brides ages thirty-five to forty-four, 40 percent are older than their grooms. Nearly a quarter of women ages thirty-five to forty-nine marry men who are at least five years younger than they are. There is no evidence to date indicating these marriages are any less happy or any more likely to end in divorce than more conventional unions.

Why is marrying down the age scale more common among Boomers than in previous generations? In part, it was a consequence of the shuffling of life markers. Women no longer expected to marry early, to a man a few years older, and begin having children within a few years of marriage. Changing expectations and expanding opportunities put women and men of different ages in the same professional and social circles. Fraternizing was bound to happen.

BOOMER SEX TIPS

If I Could Turn Back Time
(Recorded by Cher for MCA Records)

How to Make Love Like a Younger Woman
1. Rearrange the bedroom so that the bed is not reflected in mirrors. (If your ex-husband put mirrors on the ceiling in the seventies and you never got around to removing them, do it now.)
2. Invest in luscious lingerie, especially camisoles and teddies that can be left on during lovemaking.
3. Install soft lightbulbs in nightstand lamps.
4. Be adventurous. Older women are actually more sexually adventurous than younger ones are, but you'll feel younger by acting, in this case, "older."
5 Become adept at fellatio. Like the little black dress, the expertly performed blow job can take you anywhere you want to go.

YOU'VE REALLY GOT A HOLD ON ME

"I love you madly . . . I can't quit now."
(Recorded by the Miracles for Motown Records)

"I haven't had an affair in three years," Molly says. "And I don't plan on having another."

Molly, forty-two, has been married for twenty years to John, also forty-two. Until her husband found out, she'd subscribed to monogamy as casually as if it were a magazine offered at a discount. Maybe she'd read this month's issue and maybe not. Maybe she'd "honor" her marriage vows, and then again maybe not. Discovery was the catalyst for changing her behavior.

They met on the campus of the University of California at Berkeley in 1974, when both were freshmen, and married in 1978, in a lavish Episcopal wedding. Her parents gave them a small house in La Jolla, several blocks from the rocky "beach." Molly, a slender blonde from a modestly wealthy East Coast family, and John, tall, powerfully built, and a descendant of "poor coal miners" in West Virginia, were an unlikely match. Yet the attraction was instant and mutual.

"I went to Berkeley to irritate, hopefully outrage, my parents," she says. "But when I got there, I felt a little lost. I looked like a preppy. The truth is, I liked preppy clothes. The Hillary headband, the short pleated skirts, white blouses with Peter Pan collars—I liked that look. It wasn't the 'me' inside, which may be why I felt so comfortable wearing it. My clothes were my protective camouflage.

"I met John at a poetry reading. He didn't look like he fit in either, though he was trying harder than I was. A girl with a daisy behind her ear was flirting with him. I met his eyes over the top of her curly head. We smiled at each other. After the reading, we met, not by accident, at the coffee and tea table. We left together, headed for a campus hangout, and spent the rest of the day exchanging life stories over very cheap and bad wine. The next morning, I woke up with a killer headache and the realization that I had met the man I would marry.

"We had sex before we 'dated,' long before. Two days after we met, we had sex. John called and asked me if I'd like to meet him for coffee again. Sitting across from him in a booth, I took off my shoe and put my foot in his lap—more accurately, into his crotch. I felt him swell inside his pants. 'Is that what you want?' he asked me. It was.

"He was a good lover from the start. I liked the way the top of his head seemed to be blowing off when he came. He got so hot. I felt like I had tremendous power over him. And he was so eager to please me. I could tell he knew most of what he knew about lovemaking from reading books, but I liked that. It showed me how hard he was willing to try, how much he wanted to do everything right.

"We didn't exactly date the first year we knew each other because John, who was on a work scholarship plan, didn't have enough money to date. The hard part was finding places to make love. We did it outdoors, in the balcony of a movie theater, in my dorm room or his. Finally I talked my parents into buying me a car, a little blue Dodge. Then we had a regular place to do it. Nobody bothered us. We parked at the edge of a student lot and fucked like bunnies, steaming the windows. Occasionally someone would thump the car in walking past, but that was it.

"I wasn't a virgin when I met John. I never told him that. He didn't ask, so I let him make whatever assumptions he felt comfortable making. I lost my virginity when I was fourteen. By the time I graduated from high school, I'd had half a dozen partners. I was smart about birth control. I got my older sister to take me to her gynecologist, who put me on the Pill before I was fifteen. And I was lucky in orgasms. They came easily to me. I began masturbating when I was eleven or twelve and having orgasms shortly thereafter. I think I was sexually precocious. Having older sisters probably made a difference. I read their books and magazines, eavesdropped on their conversations, peeked through the bathroom keyhole and caught them playing with themselves.

"John told me he loved me after the first time we made love. I didn't tell him I loved him back for months later, and when I did, he assumed it meant the same thing as it meant to him. It didn't. I did not mean to be faithful to him—not then, maybe not ever."

Molly changed her preppy clothes for a wardrobe deemed more stylish in sunny California. She didn't change her habits. A disarmingly warm and outgoing person, she is also "secretive and controlling." Outward appearances, whether clothing or actions, may be deliberately at odds with inner thoughts and feelings.

"I let John think there was never anyone else," she says, "because I wanted him to be faithful to me. I knew he probably would be. John was devoted to me from the beginning. He's that kind of man. Some men are born to make a commitment.

"I had sex with other guys in college. When we decided to get married, I almost told him the truth, but lost my courage. For a short time, I meant to be faithful. We'd been married less than a year when I broke that vow. I didn't have affairs because John wasn't good in bed. He was. And he likes sex as much as I do. I could blame it on his job, saying he was away a lot on his rapid climb up the old corporate ladder, but that wouldn't be true. He *was* away a lot, and he *did* become successful quickly. But I didn't have affairs to fill the empty hours. I could have done that shopping.

"I had affairs for me, to keep a part of myself private. Yes, I enjoyed the sex, but I needed more than enjoyment. It was pleasure and it was personal, for me—separate from John and me, our marriage. I could never make up my mind to stop using birth control and get pregnant, which disappointed John, because I needed birth control. Without it, there was always the chance I'd get pregnant with someone other than my husband's baby."

The death of Molly's mother from cancer four years ago changed her life.

"I was really scared. My mother's dying was painful, for her, and for me and my father and brother to watch. I learned a lot about my family while we were gathered around her bedside. My father, as I'd suspected but not articulated, had been unfaithful to her for most of their marriage, until age dulled his enthusiasm for sex. She had not really forgiven him. How much of their secret drama inspired my own behavior?

"I began questioning myself and the way I lived my life for the first time. I questioned my integrity. Did I have any? Did I owe my husband the truth? Did he suspect anyway? Would telling him be a courageous act or a cowardly one designed to assuage my conscience?"

Molly put the questions aside, promising herself to face them after her mother died. She went home to La Jolla, to the much bigger house on a cliff overlooking the ocean they now lived in, and for the first time in her married life, she began to think seriously about having children. Some weeks after the funeral, she came home one day to find John sitting alone in a darkened living room, tears running down his face. She knew something terrible had happened. Another death in the family?

"He didn't look at me, but just said 'I know' in a low, scary voice. 'Know what?' I asked, sitting beside him, trying to take his hand, which he balled into a fist. 'I know about your affair,' he said. It felt like my heart dropped out of my body. My stomach turned over. I was queasy. I began to sweat. He knew about which affair?"

While searching through Molly's desk in the den for some documents their tax preparer had requested, John had inadvertently found a card from a lover she'd inexplicably saved.

"He hadn't meant anything to me," she says. "I was with him three, maybe four times tops. The card was explicit. I don't know why I saved it. I never saved things like that. Probably it got caught up in some papers and tossed into the desk. I'm not very organized or neat. My mother always said I'd pay for my sloppiness by losing something important, and she was almost right. I almost lost John."

It was 1995. Molly had just turned thirty nine. In fear of being left by her angry husband, Molly grasped for the traditional straw: pregnancy.

"I told him I'd gone off birth control and was trying to get pregnant," she says. "He was stunned. I don't know why it didn't occur to him to doubt me, but he didn't. He said he wouldn't make any decisions about our marriage until we saw if I was pregnant. Well, like some demented soap opera star, I tossed my pills into the toilet and plotted ways of getting him into my bed before my period started.

He moved into the guest room and resisted her advances. At the end of her cycle, however, she didn't have a period. No, she wasn't miraculously pregnant. It's not unusual for a woman to have erratic periods upon stopping the birth control pill after taking it for many years. She told him she thought she was pregnant. He went to the pharmacy and bought a pregnancy test. While he was gone, Molly, in "a fit of quick thinking," ran next door to borrow a cup of urine from a pregnant neighbor.

"When I came out of the bathroom and handed John the stick showing pink for positively pregnant, he was speechless. I could read the emotions playing out across his face, and I knew he was vulnerable. Crying, I put my arms around him. I sank to my knees and begged him to forgive me. We ended up in bed. Three weeks later I had a period, which I passed off as a miscarriage. By then, he was ready to forgive me and give our marriage another chance, and I was damned determined to get pregnant."

After two months of fertility drugs, Molly did get pregnant. Their son is almost two, and she is once again on fertility drugs, trying to get pregnant again. She and John, she says, are closer than they have ever been.

"I am happier than I deserve to be," she says. "My only little niggling fear is that someday, somehow, John will discover another piece of my past. I don't know how he would handle it. I believe he trusts me now. Having the baby cemented our relationship. But could he forgive more past indiscretions? Would he stay but distance himself emotionally? Or would he leave? I can't bear to think about it, so mostly I don't."

Like many women and men who have made a commitment to monogamy rather late in the relationship, Molly is both fearful of further discoveries and guilty about her past indiscretions. Would telling her husband "everything" be a good idea? Probably not. "Experts," of course, disagree, as "experts" are wont to do, but the preponderance of opinion is against confessing.

A husband who did confess all his sins after his wife had discovered one of them said, "I was an ass. Things have never been the same between us. I really hurt her, not to mention put myself in an untenable position. I'm the bad guy now."

The Boomer Facts

- Men and women can and do change promiscuous behavior at midlife. Inspired by religious conversion, sobriety, discovery, an ultimatum, a new partner, or simply a lowered libido, they commit to monogamy. It's probably easier to make that commitment to a new partner than to change the status quo in a long-lasting marriage.

- Becoming sexually active again after beginning recovery for substance abuse creates a new set of sex problems. The sober person needs new seduction rituals and an understanding partner. The performance bar will probably have to be lowered for a time. And the emotions aroused by lovemaking may seem overwhelming.

- Though there are many reasons for having repeated affairs, bad sex in the marriage is not often one of them. Sometimes, however, it is. Women who married before they had masturbated or achieved orgasm are most likely to fall into this category.
- Boomer men and women may be more likely to find their marriages to much younger partners completely sexually satisfying than their first marriages were. The sexual fit between the older man and younger woman and between the older woman and younger man may be ideal for these individuals. Older women especially seem to thrive in these relationships.

PART 4

The Midsex Point

At midlife, the long married are fairly entrenched in their marriages. The never married, or briefly married, are not likely to change their marital status either.

Both groups are more or less satisfied with their lives—or comfortable on some level with their dissatisfaction.

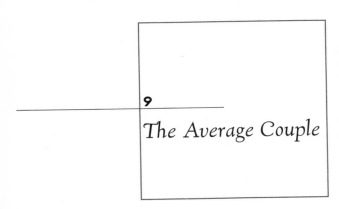

9

The Average Couple

I met a lot of couples who claimed they are "average." Most people have a desire to be "normal." They want to believe their weight is within an acceptable range, their income affords them at least a middle-class lifestyle, and they have the same amount of sex that everyone else their age is having, if not more. The desire to fit into the larger social group must be an ingrained part of human nature. Even those of us who want to be different perversely also want to belong.

As my interviews progressed, I added questions I hadn't thought to include on the questionnaire. One of those questions is: How would you define an "average" sex life? The answers varied according to marital status. Not surprisingly, the unmarried were more realistic about sex lives in general than the married were. They didn't imagine the average unmarried man or woman in their age group was having two or three times more sex than statistics show they are. Married couples were that far off base. There may be a very simple explanation for their myopia: The married talk less to each other about their own sex lives than single people do.

A forty-year-old married woman said, "I don't know anything about the sex lives of my closest married friends. We never talk about sex. When I was single, I talked about sex with my single friends. There is a taboo against talking about lovemaking with your husband. It's a betrayal. Your sex life isn't your sex life anymore; it belongs to another person, too. When a married woman starts griping about her sex life, she's thinking about getting a divorce."

Other married people agreed with her, but some thought the the reticence was only partially attributable to marital loyalty. Workplace ethics also contribute to the ban on private sex talk.

"When I got my first job as a secretary, at age eighteen," said a forty-five-year-old woman, "there was a preponderance of women in clerical jobs. They talked like housewives in a kaffeeklatsch. As the years went on and more and more women had management positions, the way women talked in the workplace changed considerably. Today they are more circumspect. Harassment concerns prevent men and women from having open conversations about their personal lives, too."

Single men and women have more opportunities to talk about their sex lives with their contemporaries outside the workplace. Over drinks, dinner, at the movies waiting for the lights to dim, they compare notes. There is also a kind of conversation common to the unmarried but rare to the married: The late night phone call in which two friends, sometimes of the opposite sex, confide all. Singles have a greater need to share experiences and seek emotional support from others, and they have the option to do so while the married really don't. When your partner is sleeping beside you, it is more difficult, and far less important, to make an intimate connection with someone else. Ironically, it is the married who are isolated from everyone except each other—and in their isolation, they form beliefs about the sexual behavior of peers, much as the man in Plato's cave gained his impressions about life outside the cave from flickering shadows on the wall.

Their behavior may not match the mythical standards, but they often pretend it does. For the most part, married men and women were more difficult to interview than the unattached until I learned to present them with sets of numbers that lowered the expectation bar—statistics like, for example, the fact that the average Boomer couple, married for at least ten years, is not having sex three or four times a week. Those who most aspired to fall within the designation "average" often were just that.

At midlife, the average long-married couple are entrenched in their marriage. They are not wanting to change their status from married to divorced. Within the category of the determinedly married are subcategories which include:

• *The emotionally alienated.* The connection between them is strong, but unresolved anger or other issues keep them apart, emotionally and often sexually. Some couples seem to have meshing neuroses, and their connecting grid filters out erotic impulses.

• *The pharmaceutically alienated.* In their forties, many people, especially the overweight and out-of-shape, begin taking prescribed medications for a host of maladies, including mild depression and hypertension. A side effect of these drugs is some degree of sexual impairment. Either libido or performance ability or both may be affected.

• *The fat and otherwise attraction impaired.* New studies report that even more Americans are overweight than was previously thought. Fat, lack of adequate muscle tone, and other physical factors may not impede sexual activity for every couple, but they do for many. If you don't feel attractive, you can't project desirability.

• *The habit driven.* Some couples make love in the same way, often on the same days of the week. Their ritualized lovemaking precludes experimentation and spontaneity. In some cases, one partner stopped being inventive after the other repeatedly rejected anything different.

• *The over-worked, over-scheduled, over-tired.* Many "average" couples are members of the sandwich generation, caught between the needs of teenagers and aging parents. Lack of privacy and personal space are issues. Some, who had their children in their late thirties or early forties, are overwhelmed by the demands of child care and high-powered careers. All frequently complain about being "too tired, too busy" for sex.

• *The bored.* They have the time and the energy, but they're out of ideas for making the sex more exciting. Many of these couples, more erotically sophisticated than previous generations, have employed the techniques suggested in sex advice articles and books. Increasingly, they are turning toward the Eastern sexual teachings to combine the physical aspects of lovemaking with spirituality. "Spiritual sex" is the hot trend among bored couples who want to remain both married and monogamous.

• *The satisfied.* A lot of "average" couples are content with their lives, their marriages, their sex lives. While they may have private sexual wish lists, they aren't tormented by unmet desires. They still find their partners attractive. They may have occasional attractions to others, but they want to stay where they are and anticipate doing so until death do them part.

Every average couple has a story, and some of the stories are more poignant than others.

GIL AND LINDA

"Oh, yeah, life goes on . . . long after the thrill of livin' is gone."
(Recorded by John Cougar Mellencamp for Polygram Records)

"Five years ago, I played spy for my friend Josie, whose husband was having an affair," Linda says. "He was going out of town on yet another business trip. She gave me all the flight information. I went to the airport to see if I could catch him in the act of boarding the plane with the other woman, a young administrative assistant in his company. I sat in an airport bar and watched him and the girl check in for the flight. He nuzzled her neck, held her hand, whispered in her ear. I hadn't seen a man so besotted with a woman since I was her age.

"I took pictures. Josie placed the photos and negatives in her private safe-deposit box. I went with her to the bank the day she did. We never talked about it again. Sometimes when I'm having trouble sleeping at night I can't get out of my mind the image of my friend's husband with his face in that girl's neck. Has my husband done something like that? Why don't I ask him?

"He doesn't know about my airport adventure. I don't know how he would react."

Linda, forty-five, has been married to Gil, forty-eight, for twenty-two years. They live in Shaker Heights, an upscale Cleveland suburb. A self-described "average couple," they agreed to a joint interview. Before I met them in their comfortable home, Linda called with a reminder: Don't tell Gil the "spy story."

"I don't get sex as often as I would like," Gil says, less than five minutes into our conversation. "I still want it more than she does. Wasn't that supposed to change for us? I'm waiting for Linda's thirtysomething hormones to kick in."

Gil and Linda needle each other frequently during conversation. Like emotional acupuncturists, they know where the pressure points are located. But they are also a couple for whom laughter comes easily. They tease. Sometimes the teasing is good-natured and sometimes it has an edge sharp enough to slice and dice. The main topics are her weight gain, smoking, Prozac, and sexual frequency. That they are willing to confront each other the way they do in front of a third party, that they laugh while saying cruel things as if their laughter and their words had no connection, that they are still together after all these years—must come as no surprise to anyone who has known or been part of such a marriage. The brief sad looks they very occasionally exchange hint at the love between them. Their eyes meet. Then each quickly looks away as if they had been braised by a laser beam. Those painful glances answer the rock 'n' roll question "How deep is your love?" It's deep. Buried under layers of resentment, anger, frustration, disappointment.

They met when Linda applied for a job at the law firm where Gil was a junior partner. She didn't get hired, but she did get a call.

"I thought he was calling to offer me a job," she says, "and I was disappointed. I'd been looking for a job for six months without finding anything other than temp work. It was 1976. I had a degree in fine arts. I couldn't type. I was living at home with my parents in Shaker Heights. Nothing seemed to be going right.

"I was disappointed when Gil asked me out, but I accepted because I didn't have anything else going on romantically. He was handsome. My mother was thrilled, because my father is a doctor and she wanted me to marry a lawyer or a doctor. She never trusted businessmen.

"Well, I fell in love with him that night. He was wonderful—smart, funny, romantic. He made me feel pretty and sophisticated."

Gil interrupts her to say, "Prozac has taken a toll on us sexually. One or the other of us has been on Prozac for the last eight years. It changes things." Then he left the room to make a business call before he could hear her response.

Linda says, "We were happy together until our son started high school. The stress of dealing with a teenage boy, a prepubescent daughter, a mother recovering from a stroke, and my own early perimenopausal symptoms were too much for me. Gil was never home. I always was. His practice was busy, and he was involved in Republican politics at the state and national levels. His favorite self-descriptive phrase about his politics, 'I was a liberal, and then I matured,' was adopted as a campaign slogan by a local politician.

"He'll tell you I retreated into the refrigerator," she says, "but it isn't that simple. He was on Prozac first; and it wreaked havoc with our sex life. He got these monster erections that wouldn't go down. No matter what I did, I couldn't make him come. He wanted to go on and on. I wanted him to stop, but once he got started he didn't want to stop until he came or I couldn't take it anymore. You know which happened first.

"I started eating to protect myself from him sexually. He says he still wants me when I'm fat, but he lies. He doesn't. The fat turns him off."

Gil returns with a gin and tonic—"better than Prozac"—and lights a cigarette. Linda smashes a half-smoked cigarette into an ashtray filled with butts of the same to slightly shorter length. She is "cutting back."

"I went off tobacco twice," Gil reports. "Once, for five months. Linda couldn't stand it. She told me to start smoking again."

"I didn't quite say that," Linda says, her cheeks flushing in embarrassment. "I said you were so irritable I couldn't stand being around you."

"You said you liked me better when I was smoking."

"You can't leave without seeing our wedding album," Linda says. Gil groans. "We were married in July 1976 under a big tent on the back lawn of my grandmother's home."

She pulls out the album. There was actually a series of tents on a vast lawn with a pool visible in some of the photos. Flowers were red and white. The bridesmaids wore royal blue. Linda was absolutely radiant in a slim white gown with long sheer sleeves and a sweetheart neck. She looked like a movie star from the forties, her thick dark hair swept up into a floral headpiece. It must have been hot in Cleveland outdoors in July, but she appears serene, cool. Her lips are glossy in the fashion of the day. The young Gil's pride and delight in her is evident.

"We were a handsome couple," he says.

"You were handsome," she says, smiling affectionately, her eyes glancing off his.

"You were beautiful," he says softly.

She was.

In the morning after Gil has left for the office, she returns to the "spy story," the day she went to the airport for her friend Josie.

"I wonder if they have sex anymore," she says, placing her hands around her coffee cup, as if to warm them. "I wonder if he's still seeing that girl or another girl, if Josie's forgiven him, if they found a way to get back to each other The questions I have for her might lead her to ask questions of me. I don't want to go there. I don't want to talk about my marriage to my friends. It seems like a betrayal. I don't know many women who do talk. When they do, it's usually a signal that the marriage is going to end. How can a man and woman live together after the trust is gone?"

In spite of their difficulties, she doesn't believe her husband has been unfaithful to her. "And if he has, it would have been a one-night stand." Nor has she had an affair.

"I'll never forget the first time he made love to me. We'd been dating three months exactly; and I could tell he'd just made up his mind, no more stalling. He prepared this wonderful candlelight dinner for me. We were too excited by each other to eat. It was a wonderful experience. I'd had three lovers before Gil, but they were boys. He made love like a man."

Gil and Linda are among the couples targeted by books and magazine articles offering sex advice, because they are, in many respects, "average." They have sex approximately once a week. She is capable of orgasm and typically did reach orgasm during lovemaking before Prozac. Gil, too, is functional. He does not suffer from premature ejaculation nor does he have difficulty ejaculating. Neither a fetishist nor a prude, he is willing to be playful in bed.

Like many other couples, they may not be having as much sex as one (or often both) would like to have and one (or both) may have complaints about the variety of lovemaking as well as its frequency. Gil, for example, would like more oral sex, and Linda would enjoy more romantic and leisurely sexual encounters than they typically have. These issues and similar ones can be addressed by sex advisers.

Unless both partners are open to erotic suggestion, nothing will change. Some couples cling to the status quo—infrequent, mundane sex— because it's easier than breaking a habit. Like smoking and overeating, unsatisfactory sex actually satisfies some deep and hidden needs. It helps the partners maintain the distance they've created between them. Maybe it protects them from the pain entailed in examining the reasons behind their quiet and mutual anger. Sexual disappointment can be a habit more comfortable than any other, because it is not accompanied by health warnings and gentle admonishments from friends and family.

If Gil and Linda reestablished the erotic connection they clearly once had, would either of them need the Prozac? When I left them, I felt a little sad. I wanted them to appreciate what they have in each other and in their marriage—and seize the moment before fate takes it away.

The Survey Says
- 78 percent of Vietnam-generation men and 83 percent of women in marriages or other committed relationships want more sex than they're having with their partners.
- 76 percent of Watergate-generation men and 79 percent of women

in marriages or other committed relationships want more sex than they're having with their partners.

- 59 percent of these Vietnam-generation men and 44 percent of the women want different kinds of sex or more variety in their lovemaking than they're enjoying now.
- 51 percent of these Watergate-generation men and 37 percent of the women want different kinds of sex or more variety in their lovemaking than they're enjoying now.

SEX TIPS FOR BOOMERS

"Do It, Baby"
(Recorded by the Miracles for Motown Records)

Hot-spot lovemaking is an easy way to reestablish a strong erotic connection between tired, jaded, disaffected partners. Men and women have a number of "hot spots" beyond the obvious two: the head of his penis and her clitoris and its surrounding tissue. These "spots," or areas, produce pleasurable sensations, often including orgasm, when stimulated. At midlife, as men's erections lose some of their firmness and women lose a degree of vaginal tone, the same ways of making love may not be as exciting as they once were because the spots aren't being hit, especially during intercourse. A shift in position or the addition or subtraction of a pillow can reestablish the connection.

His Spots

The F Spot. The frenulum is that loose section of skin on the underside of the penis where the head meets the shaft. The area is sensitive to touch in most men.

The R Spot. The raphe is the visible line along the center of the scrutoum, again a place sensitive to touch in most men.

The P Zone. The perineum, that area approximately an inch in size between the anus and the scrotum, is rich in nerve endings. A neglected hot spot, it can, when properly stimulated, trigger orgasm in some men.

Her Spots

The G Spot. You may have heard about this one. A small mass of tissue about a third of the way up the front wall of the vagina, the G spot can be located by inserting two fingers inside the vagina and making the come hither gesture. That rough patch of skin is the G spot.

The U Spot. The U spot is the tissue surrounding the urethral canal, found approximately an inch behind the clitoris in front of the vaginal opening.

The AFE Zone. The anterior fornix erogenous zone is located on the upper vaginal wall across from the G spot (Think of a chair, the G spot, and a sofa, the AFE zone, facing each other in a cozy room setting.) Stroking the area with a finger produces greater lubrication in many women.

Hitting the Hot Spots

Pay attention to the hot spots during fellatio, cunnilingus, and manual stimulation of the genitals. Vary the movements of tongue and degree of manual pressure applied to the spots. Pay attention to your partner's responses so you can gauge what is most effective.

Make adjustments during intercourse to create more friction between his and her hot spots. For example, shift the angle of penetration in the female superior position by moving slightly more forward or backward than usual. Experiment with pillows under back or hips in the female superior and missionary positions. In the missionary position, keeping her feet on the bed with knees bent or wrapping her legs around his neck may create a better hot-spot connection.

Rear entry may be the ultimate hot spot position for some couples. Many women report they feel G spot stimulation only in this position, which is also conducive to R- and F-spot stimulation for him.

DON'T STOP

"Don't stop thinking about tomorrow . . ."
   (Recorded by Fleetwood Mac for RCA Records)

"We don't have the time, privacy, or energy to have sex as often as we'd like," Lorie says, "but we hang on to the idea of tomorrow. This is temporary, a prolonged bout of temporary, but not permanent. All our friends must be in the same place. Nobody talks much about sex, except in the abstract, or in the specifically Presidential. We talk about the President's penis often, but we live inside the Beltway. We talk about Viagra. A friend went to a dinner party where one of the guests asked if any of the men had tried it. Two guys said they had. She was shocked they owned up to it. Nobody wanted to talk about anything else all evening."

Lorie and her husband, Max, are both forty-two. Like many other "average couples," they complain that their sexuality is constrained by time and energy. They haven't experienced sexual problems, just problems having sex. He says, "When we get the rare opportunity to spend a few days alone, we're like a couple of horny kids, but we're kids who know what we're doing."

She grew up in suburban New Jersey, an hour outside Manhattan, he in a rural area in southern Vermont, "several decades" away. They met as freshman at the University of Missouri at Columbia. Both were journalism majors in one of the nation's best journalism programs. They didn't hit it off on the first date—and didn't run into each other again on campus until their senior year, 1977 to '78.

"By then, we were aware of each other," she says. "Both of us had written at one time or another for the school paper. We'd been on the yearbook committee at different times. I thought he was cute. By senior year, he had forgotten the first date. I remembered. He'd pontificated on his philosophy of journalism—everybody wanted to be Woodward and Bernstein, even the girls—hinted around that he believed in sex without love, and expected me to pay for my own dinner. He thought women wanted to be treated like equals, he said."

She liked the articles he'd written for the paper enough to forgive him his freshman folly. They "expressed a growing intelligence," she says. After trying unsuccessfully to meet him "accidentally," she did just that.

"I walked out of the library one day and spotted him ahead of me on the path. I was debating whether or not to break into a run and accost him when he stopped to chat with another guy. It was my opening. I sauntered up to him and said, 'Oh, hi, I remember you. We met freshmen year, and I've been following your articles ever since.'

"The way to a man's penis is through his ego. We had dinner that evening. Before the check arrived, I reminded him of our long ago first date. He paid. We were lovers before the week was out. Shocking our family and friends, we got married two days before graduation. Everyone assumed I was pregnant, but I wasn't. We knew we were going to be together. He hated big weddings, and so did I. Why wait?"

She smiles delightedly as she recounts the story of her reconnection with Max. We are having lunch at the National Press Club, where the ambiance is Old Boys' Club and the food is English nursery bland. Over Cobb salads, she describes her hectic life. Two teenager daughters. A widowed mother in a nursing home in north Jersey. A full-time job. A Victorian house in a constant state of rehab.

"We put a down payment on the house with the checks our families gave us in lieu of the wedding we didn't want," she says. "We have been lucky. Both of us wanted jobs in the Washington area, and we got them. We've never lived anywhere in our married life except our beloved house. In the early days, before the girls were born, and even afterward, we had sex in every one of the eleven rooms in that house. Having babies slowed us down, but not a lot.

"I had enormous orgasms when I was pregnant. Being pregnant agreed with me. It was a very sensual time. I had easy deliveries, minimal postpartum blues. Max and I had matching high libidos. Now I would say we have matching libidos on hold. We talk about sex the way we used to talk about reading Proust. Someday there will be time for this.

"Sex now? Where does sex fit into the equation?" she asks. "We have more quickies than I would like to have. Sometimes it's necessary, not just for him, but for me. I can come pretty fast, especially now. If I know I want a quickie, I'll masturbate myself for a few minutes in the shower before coming to bed. Then I'm all over him like cat hair. He likes it. We also have sex in the shower. It's quick, clean, and the noise of the shower drowns out the moans. Very effective place for sex when the kids are home.

"I remember thinking, in my naïveté, that kids really didn't have to kill your sex life when ours were small. They went to bed early. That's the secret. Teenagers are awake at the wrong end of the clock. And you know they *know*. Plus, the company. They have so many friends hanging around all the time. There is no privacy. On weekends, we may have four, six, or more girls hanging around the house, spending the night. This is the hardest time to combine being a parent and having a sex life. Something about nubile girls and the horny boys sniffing after them makes parents feel old, even shameful about their sexual urges. It's like putting on a bikini at the beach when your daughters and all her friends are bopping around in their little suits. Omigod.'

If teenagers aren't enough to keep the libido in check, add the aging-parent effect and stir. Neither Lorie nor her brother live close enough to her mother to run by the nursing home on the way to or from work. For Lorie, it's a four- to five-hour drive. She makes it every other weekend.

"I still feel guilty," she says. "I'm not doing enough for her, and I know it. Sometimes I cry driving back home. She's eighty-two, and she has Alzheimer's. Some visits are terrible. She is angry at me and says hurtful things or she doesn't know me at all. She was thirty-eight when my brother was born and forty when she had me. Ideally, one should have their kids sooner so they'll be able to retire by the time their parents are incapacitated. Of course, Max and I will never be able to afford retirement, so it's a moot point anyway.

"When we aren't worrying about parents or kids, we worry about being downsized out of our jobs."

When Max joins us for coffee, he says, "We aren't satisfied with our sex life in the same way we aren't satisfied with our financial life. We want more. We think we need more, but we don't know how to get it. Sex or money."

"Right now, it isn't possible," she says. "We're hoping things will ease up in every area when the girls go off to college. They understand that we can't pay their way. We can help, but we can't do it all. They know they need to put together a financing package of jobs and student loans. If we tried to put them through college, we'd have nothing to retire on, nothing for emergencies."

"Emergencies worry us," he says. "That's a function of aging. You begin to understand that you have less control over your life than you thought you had. All around you, people your age and a few years older are losing their jobs, developing health problems.

"Ten years ago I was driving home on the Beltway planning how I would talk Lorie into having sex on the sunporch or letting me come between her breasts. Now I drive home wondering how much I should worry about a snub from one of the bosses. Am I losing my job? If I glance in the mirror, I see my bald spot and have brief thoughts about heart attacks and arthritis.

"Life isn't very sexy anymore."

They look into each other's eyes often as they talk, searching for the answers as if they will find them inside each other, and probably they will.

The danger for couples like Lorie and Max lies in turning a matter of logistics into something else again. "We started blaming each other for the lack of time, energy, and privacy in our life," one woman said. Instead of making the most of the erotic opportunities they might have had, they wasted their time and depleted their emotional resources in arguing about why they didn't have time for sex. "Don't fight," advises a harried husband who's been there. "Make quickies, not skirmishes."

Could there be better sex advice for the overscheduled Boomer?

SEX TIPS FOR BOOMERS

Please, Please, Please.
(Recorded by James Brown for BMI Music)

"Quickies" do not deserve the disdain they've been given since society discovered that women like it slow. Women, especially at midlife, like it fast sometimes, too. (Now the question is: Can men keep up?) "Quickies" may be the only form of sexual pleasure the too tired, too busy, too stressed, and otherwise *too* couple can enjoy weekdays, and many weekends.

How to Get the Most from a quickie

Seize the moment, any moment. You need not wait until the news is over, the kids are in bed, and the phone unlikely to ring. Be creative. Go in the bathroom together and turn on the shower. Use television or music as cover. Rendezvous in a storage closet during your lunch break.

Plan ahead. You'll need to keep your clothes on, so dress appropriately in loose clothing and boxer shorts for men, skirts with teddies or body suits that can be unsnapped for women.

Foreplay doesn't have to be performed on site. Fantasize and masturbate (not to the point of orgasm) before the encounter.

Don't be goal-oriented. The big misconception about quickies is that they should end in orgasm. There may not be time for the big finish. Leaving each other on an arousal high almost guarantees that time will be found in the too busy life for sex again.

SOUND BITE

From a conversation with a forty-five-year-old upper-middle-class wife: "The women I know are in the same place now, the place that I'm in. We want to stay married, but we would like to live in separate houses. One friend says she wouldn't mind living together with her husband in a palace where they each had a wing and could meet for dinner in the dining room if she was in the mood for his company—or in one of the bedrooms if she was *in the mood*."

RIGHT BACK WHERE WE STARTED FROM

"It's all right and it's comin' on."
(Recorded by Fleetwood Mac for Warner Bros. Records)

"I came back from a business trip in the middle of the day and decided to go home rather than the office," Janice says. "The first thing I noticed when I came in the door was Terry's new stack of books on the coffee table. He'd bought six books on Eastern lovemaking techniques. 'Okay,' I thought, 'we're right on target, moving into sex as a spiritual trip.' An aging Boomer couple, we're supposed to be recapturing the magic through various mind-over-body approaches."

Aging Boomer couples with empty nests are the prime customers for books and instructional videos on Eastern lovemaking philosophies and techniques. They have the money to spend for workshops and seminars on the subject. Unlike their time-squeezed contemporaries, this group can't blame external circumstances for a lackluster sex life. They have the time, energy, and knowledge of sexual practices. When boredom sets in, they consider it a problem and look for solutions, as if they were diagnosed with high cholesterol levels or handed a mediocre job-performance review. A group of people who have given high priority to sexual pleasure throughout their adult lives, they are attracted to the languorous aspects of the Eastern erotic arts.

Their motto is: We can fix anything, including the sex. We can get it back.

Janice and Terry, who turned forty-seven and forty-nine within days of each other this year, met at Rutgers University in New Brunswick, New Jersey, in 1970. He was a senior and she was a sophomore. Both history majors, she with a minor in literature and he in philosophy, they met, quite appropriately, in the library. In her stack of books, she had a copy of *The Nine Young Men*, written in 1947, by Wesley McCune, about the Supreme Court.

"It was the only copy of an out-of-print book, and he really wanted it for a report he was doing," she says. "I had picked it up because my mother knew the author. Out of the corner of my eye, I noticed Terry eyeing me in a very keen way. Then I saw he was looking at the book.

" 'Is this what you're interested in?' I asked him, indicating the book. He looked more closely at me then, smiled as if he liked what he saw, and said, 'Well, that's not all I'm interested in.' "

Later, over coffee, he told her that he was at Rutgers because they'd given him a scholarship while his first choice, New York University, hadn't. She was there because her first choice, Columbia, had rejected her. They laughed about being in compromised positions.

"He took my hand and said, 'My life stopped being a compromise when you smiled at me.' I was overwhelmed."

They made love for the first time eight days after they met. It was, she says, "passionate, tender, incredible," like nothing she'd experienced before. He proposed marriage that night. She accepted. They married in June 1971, after Terry's graduation. He found a job in Manhattan; she continued going to school at Rutgers. When she graduated, she too found a job in Manhattan. They lived on the Upper West Side—or, as Terry derisively calls it, "the Upper White Side"—in a one-bedroom brownstone flat, until 1980, when they bought a spacious older home in an integrated neighborhood in New Brunswick.

"We always liked New Brunswick," she says. "It has the advantages of a small college town with proximity to New York City. We love to travel, but neither of us has seriously wanted to live anywhere else since we moved back here."

While Terry was and has remained an attractive man, Janice was and still is one of those few women accurately described by the old-fashioned term "knock-out." It is not hard to imagine a man being knocked out by her beauty when she was nineteen. Her assets include naturally strawberry-blond hair, a body both willowy and curvy, long legs, aquamarine eyes.

"When I was nineteen, I had creamy, smooth skin," she says. "I wish I'd taken better care of it. If I knew then what I know now, I never would have gone out in the sun."

The fine lines around her eyes and the ridges from nose to the corners of her mouth bother her excessively. She will probably have a face lift soon, she says. "Another Boomer rite of passage," she laughs.

When it comes to Boomer rites of passage, she's missed a few, namely children. Married for twenty-seven years, Janice and Terry never wanted to be parents. Terry's own parents died of cancer, two years apart, when he was in his early twenties. Janice lost her father to a heart attack several years ago. Her mother, their only remaining parent, is in good health and has re-married. Remarkably free of the caretaking responsibilities for children and parents that others of their generation are facing, Janice and Terry are also financially "comfortable." If one or both of them lost a job, they report, they could live "modestly, but reasonably well" for the rest of their lives.

"We have the time for sex, but we didn't have the interest for a while," she says. "We had been going through a slump, which prompted Terry to buy the Tantra books. Like every couple who has been together a long, long time, we've had highs and lows. Sometimes sex is very important, other times it isn't. If it hasn't been for a while, one of us gets worried and makes the effort to get it back again."

Few Boomer couples, if any, have *never* experienced tough times in their marriages. When faced with major difficulties, some couples separate, have affairs, or settle into a marriage of resentful accommodation. The successful couples grow and change. As they evolve, their sex lives do too. Janice found the challenges to their relationship were not the big problems, but the minor discontents.

"I have always said I can handle a full-blown crisis better than I can a series of little annoyances," she says. "I rise to the occasion. Terry is the same way. When we lost parents, lost jobs, lost a very dear friend to AIDS, we grew closer together. Each of us knew how to comfort the other. We pulled together.

"On the other hand, it's a miracle we didn't get a divorce over his snoring or my forgetfulness. The habits we have that drive each other crazy take center stage when life is going smoothly. At those times, the sex gets boring. Around our tenth anniversary, we both had affairs. We almost split up. Each of us had talked to a lawyer. I remember walking through the house and making mental lists of the possessions under two columns, his and mine, but I could not have explained to anyone how we got to the place we were in. There hadn't been anything seriously wrong with our marriage when we both cheated on it.

"A few days later, he asked me to have dinner with him at Frog and Peach, a little neighborhood restaurant. We hadn't been seeing much of each other. Sometimes one or both of us spent the night away from home. When he asked me to dinner, it felt like a date. I put on a slinky little dress and high heels. Sitting across the table from him, I realized how handsome he was, much better looking than the man I was seeing. I felt tenderness toward him growing inside me. His eyes got soft when he looked at me. I knew what that meant. He wanted me, and I felt what he felt in my groin.

"Driving home, I snuggled against him, ran my hand up and down his thigh. He one hand off the wheel and guided mine to his erection. He kissed me at the stoplight, a full tongue-in-the-mouth kiss. My heart was pounding in my ears as we pulled into our driveway. We made love in the entryway of the house. He possessed me so completely that I called the man I was seeing and broke it off that night. We made love again afterward.

"We learned a lesson from that experience: When the sex gets boring, we're vulnerable. We almost threw our marriage away over routine sex. Maybe we wouldn't have come so close if we'd had children to consider or maybe we would have. I know a lot of divorced parents."

From that night on, Janice and Terry "worked" at their sexual relationship. They discovered her G spot and both their PC muscles, rented X-rated movies, bought a camera and made some of their own, learned how to give her multiple orgasms and delay his. After seeing Spanish director Pedro Almodovar's *Tie Me Up! Tie Me Down!* in 1990, they became sexual bondage aficionados.

"We did it in the shower, with chocolate and honey, on the beach at night, in the back seat of the car," she says. "We were inventive, creative, athletic. As good as we were, we'd once again reached the place where the sex is a little stale when Terry bought the Tantra books."

Janice scanned the books and thought, Been there, done that. Candles, scented oils, incense, techniques for multiple and delayed orgasms. Was there anything they hadn't tried?

"I briefly considered manufacturing a crisis," she says, "like carrying on a heavy flirtation with another man. I thought we needed a crisis, something to jolt our libidos. Terry persisted in quietly reading the books. He signed us up for a four-day workshop with a guru in Northern California. I thought it was as good an excuse as any for a trip to wine country. Besides, a change of scenery always revved our engines."

She went to California with her husband "open to the possibilities," but not expecting the life-changing experience they did have. Many people at midlife become more spiritual. For previous generations, attending church was the primary means of expressing their new spirituality. Boomers, who haven't returned to organized religion in tremendous numbers, have other socially sanctioned spiritual outlets, including sex with one's lifelong mate.

"We learned a few new techniques, but the workshop was not about manual dexterity. It was a given that the couples attending probably had achieved a respectable level of skill. There's nothing wrong with the standard advice: Date your mate, read erotica out loud to each other, communicate your desires. Fine. You've done all that. Twenty years of making love to the same person, even in different ways, is a prescription for boredom. Most couples who stay together, in my estimation, accept the trade-off— the sex may be boring but it's regular and there are other benefits to marriage.

"It's like the old joke my Jewish friend's mother tells: Two women complain about the food at a restaurant under new management. The food is bad, one says. The food was always bad, the other counters. Yes, the first one says, but there was plenty of it. Now it's bad and there isn't enough.

"The sex may be boring in marriage, but there isn't enough of it if you're single.

"Tantric sex teaches you how to make a spiritual connection through your genitals. The breathing techniques are helpful, but the most important aspect is keeping your eyes open. It sounds simple, but it's amazing the difference it makes. You open your eyes, and your heart follows.

"The first time Terry and I made love in the Yabyum position, we didn't have our breathing coordinated but we had an astonishing experience anyway. Looking into each other's eyes as we made love, we came closer to one another than we had since the early days of our marriage."

Tantric devotees, Janice and Terry regularly meditate together, often make love without penetration, and sometimes without the expectation of orgasm. Tantra is the sexual philosophy outlined in *The Kama Sutra*, published in India thousands of years ago. Tantra and the Tao, the sexual philosophy of ancient China, form the basis of the Eastern erotic arts, newly popular among today's educated Western couples like Janice and Terry. While Tao places more emphasis on male ejaculatory control, both teach prolonged and intensified lovemaking as a way of achieving a closer, more spiritual union of man and woman.

It is an approach to sex most easily adapted by the midlife couple in reasonably good physical condition. Young men find ejaculatory control more difficult than mature men do. At forty or fifty, a man may not feel the urgency to ejaculate every time he makes love. In fact, he may not be able to do so. Emotionally investing in Tantra gives him the erotic framework he needs to shore up his ego. If, by the standards of his youth, he isn't as potent as he once was, he is, by the standards of his maturity, a better lover, more capable of achieving and sustaining a deep intimate connection with the woman he loves. Women reap the benefits of prolonged lovemaking just at the point in life where they are more likely to be capable of multiple orgasms.

"This is exactly what we needed," Janice says. "We've never been closer. In many ways, Tantra is the fountain of youth."

Pleasure-oriented rather than goal-oriented, the Eastern methods of lovemaking have a unifying principle: Sustain arousal at the lower levels by using minimal stimulation for prolonged periods of time. That increases pleasure and creates stronger orgasms when they eventually occur. The one significant drawback for many "average" couples: time.

BOOMER SEX TIPS

"Oh What a Nite"
(Recorded by the Dells for Atlantic Records)

A mere introduction into the sensual world of the ancient East, this is not going to be a quickie. Allow plenty of time for lovemaking. (Remember: You are adopting the style of a people who lived without fax machines and E-mail.) Light candles. Burn incense. Fill small vases with single blossoms. Devote as much time to kissing, caressing, cuddling, and stroking as necessary to reach the point where you are aching for genital contact. Then perform:

The Eyelock

Look deeply into each other's eyes as you are caressing. Hold the look. Do this more than once. You won't realize how little you have been looking into each other's eyes until you do this. Now assume:

The Yabyum Position

Sit in the center of the bed facing each other. Wrap your legs around each other so that she is "sitting" on his legs. Place your right hand at the back of your partner's neck, your left hand on your partner's tailbone.

Each press your palm firmly at the base of your partner's spine. Slide your hand up his or her back to the back of the neck, and to the top of the head. Imagine you are channeling sexual energy up through the body, warming the body from genitals throughout heart through head. Repeat the stroke over and over again until you are both feeling very aroused.

Insert his penis into her vagina so that the shaft exerts as much indirect pressure as possible on her clitoris. Rock slowly as you rub each other's back and perform the eyelock.

Now, perform:

The Tantric Kiss

When the woman feels her orgasm is imminent, she should signal the man. They remain as still as possible in the Yabyum position. Pressing their foreheads together, they breathe into each other's mouths. As he exhales, she inhales and vice versa. Prolong the kiss as long as possible. At some point, remaining still will not be an option.

You are free to have an orgasm now.

The Boomer Facts

• At midlife, Boomers who have been married for twenty or more years are fairly entrenched in their marriages. The national divorce rate continues to hover at 40 percent, but most studies place it somewhat lower, from 25 to 30 percent, for this age group. Entrenchment does not necessarily equate with happiness. Some of the strongest marriages are between a man and a woman with meshing neuroses.

• The number-one sex complaint of the average couple is not enough sex, closely followed by "boring" sex. They cite reasons for the situation which include physical factors—from overweight to the libido-dampening effects of prescription drugs—time constraints, the demands of jobs, children, aging parents. Couples handle these problems in a variety of ways, some positive, some less so. They may practice avoidance, argue, or learn new sex techniques. The Eastern lovemaking arts are enjoying a revival in our society, largely thanks to aging Boomers' need for new ways of improving their sex lives.

- Experiencing at least intermittent dissatisfaction with their sex lives is "average" for long-married couples. But most of them remain optimistic about their sexual futures. They know the dangers inherent in prolonged sexual boredom or avoidance of lovemaking. Most do what they can to spice up their lovemaking, at least occasionally, and look forward to a future when they will have more time and energy to devote to each other.

10

Middle-Age Single

Men and women who don't want to get married eventually—and are, in fact, closed to the possibility—are not in the majority in any group of singles. I interviewed women who had been dating for more than twenty years, yet still expected Mr. Right to be waiting at the altar someday, the last man at the end of the procession of the Mr. Wrongs through their lives. It's a long time to delay choosing a decorating scheme. But many singles, male and female, persist in the belief that they will find "the one" as they lead prolonged temporary lives.

A fifty-year-old Manhattan woman who had never been married said, "I think I am finally ready to meet the right man. I've made a lot of dating mistakes in the past, but I know what I'm doing now. I play by the rules. Women who say there's no one left at this point are too negative."

She hadn't had a date in five years when we met for coffee at a café in a Barnes and Noble superstore where she shared her philosophy of dating with me. Women compose 59 percent of single Boomers in New York City. Of the 41 percent who are men, many are surely gay. Yet she and a small group of single female friends talk about the day when they will walk out of their rent-controlled studio apartments into the waiting limos that will get them to the church on time.

At the opposite end of the spectrum, occupying a different emotional plane, are the women and men who have built a single life like a comfortable home, the plans drawn exactly to their specifications. Increasingly, the person who chooses to be single is a woman, and she may, or may not, be what we would define as a "career woman." For a previous generation of women, the choice of a career was tantamount to relinquishing the rights to husband and children. Though that's certainly not true today, some women do make the conscious choice of a consuming career over marriage and family. They don't want to put the time and effort into being a wife and mother that they know those roles require.

A San Francisco surgeon in her forties said, "I've watched other women try to have it all. Something has to give, and it's their private time. I have chosen to make a life around my work and my private time. I have good friendships, hobbies and interests outside my work. If I had a husband and children, I wouldn't have me."

Not everyone who opts for a lifetime of single occupancy has a demanding career. Single by choice people include:

- *Self-sufficient personalities.* Often very outgoing and gregarious, they need more personal space than most others. Many of the people I interviewed in this category worked in creative fields or were entrepreneurs, some financially successful, others just getting by. They often had long-lasting love relationships and were typically serial monogamists. A few juggled two or more long-lasting love relationships at the same time.
- *Rigid personalities.* Some people, more often men than women, are single because their narrow views and rigid tastes and habits make it difficult for them to accommodate another person sharing their physical space. (Are women taught in childhood to be more accommodating and compromising?) They, too, may have long-lasting love relationships. It's easier to love than live with someone who has many and specific needs and doesn't know the meaning of compromise.
- *Secret-keepers.* Some never-marrieds are exactly the men and women your mother thinks they are. They are alone because they can't, or won't, share their secret lives with a significant other. They may drink too much, abuse prescription or other drugs or their credit cards, indulge only in kinky sex practices and preferably with prostitutes, or have some other aberrant or not socially acceptable behavior, like smoking. To be fair, probably more married than single people fit this description, but the single by choice within this category are consciously protecting their behaviors from the scrutiny and interference of a mate.
- *Cohabitators.* The Boomers made cohabiting a viable alternative to marriage. Though many have used living together as a marriage tryout, others view it as preferable to the legal and financial entanglements of

marriage. Men and women who choose cohabitation over marriage may have significant property to protect, money issues, or other family obligations. Or they may be romantic rebel spirits who simply never stopped believing that the little piece of paper isn't what makes a commitment a commitment.

The Survey Says

- 19 percent of Vietnam-generation men and 27 percent of women either have never been married—or were married less than three years when very young.
- 23 percent of Watergate-generation men and 28 percent of women either have never been married—or were married less than three years when very young.
- 15 percent of Vietnam-generation men in this category and 64 percent of women are satisfied with their lives.
- 24 percent of Watergate-generation men in this category and 53 percent of women are satisfied with their lives.

I NEED A LOVER

"I need a lover who won't drive me crazy."
    (Recorded by John Cougar Mellencamp for Polygram Records)

"I could be married if I wanted to be married," Katie says. She is the lover John Cougar Mellencamp sang about. "I was married for three years a very long time ago, and I could have married someone else. By age twenty-two, I was a divorcée, with no kids. It was like it never happened. Everyone said to me, 'You can start over,' but they missed the point: If I'd wanted to be married, I would have stayed with my husband. He was a good guy, my sweetheart from high school in Darien, Connecticut. I like being single. What I've lacked in quantity of sex, I've made up for in quality of experiences. I have a full life."

Unlike people who gradually adapt to being single because they can't find the elusive "perfect" mate, Katie, forty, knew before her divorce decree was final that she never, ever, wanted to marry again. Women, and men, who are sure they don't want to marry—and say so—probably make up less than a third of Boomer singles. In a society based on double occupancy, acknowledging that one has actively chosen to remain single for life is tantamount to backing a fringe political candidate. If you're against "intimacy," you must be for cigarettes, handguns, and illegal drugs.

"Acquaintances feel they have the right to ask prying questions," Katie says. "Basically, they want to know what's wrong with me. Am I neurotic, lesbian, repressed, a victim of childhood sex abuse, or all of the above? Married friends want to hear about my sex life. They say they live vicariously through me. I know more married people on Prozac than not at this point in our lives. Living with someone is harder than living alone."

Katie, an artist who works as a waitress to supplement her income, has lived in Manhattan's East Village area for the past fifteen years. ("The West Village was getting too expensive.") Thin, tall, and very pale, she has "wild raven hair" and large dark blue eyes perpetually outlined in navy blue liner, the lashes enhanced by two layers of mascara meticulously applied. She favors black clothing cut in simple lines accented with dramatic accessories like the necklace of African trade beads she wears to lunch at Cassini's, a tiny French bistro at First Avenue and First Street in her neighborhood. While she looks distinctively "New York," Katie is part of a sisterhood of Boomer women in urban neighborhoods throughout the country, women who live happily alone.

"My sister says I got married at nineteen as a form of inoculation against wanting to get married when I was old enough to know how to do it right," Katie says, laughing. "She is the quintessential Connecticut soccer mom. Her uniform is blue jeans, white shirt, white Keds. At thirty-six, she's in the thick of carpooling, room-mothering, and soothing the savage brows. Her three kids are eleven, nine, and seven, two girls and a boy. If the boy hadn't come along in the number three slot, she'd have had four kids. She was determined to have a son to keep her husband's name alive, but she had set four as the cap. Her life is so foreign to me, it's exotic. When she comes into town to have lunch with me, she walks around the Village like a woman visiting a zoo where the security isn't too good and the bears might storm the barricades at any moment.

"But she's the one with the strange and unusual life, not me. I give her a lot of credit for visiting me here. Her husband hates the idea."

Katie's collages and oil paintings feature strong, often erotic, images and vibrant hues. Her watercolors, by contrast, are pale illusory glimpses of mermaids at play. They fill the walls of her apartment, a sunny two-bedroom, fourth-floor walk-up, also her studio.

"The mermaids," she says, putting up her hands, "perplex even me. I don't know why I paint them. Or maybe I do. They seem to bring me sex.

When I feel myself drawn to the watercolor box, I know I am going to paint mermaids, and sooner or later, the sex will come."

She is also perplexed by the complaints of other Manhattan single women her age, namely that they can't find a date. The men, she says, are "everywhere." If a woman can't find one, she either isn't looking or has unrealistic criteria.

"Women eliminate men as prospective lovers based on their job titles and salaries. Then they whine because men want youth and beauty. Women, at least in New York City, are less interested in finding a lover than a solvent life partner. They want financial security, but security, financial or emotional, is basically an illusion. In a second, your life can change, and your security can slip out from under you like sand when the tide comes in. I like sex. When I want it, I can get it. That has been my security."

Katie's lovers have included married men, bisexual men—"I know how to protect myself"—younger men, black, Asian, and Hispanic men, and men her own age and race. She has found, however, that for white middle- and upper-middle-class men, single is more likely a waystation than it is for men of other races or social classes. White men expect to be married, and she believes they need to be married more than women do.

"An important part of the relationship with these men is listening to their innermost thoughts," she says, spearing an escargot with more interest than she apparently has in the private thoughts of the Boomer male. "They're spilling; and I'm thinking 'yadda, yadda, yadda.' I don't care. I really don't care. Women have friends for this stuff. Men should, too, but they don't, unless they're gay."

But she isn't "cold, heartless," as women friends have accused her of being. Behavioral studies from Alfred Kinsey through Shere Hite in 1976 and beyond have repeatedly told us that almost no women want sex for the sake of sex. Women—even the single, urban, feminist, economically dependent women of Hite's survey—crave sex with emotional attachment. Is there something wrong with Katie? No, she insists. She attaches, temporarily. "I sometimes get into a man, a relationship, intensely," she says, but the period of intense feelings has never lasted, and she expects it never will. Women, she believes, feed the emotions surrounding sex to justify their lusts, like a camper working to build a fire from a spark. If they didn't work hard to fan the flames of their emotional fires, they would have to acknowledge their true natures are less monogamous than they want to believe. Naked female desire is as shameful as naked female bodies once were.

"I crave balance," she says. "My attachments are fleeting. I will always get back to the balance, between love and work, friends and family and lovers, personal space and emotional sharing. It's not in me to build my life around someone other than me. I am my center, not someone else. Granted, I need more space than most people, but I am far from shy and withdrawn. I can talk to almost anyone. Actually, I think people who cannot make acquaintances easily are most dependent on having a partner. They feel naked alone. I can go out by myself and not give it another thought, especially in New York. It might be harder in Salt Lake City. I don't know."

Katie attracts men. They smile at her across crowded rooms, send over glasses of wine and their business cards. Striking, not beautiful, and trim, not model thin, she looks good for forty, but she doesn't look thirty. What she does look is confident, approachable, sexy.

"I love the male body," she says. "I adore the male genitals. Each man is unique. He tastes, looks, smells, and feels different in my mouth. I've learned so much from making love to many men. If I'd spent my whole adult life in the same marital bed, I wouldn't love and appreciate men the way I do. Every new man opens another window of erotic opportunity."

Many of her lovers have remained friends, or at least acquaintances. Last Christmas she received three floral arrangements, an orchid plant, and a bonsai tree from former lovers.

"There have been men who've forgotten me and some I've wanted to forget," she says, laughing. "Every single woman has her list of men who inspire the question. What was I thinking? Cringe and move on. None of them, not one, has ever been violent, verbally or physically abusive. A few geeks, yes. Some self-absorbed urban assholes. No one is more boring than the urban male bent on self-actualization. Yech. One who stuck me with the check. More than one who was cheap. I hate cheapness in a man. But I've never had a violent, angry man in my bed."

Does she worry about the day when the men will no longer look her way?

"I'd be lying if I said it never crosses my mind," she says, and crosses her legs as she does. "We all wonder if we'll end up alone and unloved. Even my sister has to wonder that sometimes. But, no, I do not think I will be without options, no matter how old I get. My role model is a woman who may be in her late sixties or older. She is wonderful. Men still take her out to dinner. She wears these fabulous hats. I tell her I am getting to the age of wearing hats soon.

"I believe in the theory of abundance, of the half-full versus the half-empty glass. Maybe my lovers will all be married. Maybe when I'm ninety, my dates will be seventy-year-old gay men who are as alone as I am. There will be someone."

Does she have lovemaking secrets?

"Secrets, tricks, yes—doesn't everyone who loves sex?"

<hr />

BOOMER SEX TIPS

Black Magic Woman
(Recorded by Santana for CBS Records)

Katie's three best "tricks":

The Soft Touch
Ancient Chinese courtesans were trained in the art of the soft insertion. If a man has difficulty achieving a firm erection, take the pressure off by taking him just the way he is. The "trick" is in grasping the penis firmly and first using the head of it to stimulate the vaginal lips. Insert an inch at a time, maintaining a firm grasp on the base. Good PC muscles help. Katie says, "It is extremely arousing to feel a man grow hard inside you."

The Silken Swirl
Katie's favorite fellatio technique is easy to master. Swirl your tongue lightly and repeatedly around the head of his penis. Alternate the swirl with gentle sucking of the head. Flick your tongue across the corona. And swirl again.

The Erogenous Zone Hunt
"Everyone has at least one hidden erogenous zone. Women are conditioned to go for the penis in foreplay. There's more to a man than his penis. Explore his body with your mouth and hands. Nipples are surprisingly sensitive on many men. When you find his spots, lavish attention on them."

(I'M A) ROADRUNNER

"When I get restless, I gotta move somewhere . . ."
(Recorded by Jr. Walker & the All Stars for BMI)

"When I was twenty-two, I bought a diamond ring," Rodney says. "I was in love with the prettiest little white girl I'd ever seen." Rodney is a light-skinned mixed-race black man with Cajun heritage. "I was a brand-new lieutenant in the United States Army, stationed in Germany. She was a nurse. I fell hard. I thought she did, too. The ring was in my pocket the night she broke up with me.

" 'Rodney,' she said, 'you know I've really enjoyed being with you, but my family is from the South. I can't do this anymore.' Now, I'm not telling you this story so you'll get the impression I never got over a broken heart. I look back on that little gal with real fondness. She was right. It was 1975. Neither one of us could have gone back to our Southern families with a husband or wife of a different race. More important, I was too young to know I didn't want to be married then. My broken heart lasted just long enough for me to figure out what a big favor she did for me."

Rodney, forty-five, estimates his lifetime partners must number in the "high two digits, maybe seventy or eighty. I didn't keep track." A self-described "sexual cowboy," he was more promiscuous in his twenties than he's been since. For the past ten or twelve years, he's been a serial monogamist, staying in each relationship until the woman presses for commitment or leaves him because he won't commit or until he's transferred to another country, whichever comes first.

"I've been seeing a woman for the past year who seems as happy being single as I am," he says. "She was married, but she's been divorced for twenty years. I consider that a good sign. If she'd wanted to be married again, she would have done it by now."

Born on the Fourth of July in 1953, to parents who were happily married, Rodney says he has disappointed his mother by remaining single. She tells him he's "part of the problem, black men not marrying black women" and wishes he would become part of the solution. Both his parents, children of poor sharecroppers, taught in the New Orleans public-school system until retirement. They are proud of being middle class, and Rodney's rejection of the most basic middle-class value, marriage, dismays them.

"They blame my career," he says. "After the Army, I joined the State

Department. I've traveled all over the world, seldom living anywhere for longer than three years. It's easy to blame my lifestyle on the travel."

Rodney is mostly satisfied with his life, and the areas of dissatisfaction center around his career achievements, not his personal living arrangements. He can't imagine being married, and having interviewed him in his Crystal City, Virginia, apartment, I can't imagine him being married either. Crystal City is a a virtual high-rise dorm for Pentagon and other government employees. The impersonal box within a stack of boxes suits Rodney, who was serving his first "stateside" assignment in a decade. (A week after I interviewed him, he called to say he'd just received notice he was on his way to Asia in two months.) His apartment looks ready for a white-glove inspection at any moment. I ask him to bounce a quarter on his bed, and he does. Yes, it bounces. Even the reading material on his coffee table and bedside tables is aligned uniformly to the edges of the tables.

"A woman spent the night last night," he says. "I told her she could sleep in because I had to leave for work by seven-thirty. When I got home, I saw that she'd tried to make the bed."

Tried?

"It was all wrong. I remade it, of course."

Of course.

"My sister used to tell me I was 'anal retentive.' I haven't heard that phrase in a while. Now I think they say 'obsessive-compulsive.' I do have those traits, I suppose. I do some things I wish I didn't do, like counting. When I'm walking, I'll count my steps. I can tell you how many steps from the elevator to the lobby door, things like that. Compulsive?" He raises his eyebrows and laughs. "Probably. I dated a woman who told me how cute my butt was. She said it thirteen times over a weekend we spent away together. I didn't see her again. Okay, she liked my butt. But thirteen times? Women talk to fill the silences, and I don't mind talking, but not if I have nothing to say."

Rodney has dated white women exclusively when he's in the United States. He blames this only partially on "early imprinting." His first crush was on a little white girl. The centerfolds in *Playboy* and *Penthouse* constituted his initial exposure to "pussy." At the time, they were all white, except for the occasional Eurasian woman.

"*But,*" he says, pointing his finger to emphasize the word, "that's only part of the story. I did date black women in my twenties when I lived in Chicago and Washington, D.C. They were more interested in the size of my paycheck than the size of my cock. Afro-American women are golddiggers. As they get older, they get bossier—and fatter. Show me an Afro-American woman my age and I'll show you an angry, loud, fat woman. I don't care how much education she has. She'll fit the pattern.

"White women are more likely to keep their shape, pay their way, and speak in well-modulated tones. Call me a racist pig, if you like, but that's where I am. It's not a skin color issue. I have dated black African and Haitian women, as well as Asian women. I am open to any race, class, or type, except the African-American woman."

When Rodney moved back to D.C. last year, he ran a personals ad in *City Paper*, the alternative weekly paper. He described himself as a "cosmopolitan world traveler, a black man in search of a relationship with an American white, Asian, European, African, or Hispanic woman. No African-American women please." Some African-American women left angry messages on the voice mail. If they included numbers, he called them back and explained his position.

"That was only common courtesy," he says.

Did they receive it in the courteous spirit in which he intended it?

"No!" He laughs. "I got my share of lectures. Maybe what I said made one woman think. If I accomplished that much, I did some good."

In addition to having rigorous housekeeping standards, Rodney has a set of limited personal tastes that take on an almost religious significance in his life. They are requirements, rather than preferences, and they include: meat, largely beef, at all meals; cigarettes, one and a half to two packs a day; two to three "perfect" dry vodka martinis prior to dinner each night; and no interruptions while he's watching television. Rodney is a fan of *Star Trek* in all its incarnations, the Dallas Cowboys, an assortment of sitcoms, and action films. When he is at home alone in the United States, he parks himself in front of the television, remote control in one hand, cigarette in the other, from the evening news to the last syndicated repeat of *Star Trek*. He will not answer the phone when "his shows" are on. When he reads, it's probably a book he's read before, like *Beau Geste*, a novel about the French foreign legion he's read thirty times.

"I am not the most interesting man in the world," he concedes, "but I am content."

Rodney does have an enlightened sexual attitude. He realized at a young age that he was a man of "average" endowment. Such a man, he reasoned, needed an erotic specialty to stand out in a woman's mind as a good lover. He made cunnilingus his sexual calling card.

"I really get into it," he says. "I enjoy doing it. I love what I can do to a woman with my tongue. More than one woman has told me how good I am at oral sex." He grins. "A man has to have something to fall back on in his old age. My penis doesn't get as hard as it did. That's life."

Rodney began perfecting his cunnilingus technique at an early age, fifteen, on his own hand. ("I shaped my like the hand puppet character Señor Wenslas or a name to that effect.") He was inspired by a cartoon in *Playboy*. The woman in the drawing was spread-eagled on the bed; the man had his face between her legs.

"I don't remember the caption. I wasn't sure what the man was supposed to be doing to the woman, but I aspired to find out. Nothing had ever captivated my interest like this cartoon did. Luckily, I found some dirty books in a used-book store in the French Quarter. My parents were believers in reading. They never censored our reading material, never even looked at the books we brought home unless we offered to share them. I taught myself the intricacies of pussy eating. Though I didn't get the opportunity to practice until I was almost seventeen, I can honestly say I knew what I was doing before my tongue hit the velvet."

In general, Rodney is satisfied with his sex life. He wishes he had the rock-hard erections of his youth. And he wishes women who were like-minded on the issue of marriage were easier to find than they have been throughout his life, and particularly during the past year, in Washington.

"I could not have enjoyed the range of experience with one woman that I've had with many," he says. "I love women. I've learned a lot from each woman I've been with. Occasionally I hear from an old girlfriend, and I enjoy that. It's nice to know I haven't been forgotten.

"Last year, when I was in India, a woman I'd known in France came to see me. She was recently divorced and wanted to renew our sexual acquaintance. Getting to know her all over again was wonderful. She told me no man had ever eaten her pussy like I had, and that kind of flattering is what keeps me warm on lonely nights."

BOOMERS SEX TIPS

"ABC"
(Recorded by the Jackson 5 for Motown Records)

Lifelong bachelors frequently pride themselves on their lovemaking abilities. Rodney, like his female counterpart Katie, has a few tricks.

He says, "If a man isn't paying a woman's bills, he has to give her something she can't get everywhere." His three best "tricks" are:

Cunnilingus

In addition to mastering the techniques described on page 24. Rodney advises: Use your nose. He alternates licking and sucking with massaging the area around the clitoris with the bridge or the tip of his nose. Women, he says, love the nose.

Hand Kissing

"Hand kissing is a lost art," he says, "and women love having their hands kissed. Hold her hand. Lower your lips to the back of her hand while maintaining eye contact."

I shared with Rodney a thrilling variation on hand kissing taught me by a French gigolo: the wrist kiss. Turn her hand over. Lower your lips to her wrist while maintaining eye contact. Then close your eyes and use your tongue on her wrist as you would her clitoris. Open your eyes. Make eye contact with her while keeping your lips on her wrist. If you don't feel her pulse now, she may not have one.

The Flower Petal Massage

Buy a dozen roses. They need not be expensive. The roses available on the street in big cities or in the supermarket flower sections in suburban areas will suffice. Take all the petals off and place in a bowl in the refrigerator. (Don't do this too far ahead of time. While she's sipping her wine and waiting for the foreplay is good timing.) When she is aroused and naked on your bed, take the flower petals out of the refrigerator, sprinkle them on her body, especially breasts and genitals. Using the pads of your fingers, massage gently.

THE OLD HEART OF MINE (IS WEAK FOR YOU)

"When we kissed, you reminded me of what I missed."
(Recorded by Isley Brothers for BMI)

"In your twenties, living together is part grand adventure, part economic necessity," Christine says. "And in your forties, living together is part grand adventure, part economic conservatism. You're in love, you want to be to-gether, but you don't want to lose what you have in a breakup."

Christine, forty-two, has been living with Mark, forty-six, for two years. Neither of them wants to marry again. They each owned a house and had investments and retirement accounts when they met at a bar mitzvah in suburban Maryland in 1995. He is a friend of the boy's father, she a business partner of the mother. They'd heard about each other, but had re-sisted "the fix-up." His marriage ended in divorce when his wife left him for another woman. Her husband died of cancer. Pleasantly surprised to find one another likable and attractive, they made a dinner date for the fol-lowing night.

"We had *fun*," she says. "I didn't realize how much I'd missed having fun with a man until I started seeing Mark." After stressing the "fun" as-pect of her relationship, she adds, "He's only the second man I was physi-cally attracted to after my husband died. The first one was fifty, and he didn't have a job. I looked at him, saw a man without an income, and willed my hormones to bubble back down. With Mark, everything came together."

Christine, the third of three daughters, was born in 1956, in Bethesda, Maryland. A decorated war hero, her father worked for the State Depart-ment, and her mother was a housewife, apparently a happy one. Christine can't recall any evidence to the contrary.

"They were everybody's ideal parents," she says, "youthful, attractive, energetic. We lost my mother to breast cancer in 1973, when I was sev-enteen. I was devastated. My father never really recovered. I remember every song from that year, especially 'Tie a Yellow Ribbon Round the Old Oak Tree.' My sisters and I tied yellow ribbons around the bushes and trees outside my mother's hospital room window. She was too sick to re-alize it.

"After she died, I lost my virginity to my steady boyfriend, Curtis. It was an okay experience, but I cried afterward, thinking about my mother. The next year I went away to college. After a year at Swarthmore, I trans-ferred to American University in D.C., because I missed my father and my sisters. The oldest one was married and living in Bethesda; the middle one was going to school at the University of Maryland in College Park."

Christine met the man she would marry at a private party at a disco club in 1979. She was twenty-three, and he was thirty-seven, a diplomat from a European nation, a widower with a teenage daughter. It was love at first sight. They were married the following year.

"The sex in our marriage was always good," she says, "but, after the first year or two, it wasn't a matter of great urgency. We had so much else. Our only child, a son, was born before our second anniversary. We were posted to South America. I had so much to do, with a baby, a stepdaughter, and social obligations.

"We had a wonderful life together. He retired in 1992, at age fifty. We bought a house in Bethesda and kept the apartment in Paris. He was going to write books. We had so many plans. And then he got sick and was gone. I felt like I had when my mother died, only worse. People kept telling me, 'You're young; you'll marry again.' In their haste to offer superficial comfort, people can be stupid and cruel. I never want to marry again.

"I love Mark, and I enjoy being with him, but I won't marry him or anyone else."

After they decided to live together because "the commute was killing," Mark rented out his house in Fairfax, Virginia, and moved into hers. He pays rent to her. They divide the utilities and other expenses, such as groceries. When they go out to dinner, he pays. Neither knows exactly what the other is worth. They keep their finances separate and strictly private. Photos of her late husband are in almost every room of the home she now shares with Mark. His furniture and most of his personal effects are in storage.

Does he mind living inside a shrine to another man?

"If he does, he's never mentioned it," she says. "I don't think he sees it that way. He understands that my husband died. He didn't leave me. It would be different if Mark kept pictures of his ex-wife around. I would have to wonder why he didn't just stay with her."

Mark didn't stay with his wife because he finally tired of her alcoholism. Their son, twenty-two, encouraged him to leave. The divorce brought them closer together. Mark's son and Christine's son, seventeen, are cordial but not friends. No one is pressuring them to become friends.

"We aren't trying to turn ourselves into the Brady Bunch," Christine says. "Things are fine the way they are."

And the sex?

"Oh, that's good," she says. "We had a fight about sex after we first got together, specifically about oral sex. That's something I won't do. He tried to persuade me, but he couldn't. I never have done it, and I'm never going to do it. I think it's cheap. If a woman has any pride, she won't perform that service for a man."

The Survey Says
- 40 percent of Vietnam-generation men who cohabit and 63 percent of women report having sex 1.8 times a week, the average for married couples their age.
- 42 percent of Watergate-generation men who cohabit and 56 percent of women report having sex 1.9 times a week, the average for married couples their age.

Other Surveys Say

According to many surveys, cohabiting couples have more sex than married couples. However, the surveys typically include more respondents in their twenties than Boomers of either generation. For example, a study reported in *the Journal of Marital and Family Therapy* found that cohabitants had sexual relations an average 3.1 times a week, compared to 2.4 for married couples. The ages of participants ranged from twenty-one to fifty-four, but 75 percent were between the ages of twenty-one and thirty-one.

I recalled the conversation with Christine about oral sex when I was introduced to Mark a few weeks later. He looks and acts older than his forty-six years, his laconic style a contrast to Christine's ebullience. They are affectionate in a manner reminiscent of older couples who've been together a long time. She calls him "Pie," short for "Sweetie Pie." He calls her "Teenie," a funny nickname for a woman who is nearly six feet tall and robust.

"He won't talk to you about sex," she confides after the introductions are made. "He's uncomfortable with the subject."

She was right. He didn't, and he was. If I'd thought she was limiting his sex life by her views on oral sex, I changed my mind after meeting him. They seemed well suited to each other.

I met several cohabiting couples in both the Vietnam and Watergate generations. Most of them, like most single and married Boomers, are practicing, or have practiced, oral sex. Otherwise, they have something in common with Christine and Mark: Unlike younger cohabiting couples, who tend to pool their resources more generously, these men and women keep their money separate, and they keep financial score.

Why do they live together when they could afford to live apart?

They cite as their primary reasons companionship, mutual emotional support, and the pleasure of not sleeping alone.

The Boomer Facts

- The determinedly single are in the minority of singles, but their numbers among the Boomer generation are surely larger than they were among previous generations. Women are more likely now to choose the single life, especially if they are financially independent. These singles don't fit the stereotype of "old maids" and "committed bachelors." They are more often than not gregarious people with strong social support systems of family and friends.
- More single women than has been previously acknowledged can have sex without "love," i.e. the kind of love that leads to commitment, marriage, and the sharing of domestic chores. They can fall in and out of love with their sex partners without feeling the need to commit. And they are more likely to describe themselves as "happy" and "satisfied" with their lives than their single male counterparts. Single men in general tend to be more rigid and isolated than women.
- The motivations for and the rules of cohabiting differ among Boomers and the younger generations. Younger couples typically see living together as a marriage tryout and more generously pool their resources than Boomers do. Since 1970, the rate of living together has increased fivefold, with more than a third of adults twenty-five to thirty-five cohabiting before marriage and 61 percent of people ages twenty-five to forty-four living together before getting remarried. Boomers have reasons for living together, but they don't always include testing the marital waters and financial pooling of resources.

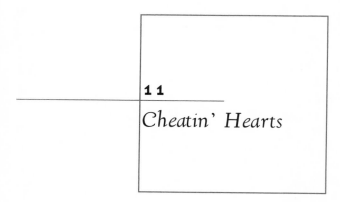

11

Cheatin' Hearts

According to the conventional wisdom, women can't have sex without loving, can't love more than one man at a time, won't have affairs unless their marriages are bad, and will suffer pangs of guilt about them even if their marriages *are* bad. Men, on the other hand, can do all of the above, hold the guilt. In this popular view of men, women, and adultery—nourished by film, television, books, music, and mothers—the "cheating" wife usually pays by losing husband, lover, or both, and often the "innocent" wife pays, too, by losing her husband to another, probably younger, woman.

Real life often defies conventional wisdom. The men and women interviewed for this section, unlike other married people who'd had affairs, accept themselves as nonmonogamous beings. Rather than labeling their affairs "mistakes," "indiscretions," or something similar, they see sexual relationships outside marriage as their own private indulgences, not a betrayal, a sin, a reason to rush into marital therapy. They've done it before and may well do it again, they say, and so what?

Statistics vary widely about the percentage of married people involved in affairs though most show that more men than women still admit to having extramarital affairs, sometimes by two to one. The gap, however, is closing, now that the Boomers own the cheating years. More women have affairs in the same way men do—with no intention of leaving their partners for their lovers—and for the sex, not the emotional sustenance.

"Cheating" has become more difficult to define in the electronic era, too. Some husbands and wives don't have physical affairs. They participate in cybersex or phone sex. Does a cybersex affair have the same potential impact upon a marriage as the real thing? Is it really even sex if you never touch?

The Survey Says

- 62 percent of Vietnam-generation men and 49 percent of women have had (or are having) an extramarital affair. 25 percent of men and 24 percent of women report the affair was discovered, leading to problems within the marriage. Only 9 percent of men and 12 percent of women left their spouses over the affair, and less than 5 percent of men and 10 percent of women married the lover.
- For 26 percent of Vietnam-generation men and 22 percent of women, having an extramarital liaison is an ongoing part of life. In other words, more of them plan to continue leading a double life than have divorced and married their lovers.
- 59 percent of Watergate-generation men and 52 percent of women have had (or are having) an extramarital affair. 14 percent of men and 18 percent of women report the affair was discovered, leading to problems within the marriage. Only 7 percent of men and 8 percent of women left their spouses over the affair, and less than 5 percent of men and 6 percent of women married the lover.
- For 20 percent of Watergate-generation men and 22 percent of women, having an extramarital liaison is an ongoing part of life. Again, more of them plan to continue leading a double life than have divorced and married their lovers. More women than men left a spouse to marry a lover.

Generally, there are two types of affairs, the emotionally superficial and the emotionally involved. Obviously, superficial affairs, the more common variety, pose less risk to the marriage, particularly if the affair is never discovered. The majority of men and women who have affairs have casual dalliances, sometimes only one or two in a lifelong marriage. Moralists and marital therapists don't like to acknowledge this, but there may be no consequences at all to such lapses of monogamy. When lovers begin to think of themselves as soul mates, trouble may lie ahead. Or again, maybe not. Some people can balance the double life. For others, the passion peaks and declines, much as it did in the marriage or in past affairs, and, if the thrill is gone before they're found out by their mates, they lose nothing.

Men and women have affairs today for much the same reasons they always did. The primary reason Boomers in both age groups gave for having an affair: sex. They went outside the marriage to get more sex or a different kind of sex than they'd been getting at home. Often nonsexual issues get in the way of sex. Rather than resolving the issues, the partners look for the sex elsewhere. Since Kinsey asked the first sex-survey question, men have been saying they have affairs to get more sex. The surprise is that now women increasingly have the same answer. More women than men cited emotional needs, such as the need for attention, romance, an ego boost—but the hard answer, sex, was more often than not their answer, too.

A forty-year-old woman married for fifteen years, said, "I have occasional affairs. I don't want them to go anywhere. If they look like they might, I end them. I'd only been with two other men when I got married, and I got the itch before seven years. I could not imagine living my whole life without experiencing more."

Like this woman, a forty-four-year-old man said he didn't fall into extramarital affairs. He planned them. "People who had never planned to cheat end up falling in love and messing up their lives over it," he said. "A few years into the marriage, I knew I would have affairs. I also knew I would stay married."

The desire to remain married while having affairs characterizes the "cheatin' hearts" I interviewed for this section. They are satisfied with their lives. They like the emotional, social, and economic comfort of their marriages. And, yes, many say they also like the sex. Maybe they need the element of risk, the romantic tension, the sex they just can't get in their own beds. Some say the affair improves the marriage, including the sex. The straying spouse returns sexually charged and just guilty enough to be kinder than he or she might otherwise be. Most have few regrets and fewer excuses. The uncertainty about tomorrow that surrounds illicit lovemaking imparts an aura of fond regret even before the good-byes are said. If orgasm is a "little death," as the French say, then orgasm outside the sanctity of marriage has a special, more mortal, status.

"This is not my mama's affair," one woman said.

AMERICAN GIRL

"She was an American girl, raised on promises . . ."
(Recorded by Tom Petty and the Heartbreakers for MCA Records)

"I am the lady of the manor," Meredith says, "the queen of my castle. I grew up in a very comfortable north Jersey bedroom community, and I expected to marry well. This," she says, indicating the two-story great room on the first level of her house, "is more than I expected."

Meredith, forty-one, is the ultimate upper-middle-class wife. Groomed, toned, taut, and glossy, she lives with her husband and two children in a luxurious suburban community outside a major city on the East Coast. There are no street signs in her neighborhood. If you don't know where you're going here, you can't get there—and that is surely the point. Markers indicating directions to major highways are ultra-discreet, printed in small letters on tasteful signs half-buried in the foliage. On my way to Meredith's house, I got lost. Passing mansion after mansion set like jewels in little parks well back from the tree-lined roads, I felt like Dorothy in Oz. This wasn't Interstate 70 anymore. Judging from my informal research, cheaters are more likely to abide here than they are within the middle-class communities where both spouses typically work and someone, be it neighbor, relative, colleague, or friend, can testify to their whereabouts most of the time. Adultery may be a game more often played by the rich or the very poor, who in different ways have time and access.

Meredith's husband, Jonathan, is—you must have guessed by now—the CEO of a corporation. He is rarely at home. She estimates he has spent less than a dozen full evenings at home with the family, from dinner through bedtime, in the past year. Typically, he arrives home after their children, boys aged thirteen and fourteen, are in bed, at least on school nights. He also travels frequently.

"If he's in by eleven, that's a good night," she says. "He has a company limo and a driver, of course. Otherwise the ninety-minute commute each way would wear him down. You don't live this kind of life with a man who has a nine-to-five job, unless he's inherited money. We all make sacrifices in exchange for the kind of pleasures only money can buy. He isn't doing it for our sakes alone. No. He would do it anyway. When he's angry at me about something, he says, 'I do this for you and the boys,' but it isn't true. He knows it isn't true. We are the beneficiaries, but we aren't the motivation.

"I am very satisfied with my life. I'm one of the world's most fortunate people, and I know it. And I'm very satisfied with my sex life. When my husband has time for sex, he's a good enough lover—not the best I've ever had, but good." She pauses for effect. Dressed in a black lycra jumpsuit and high black wedge sandals, she inhales deeply to emphasize her figure, expels the breath, and says, "I have affairs. If you have a marriage like mine and you don't have affairs, you're going to end up angry and resentful. I don't get what the average woman gets from her husband: time, attention, emotional support. He was in Brazil when our second son was born, in Thailand when my mother died. If I need reassurance about something, he's in a meeting. He tries to be there for me and the boys, but it's seldom possible. That's the reality of his, *our*, life.

"But he is a good lover. There is something incredibly sexy about money and power. It stays sexy. The dirty little secret is that money and power remain sexy, no matter how long you're exposed to them, while beauty, a particular beauty, can grow tiresome."

Meredith was groomed for marrying a man like Jonathan. Her mother, who bears more than a passing resemblance to Jackie Kennedy toward the end of her life, married well and was determined that her daughter, the inheritor of her dark beauty, would marry better. She did. Ironically, no one thought it would be Jonathan, a friend of her older brother's.

"My brother and Jonathan were pals from nursery school," she says. "Jonathan was around our house so much he was an honorary sibling. We teased each other like brother and sister. I didn't think about him as a romantic partner until I came back from Europe at the end of my sophomore summer. Jonathan and my brother had graduated from Yale that June. It was 1977. Jonathan had a job in another city, but he was home for a wedding. He needed a date for it, and I had a great new dress I'd bought in Paris.

"We went to the wedding together. My mother took pictures of us before we left the house, like we were going to the prom. When I walked out the door with him, I took his arm, the way women do in Europe. He told me later he saw me in a different way from that moment on. We had a wonderful time at the reception, dancing and flirting with each other. I looked better than I ever had, and the effect wasn't lost on Jonathan. People treated us as though we were a couple.

"There was an awkward moment when he turned off the car's engine in my driveway. I sensed that I would be like Cinderella at midnight turning forevermore back into his best friend's kid sister if I didn't seize the moment. He turned toward me as if he wanted to kiss me, but he hesitated. I leapt into the hesitation by leaning toward him. Nothing else was required. He took my face tenderly in his hands and kissed me full on the mouth. I Frenched him. He asked me to have dinner with him the following night.

It was the beginning of a whirlwind bicoastal courtship that culminated in a beautiful wedding on New Year's Day 1978.

"My mother thought it was a bad day for a wedding, but she didn't put up much resistance. It was clear that Jonathan was going places fast. She was delighted to see me catch that train. From the beginning, he was insanely busy, substituting gifts for time, quickies for the real deal. But we came into the eighties like the kids in the first car of the biggest ride at the amusement park. He gave me a sable coat when our first son was born. How many women get sable in their twenties?"

Meredith didn't have her first affair until after her children were born. The boys were two and three. She had a group of female friends, all well-married young wives, who met at one another's home once or twice a week for wine and emotional bonding. Their angst fed hers.

"I felt sorry for myself because my husband was neglecting me," she says. "In that wounded frame of mind I did something that could be considered stereotypical behavior for a woman my age now: I had a little fling with the pool guy. I was discreet. The first time it happened the boys and their nanny were at a play date. Serendipity. I arranged pool treatments to coincide with play dates until I got tired of the pool guy."

That "fling" liberated her. She eased away from the group of women friends whom, she realized, she didn't trust enough to share her secret with. More important, she stopped being resentful of her husband.

"Partly out of guilt, I started being a lot nicer to Jonathan," she says. "He appreciated the change enough to take four days off and whisk me away to Paris."

The pattern was established. Whenever Meredith feels neglected, resentful, unhappy, or restless, she has a "fling." Lovers have included her personal trainer, poetry teacher, a "Mr. Mom" she met at a nursery school function. She is careful to choose "discreet" men, leaves no paper trail, and never confides in her friends.

Does Jonathan suspect? Does she suspect he has affairs of his own?

"I don't think he suspects, but I can't be positive," she says. "No, I don't think he has affairs. He doesn't have time. I guess he's had a few quickies with other women over the years, or more likely received blow jobs from subordinates. Young women are willing to go down on their knees for the boss. I know he's not had an emotional involvement with anyone else. Nor have I.

"I love my husband. I love my life. The only thing that scares me is aging. When you turn forty, you can feel the breath of the wannabe trophy wife on your neck. I don't really think Jonathan will leave me for another woman some day, but I can't realistically say that would never happen. What women in my position can?

"I spend a lot of time and money on my body, my hair, my skin. Yes, I'll get a face lift as soon as I need one, probably in four or five years. I'll do everything I can. When I'm fifty, I'm not going to look like thirty anymore." She holds a hand out in front of her. "Hands, for example. I've read about treatments that can zap age spots and deflate veins, but I'm skeptical. Whenever I meet a middle-aged woman whose face lift looks very good, I check out her hands. I'm not seeing evidence of miracles being worked on hands yet."

SOUND BITE

From a conversation with a thirty-nine-year-old woman: "Affairs aren't for women who have to tell every little thing to a girlfriend. My friends would be shocked if they knew about my other life. Women are so judgmental, especially of each other. I know a woman who bragged at work about telling a friend's husband that his wife—her *friend*—was cheating on him."

BOOMER SEX TIPS

Travelin' Man
(Recorded by Ricky Nelson for Atlantic Records)

The "How To Tell If He's Cheating" article is a standard feature in women's magazines. Perusing the contents page of a men's magazine would leave a reader suspecting that women never stray. They most certainly do. Some clues that may indicate he or she is cheating: You're having more (or less) sex than usual, he or she is kinder (or more hostile) than usual, and so forth. It couldn't be clearer.

More to the point, a polling of marital therapists concluded that there are numerous factors that will predict whether or not an affair leads to divorce. They include:

• The strength of the bond prior to the affair. Couples who have drifted apart emotionally are more susceptible to emotional involvement in affairs.

• The quality of their sex life prior to the affair. A man or woman

> won't necessarily leave a spouse for better sex with a lover—unless
> the sex had been bad, or missing, for some time.
> - The straying spouse's basic value system. Remaining faithful is
>   more important to some people than to others. The strength of his
>   or her commitment may not prevent him or her from having an
>   affair under any circumstances, but it will cause him or her to end
>   the affair and return to the marriage.

DARLING, BE HOME SOON

*"Come and talk about the things we did today and laugh about our
funny little ways."*
(Recorded by the Lovin' Spoonful for the Special Music Company)

"I love my wife," Phillip says. "We have a good life together. She is my
partner in every sense of the word. I would never be happy with anyone
who isn't a true equal, and Cassandra is. Her career has always been as important as mine. We are friends."

Don't nominate Phillip for husband of the year until you hear the rest
of his story.

"I haven't had intercourse with anyone else since I married Cassandra,"
he says.

Back after an absence of several weeks at Blueberry Hill in University
City, my Boomer shrine, I had to ask the obvious question: If not intercourse, then what form of sexual expression might he have been sharing
with other women outside marriage?

"Oral sex, phone sex, mutual masturbation—nothing that constitutes a
violation of my marriage vows."

Here is the truly shocking news about Boomer affairs: More married
men than women have sexual relationships that stop short of intercourse.
When a woman has an affair, she has an *affair*. In other words, she has sex
the way adults have sex, and that typically includes intercourse. A lot of
Boomer men have extramarital sexual relationships that mirror their high
school escapades. They don't go "all the way." But they expect the added
bonus, the sexual favor due to men of their stature: fellatio. Surveys of call
girls in the past decade have indicated that men more often pay for fellatio
than intercourse. My research leads me to conclude it's also their sex play of

choice when they aren't picking up the tab. Bill Clinton is not the only man who doesn't consider fellatio *sex*.

"I don't feel like I'm cheating on Cassandra," Phillip says, "if I'm getting a blow job from a girl who means nothing to me. It's not a betrayal." He has not asked his wife if the receiving of blow jobs is included in her definition of "betrayal." "Oh, come on," he chides. "Who would do that? You're asking for trouble when you bring up the subject."

Phillip, who turned fifty this year, has been married to Cassandra, forty-five, for twenty years. When they wed in 1978 in Jamaica, he was an idealistic young public defender in St. Louis County, and she was working toward her master's degree in social work and employed by a social-services agency. They were, he says, "going to change the world," but, as often happens, the world changed them.

"My clients were basically all guilty," he says, "and more often than not, guilty of heinous crimes. I'd had this vision of myself defending the unjustly accused, being the spokesperson for the powerless and the downtrodden. It wasn't like that. Cassandra was learning a similar lesson in social work. Day after day, she was confronted with people who would lie, cheat, and steal to get the government benefits that allowed them to stay home, sleep all day, drink, and do drugs. We got jaded fast.

"I got out of the public defender's office and into a firm that represents a lot of white-collar criminals. They are all basically guilty, but the crimes are less heinous, and I am well compensated for my efforts in their behalf. The bottom line: I'd rather defend some guy who ripped off his employer than one who stabbed his grandmother to death because she wouldn't give him her last five dollars for a crack buy. Cassandra is part-owner, with another woman, of a clothing and accessories boutique. They do quite well with it, largely because they pioneered the idea of the personal shopper in this area.

"I am proud of her," he says; and he seems sincere. "She's a smart businesswoman, a good mother to our two kids, a good wife, a lovely, sexy woman."

Won't she perform fellatio?

"Of course she will," he says, laughing. "That's not the point. In marriage, everything is quid pro quo, with oral sex being a little more my responsibility to dispense than hers. It's understood that women need cunnilingus to have an orgasm, while men don't, strictly speaking, 'need' fellatio. I get it. I'm not a caveman.

"Cassandra is good, though seldom enthusiastic, at fellatio. Look, I don't expect her, after twenty years, to get all hot and bothered over putting my cock in her mouth."

Phillip leans back against the wooden booth. His little pot belly is more noticeable now. I look at him closely and try to imagine what would inspire a woman to crawl under the booth, unzip his pants, and get 'all hot and bothered' by taking his penis into her mouth. I can't. He is a typical middle-aged professional white male, a little paunchy, slightly balding, eyes more weary than piercing behind wire-rimmed glasses.

"Younger women," he says, "get more excited about giving a blow job. They get all caught up in their own feelings of power. Giving head makes them feel powerful. That's what excites them. It's really more about them than me, or the man."

The waitress, who appears to be a college girl, brings our burgers. She doesn't notice him at all.

Phillip and Cassandra met in the fall of 1976 at Culpepper's, a restaurant-bar known for its spicy chicken wings in the the city's Central West End section. He was with a group of young lawyers from the public defenders's office; she was with four friends. It was happy hour.

"The guys struck up a conversation with the girls," he says. "There was a lot of laughing and teasing going on between the tables. I didn't notice her particularly at first. She is small, with brown hair, not the kind of woman who jumps out at you at first. Another woman at the table, a buxom redhead who was very lively, had everybody's attention, including mine. It was soon clear to me she was throwing her best lines at another guy, so I looked around the table more closely. I settled on Cassandra. I liked her poise. Under their giggly demeanor, the other girls were agitated that the redhead had the floor. You could see them struggling for place. Not Cassandra. She was sure of herself, not competitive. I liked that. I pulled my chair closer to hers and introduced myself. Later she gave me her card. I called her the next day and made a date for the weekend.

"We had sex on the first date, and we were immediately sexually compatible. Whenever I hear women say you should hold out to get a man to marry you, I laugh. Sex and marriage are separate. I knew I was going to marry Cassandra right away, whether we had sex sooner or later."

He proposed the following month at a Democratic Party celebration following Jimmy Carter's election. They were at Kennedy's, a restaurant-bar on Laclede's Landing, the rehabbed riverfront district. The room was so noisy, he had to yell, "Will you marry me?" She screamed back, "Yes!" They were engaged for more than a year before the wedding.

"The last few months before we got married were the most stressful in our relationship. Everybody had to throw in their two cents' worth about the wedding. Finally we scrapped the big wedding plans and arranged to get married in Jamaica, where we'd already booked the honeymoon, with only our bridesmaid and best man in attendance. The families were furious. Once we made that decision, we were tight with each other again. Nobody came between us. The honeymoon sex was great. We made love on the beach at night, something I'd always fantasized doing."

Neither career crises nor the demands of child rearing have put a serious crimp in their sex life, Phillip says. Their lovemaking remains satisfactory, sometimes better than that. They suffer the occasional doldrums of routine sex, he concedes, but, he asks, "Who doesn't after twenty years?" Yet only five years into the marriage, Phillip was playing sex games with other partners.

"I don't consider them affairs," he says. "I had my first little dalliance with another lawyer, a married woman, who was also a junior partner at the firm. We used to make out in the supply closet. It never went any further than groping, kissing, dry humping. I fondled her breasts, put a hand between her hot thighs, not inside her pantyhose. It isn't all that easy to get a hand inside pantyhose. She rubbed me outside my trousers. I came with her a few times, but I preferred to avoid that. It's messy.

"When I went home, I was so hot for Cassandra, I had to have her as soon as I could get her alone in a corner. It was good for our marriage. I saw it was. That opened my eyes. Everything we're told about monogamy and sexual fidelity is half wrong. Playing around to a certain extent improves the marriage. You take the outside stimulus home, and your partner is flattered as hell to be that desirable to you."

After his "eyes were opened," Phillip was alert for other erotic marriage-improvement opportunities. As he grew older and more powerful within the firm and the community, he discovered that younger women found him attractive. They were eager to share erotic time with him, on his terms, at his convenience.

"When the TV series *L.A. Law* went on the air in 1987, lawyers got sex appeal. Women expected me to be Corbin Bernsen. I've been told there is some resemblance." He smiles. There isn't. "Well, anyway, it gave my reputation a boost. One week in the fall of '88, I got blow jobs from a legal assistant, an attractive client, and the ex-wife of one of the partners. That was particularly satisfying. The eighties were heady times for me and Cassandra. She was dressing everyone who came into her shop like a *Dynasty* character. We had money to spend. The kids were in a good groove. Everything was good. We built a sunroom with a hot tub and a deck on the back of the house."

If everything was good, why the blow jobs?

"Why not the blow jobs?" he countered. "You have sex when you're high, when you're on a roll. Why not have sex play under the same conditions? If I'd been worried about my job or my marriage, I might not have had the enthusiasm for playing around that I had.

"I reiterate: It has nothing to do with Cassandra, with our marriage, with how much I love her or how good our sex life is. This is my thing, my little corner of the world."

He has not entirely lost the enthusiasm for the game, but he has slowed down from the late eighties and the high of a three-blow-job week. In recent years, he has become a devotee of phone sex, particularly when he's out of town.

"I have been traveling more since I was made a senior partner," he says. "If I meet a woman who excites me in a hotel bar, I'll talk to her, buy her some drinks, maybe kiss and canoodle, then I'll go to my room and she'll go to hers. And I'll phone her. You'd be surprised how many women welcome the opportunity to talk dirty. Phone sex is liberating. I masturbate. She masturbates. When we're finished, we hang up. No mess. If her husband calls or Cassandra calls me, they get the message that their spouse is in the room, on the phone, presumably doing business into the wee hours.

"Cassandra knows I'll check my voice mail and return calls to my partners, if it's important, twenty-four hours a day."

Is he satisfied with his life in general?

"Yes, very much so. My position in the firm is solid. The financial rewards have been more than I anticipated they would be. I truly enjoy my kids. And, most of all, I could never find anyone who suits me as well as Cassandra does."

And he is satisfied with his sex life?

"Yes. One always wants more, of course, but yes, I'm satisfied."

SEX TIPS FOR BOOMERS

"That's the Way (I Like It)"
(Recorded by K. C. & the Sunshine Band, for T. K. Records)

The Instant Vibrating Mouth

One of Phillip's enthusiastic younger playmates surprised him with this variation on fellatio: She held a small vibrator at low speed under her tongue as she licked him, then moved it to beneath her chin while sucking. A man can employ the vibrator in the same way while performing cunnilingus.

YOU CAN'T ALWAYS GET WHAT YOU WANT . . .

"But if you try sometimes you just might find you get what you need."
(Recorded by the Rolling Stones for Atlantic Records)

"Affairs are going to happen in a long-term relationship," Mary says. "People don't talk about it much anymore, but that doesn't mean it isn't happening. I can't speak for Dick"—her husband—"but I am happy to tell you my story, and he'll tell you his. We have a 'don't ask, don't tell,' policy in our marriage. It wasn't always like this. We almost broke up over affairs, and we don't want that to happen again."

Mary, forty-five, and Dick, fifty-one, have been married for twenty-five years. Their only child, a boy, was born with cystic fibrosis and died in 1981 at age six. Both refuse to talk about his short, sad life and death. "It's too traumatic," Mary explains. Many couples divorce following the death of a child. They stayed together, but had affairs.

"We were too sensitive to each other's touch," she says. "Making love was raw and painful for a long time. It was like my skin hurt when he touched it. I didn't feel that way with other men, and I'm sure he didn't feel that way with other women. Sometimes in bed at night, one or the other of us would flinch if we accidentally made physical contact. We were careful to sleep without touching."

When they got married, in 1973, she says, "we couldn't keep our hands off each other. If you had told us that we'd spend our tenth anniversary on opposite sides of the bed, we wouldn't have believed it. We were so romantic and idealistic, I'm sure we would have said, 'No, divorce would be preferable to living like that.' But we lived that way from 1981 to 1985."

Mary implies that the affairs, begun as a means of dulling pain, continue, albeit sporadically, because of their tragic loss. Dick has a different perspective. Affairs, he believes, are as common to marriage as shared mortgages and family holiday celebrations.

"Mary and I went through a difficult period where we couldn't give each other comfort, sexually or otherwise," he says. "We would have divorced if the bond between us hadn't been as strong as it was. Our affairs were the catalyst for getting our marriage back. We hadn't been able to make love for years after we lost our boy. She had affairs, and I had affairs. We caught each other out and decided to divorce. Then we realized how jealous we were of each other, how much we wanted to get back together. We started making love again, and we're still together, after all these years.

"I would have had affairs anyway, not because I don't love Mary, and not because she doesn't satisfy me. I do, and she does. Affairs happen anyway. My father had them, and my grandfather before him. The difference now is that women cheat, too."

Dick and Mary met when she interviewed him for a college term paper. He was a young physician volunteering at a storefront clinic in the Bronx on his days off. She was majoring in social work at Hunter College in Manhattan.

"I only got a C on the paper, but I got Dick," she says, laughing. "We started dating in 1974, when I was twenty. He wanted to get married a year later, but I wanted to wait. It was important to me to live alone in the city for a while before marriage, and I did that."

She knew when they got married that his father's infidelities had caused problems in their marriage, but she didn't anticipate having a life like the one her mother-in-law had.

"A few days before the wedding, I almost had intercourse with an old boyfriend," she says. "We came this close." She holds her fingers a millimeter apart. "I understood there would always be temptations for both of us, not merely for him."

In 1987, Mary and Dick allowed another couple to persuade them to attend a "swinger's party" in the suburbs outside Philadelphia. Neither of them chose to participate that night. They indulged in a little voyeurism and slipped quietly away. When the couple called to invite them again, they declined.

Dick says, "Aside from the disease question swinging raises for me, I found that evening a curiously antiseptic experience. It wasn't sexy. Impersonal sex is rarely erotic."

Mary agrees, but adds: "We talked all the way back to Manhattan about extramarital sex. In that conversation, we developed our 'Don't ask, don't tell' policy. My bottom line is: I'd rather you didn't, but if you do, don't get involved and don't tell me about it."

And Dick's bottom line?

"I feel the same way Mary does, except I wish more strongly that she wouldn't. I'm a little old-fashioned. To my mind, women are more likely to get emotionally involved than men are."

Each privately admitted to having had one affair in the past five years. His lasted the duration of a ten-day medical conference in Europe, hers for six months.

The Boomer Facts

- Affairs are more common among Boomers—especially women—than they were among previous generations. As women moved into the workforce in great numbers, could equality in adultery be far behind? Contrary to the prevailing theories, women don't necessarily get emotionally involved with their lovers and men don't necessarily leave a "cheating" wife.

- Some Boomers, especially men, have redefined "sex" to exclude fellatio, cybersex, phone sex, and mutual masturbation. Under their new definition, they aren't having affairs. Few, however, share that definition with their partners.

- Couples in higher socioeconomic brackets seem to be more willing to tolerate extramarital affairs without considering divorce. Women in this group sometimes feel "entitled" to have affairs to compensate them for the time and attention they don't receive from their husbands. The men sometimes treat affairs (or "blow jobs") as perks.

- Few marriages are truly "open," with the partners accepting, even condoning, each other's affairs. Typically, one or both partners have made the decision to have affairs without consulting the other. When couples do acknowledge each other's affairs without wanting or expecting the practice to end, they may be avoiding the exploration of serious issues within the marriage. Or, they may be rich people, who aren't like you and me.

PART 5

The Way We Are

Two qualities separate aging Boomers from their elders when they were at this point in life: the continuing sense of sexual entitlement and the feeling of erotic hope. The Boomers still feel entitled to sexual satisfaction. They are filled with a sense of erotic hope. They may not be having as much sex as they want in their relationships. They may not have sex partners now. But they hope. And they believe they will realize their hopes.

12

Hope

A married woman, an older Boomer, told me that her friends don't care very much about sex anymore. Either, she said, they were long married— "and sex isn't important, a minor thing"—or they were single and "getting sex is problematical." This is the kind of remark friends make to each other about sex. She may mean: Sex isn't very important to me anymore. The message is filtered through the comforting screen of "they say."

On the other hand, it may well be true for her friends—or, at least, true that they said what she says they did. Married people who aren't satisfied with their sex lives and single people who are disappointed in not having a sex life often downplay their feelings of sadness and frustration when talking to friends. I don't believe the statement "sex isn't very important anymore" to be true at all. It's just the kind of thing one says over white wine and a designer salad when the days of shredding cocktail napkins and pouring our personal pain as freely as the jug wine are past. We have learned a measure of discretion and acquired an air of insouciance.

Taking the academic approach, I don't believe it's true because the numbers tell me it isn't.

The Survey Says

The question was: How important is sex to you?

- 33 percent of Vietnam-generation men answered "Very." 49 percent said "Moderately," 10 percent said "Somewhat," and 8 percent said "Not very."
- 41 percent of Vietnam-generation women answered "Very." 43 percent said, "Moderately," 8 percent, "Somewhat," and 6 percent said "Not very."
- 41 percent of Watergate-generation men answered "Very." 39 percent said, "Moderately," 15 percent said, "Somewhat," and 5 percent said, "Not very."
- 40 percent of Watergate-generation women answered "Very." 48 percent said, "Moderately," 7 percent said "Somewhat," and 5 percent said "Not very."

Other Surveys Say

When *Men's Health* magazine posed the same question to men in various age groups, they found that of Boomer respondents, 18.8 percent considered it absolutely critical, 53.1 percent said very important, and 24.4 percent said moderately important. Only 1 percent said sex wasn't very important at all.

More compelling to me than the numbers is the palpable hope I sensed in the people I interviewed. Younger and older Boomers, long married and remarried, reformed and unrepentant adulterers, happily single and still waiting to get to the church on time—they have not forsworn erotic hope. They have not forgotten what it feels like to desire. Sex is still important to them, even if they don't have a regular partner now and haven't had one for months or years. After all this time, they are sex dreamers.

"I want to have one last great affair before I die," a forty-year-old single woman said. "Preferably more than one," she added, "but one at the very least."

She is "90 percent sure" that will happen. I would give her better odds than that.

BORN TO RUN

"We sweat it out in the streets of a runaway American dream."
(Recorded by Bruce Springsteen for CBS Records)

"I won't settle for boring sex again," Jill says. "I just need to go out and ask for what I want, and I'll get it. When you ask, you receive."

Jill is one of the world's cockeyed optimists. At forty-two, she is the mother of five children ranging in age from three to fifteen. She and her "emotionally divorced" husband, Matthew, share the same house. They have no specific plans to divorce for "financial reasons." Five years ago, Matthew wanted a divorce to be with someone else. He moved out. After a year, Jill met Clark, with whom she had "the best sex" of her life. Matt came back. She got pregnant with their fifth child. Clark moved on. And Jill caught Matt cheating again. The average soap opera plot is less convoluted.

"Five years ago Matt had a major midlife crisis," she says. "Women should watch the thirty-eight-to-thirty-nine-year-old time period. I wasn't paying enough attention. He met another woman at the same time his career was falling apart. He was wounded and vulnerable, and I was unaware of what was going on with him."

Jill and Matt met on Wall Street in 1981. Young, successful, and hard-driving, they were instantly attracted to each other. Three months later they married. He gave up his apartment and moved into hers because it was bigger.

"At the time I thought the sex was good," she says. "Knowing what I know now, I realize it was only average. We had the first two kids early in the marriage. I wanted to have my babies before I turned thirty. Living in a city apartment with two kids was challenging. We wanted more space and a healthier environment for the kids. Without realizing what we were getting ourselves into, we bought a big, beautiful house in New Jersey, a nearly two-hour-each-way commute to Wall Street."

They agreed that Jill would stay home and raise the children while Matt, who was earning a lot of money at the time, would make the daily commute to his job. Jill had grown up in a traditional family of four siblings, working father, and stay-at-home mother in a nearby New Jersey suburb. She and the children acclimated to their new life almost immediately. Jill wanted more children, and in rapid succession, two more were born.

"The move to the suburbs created a big change in our marriage, but I was in denial about the implications of that change," she says. "Matt was physically and emotionally drained from the days he was putting in. A four-hour commute, ten hours on the job. The schedule was abusive. We saw him basically on weekends. I didn't know that the responsibility of being the sole breadwinner was a heavy one for him, because he didn't tell me until too late. I didn't even know things weren't going well for him at work until he lost his job."

Jill concedes she should have been paying more attention. She enjoyed her life as a full-time mother and part-time dabbler in the literary arts so much that she didn't want to see a threat to it. When he became unemployed, however, she rallied. Within months, she'd started her own business and was making a considerable amount of money at it, enough to keep up their lifestyle easily.

"I have a facility for making money," she says. "I have a positive attitude about it, an attitude I got from my family. I was raised in a devout Catholic home by parents who had very positive values. Matt, however, was raised by Catholic parents who hated the Church and distrusted money and success. When his mother first saw the house after we bought it, she turned to Matt and said, 'How many people in this neighborhood have lost their homes?' That was her signal to him to lose the home, and he almost did lose it for us."

In retrospect, Jill says Matt should have made a career change when they moved, a change that "would have supported our lifestyle and his overall health needs." Like many couples who take on the burdens of large, expensive homes and the lifestyles they create, Jill and Matt set themselves up for trouble. Both ignored the signs of impending disaster as long as possible. One of the signs predictably was the decline of their sex life.

"He was always too tired," she says. "I accepted that. After he lost his job, I was too busy and tired getting the business going, and he was too depressed. There were a lot of reasons for not having sex, and they began with 'too.' "

Then one night around midnight, someone called. Jill answered. A woman burst into tears. Without having to ask, Jill knew who the woman was: her husband's lover.

"Until that night, I'd been berating myself for not recognizing his pain and suffering," she says. "I knew he was going through an emotional breakdown, and I suppose the other woman was a symptom of that. But once I knew she existed, I wasn't so understanding anymore. I saw his problems. His inability to admit failure to me had jeopardized our children's lives. His inability to express himself had cheated me of a full, loving relationship with my husband. His lack of courage and self-confidence had shortchanged all of us."

Matt moved out to be with the other woman. It was nearly a year before Jill met Clark, who was five years older, a confirmed bachelor, and a modestly wealthy man. By this time, Matt's relationship had fallen apart, and he was asking to come home.

"For the sake of the children and for financial reasons, I was considering it," she says. "We simply couldn't afford two separate lives without him working. Then I went to bed with Clark, and I was amazed at how sex could be. It was exquisite. I felt more female, more totally a woman than I'd ever felt in my life. With Clark, I was more into sex as an event. He brought out the best in me as a lover."

And what does that mean in more specific terms?

"Communication. We communicated, verbally and nonverbally. He told me what he wanted me to do, how he wanted me to suck him, how he wanted me to move on top of him. After we'd been together a while, he said, 'I never asked for what I wanted before. When I started asking, I got you.'

"We also had a kind of communication you can't work at developing. It's there or it isn't. When we made love, we created another energy between us. With Matt, it was always my energy and his coming together. We didn't create a new energy field—babies, yes, but no energy field. Clark and I did.

"The sex was very intense. Because he was specific and instructive, I got better and better at giving him what he wanted in bed. He got hooked on me for what I could do to him. It was incredibly satisfying to me to have this kind of erotic power over a man. We were a perfect match."

Then what happened?

"Matt came back. He sensed I was having the best sex of my life with Clark, and he couldn't stand it. I let him move back in, and he got me pregnant with our fifth child. He did it deliberately. He manipulated me to get me away from Clark."

Jill is convinced that Matt "manipulated" her into the last pregnancy by making love to her without protection. Their method of birth control had always been condoms. She got pregnant "on the first try" with each of their previous four children. He knew what he was doing, she said, and he got what he wanted. She was pregnant. Clark left.

"There was no good reason to have an abortion," she says. "I was healthy and financially stable. I had the child and lost the lover."

Why was she having sex with Matt in the first place?

"We were just having sex," she says. "He was living there, and we were just having sex sometimes."

Shortly after the baby was born, Jill picked up the phone to hear another woman sobbing.

"She told me, 'I'm so sorry. I didn't know he was married.' I told her, 'Oh, he's married, and he has five kids, including a baby. Come on over. We'll talk. You aren't the first, and you won't be the last.'

"We're still living together. He has a job in a new field. It pays a fraction of what he made on Wall Street, but at least he is finally starting over. We don't have sex anymore. We tried counseling but it didn't work. He lied to the counselor, and I couldn't sit there and listen. Clark is living with someone, but I don't think it's going well. We talk occasionally but we don't see each other. He was the love, or the sex, of my life."

Are she and Matt finally considering divorce?

"That's the question. It's so complicated. The kids are at tender ages. He was unemployed for so long, and he's so new to this job. He had the luxury of a breakdown, and I had to pick up the pieces. This is what men do, isn't it? They avoid responsibility by having sex with another woman. They don't see that it will have a domino effect and knock over the whole family. If he could go back and do things over, I know he would.

"I have asked myself, 'What did you do to bring this into your life?' I was ignorant, trusting, innocent. I believe the best of people. I was taught to win, and Matt was taught to fail. Our value systems are different. I see that now.

"I don't know if I still love him. I do know that I want to have the kind of sex and love I had with Clark. It's out there. I just have to know how to ask. Sometimes I get discouraged, especially by aging. I look in the mirror and see the sags. But I still believe. It's out there, and I can find it. I have a longing for that kind of sex now, a longing I didn't have before."

Is Jill deluding herself? One need not be a cynic to think so. But her words printed on a page do not convey the strength of her hopefulness. Quiet determination underscores her energy. The same optimism and faith that have enabled her to create a successful business may bring love, and sex, back into her life.

And then there is Matt.

"She didn't want me to talk to you," he said when I talked to him. "So I'll keep it short. I love Jill. I have loved Jill from the beginning, and I always will. I've failed to live up to her standards, disappointed her, cheated on her, but I love her.

"She wanted our last child. It's disingenuous of her to say I tricked her into getting pregnant. We were having sex. If she didn't want to get pregnant, she could have insisted on the condom. She could have been using something else. Why did she get pregnant with me and not him? She wanted my baby—our baby. And she wanted an excuse to get out of the relationship with the other guy. If he was the love of her life, why didn't she run to him?" He pauses, either to get his emotions in check or to take a drag on a cigarette. "If I pull my professional life together, we'll get back together. That's what I want. I think that's what she really wants, too. If she didn't, she'd divorce me, wouldn't she?"

Like Linda and Gil, the Shaker Heights couple, Matt and Jill left me with the strong feeling that they were good prospects for a passionate renewal—if only they could get past the pride and pain and sort out their grievances against one another.

SEX TIPS FOR BOOMERS

Magic Carpet Ride
(Recorded by Steppenwolf for MCA Records)

The Male G Spot

Jill's lover taught her how to tap into the erotic potential of the prostate, sometimes called "the male G spot."

A woman can reach that spot by inserting a lubricated finger into the anus and probing the back wall. Many men and women aren't comfortable with that approach. It can also be reached in the following way: Gently press her thumb into the perineum, the space between the scrotum and the anus. Experiment with different strokes and degrees of pressure. For many men, the perineum massage can strengthen the erection, induce orgasm, or make the orgasm feel more intense.

After talking to many hopeful Boomers, married and single, I wondered: Is it easier to have hope when you're alone and lonely or in a relationship turned sour?

"Women find me more attractive when I'm with a woman," a forty-year-old bachelor says. "I've lived with two women, one for three years, the other for four years. Other women were more interested in me during those years than they had been or are now that I'm alone. It's perverse, but true. I feel more hopeful when I'm attractive to women, no matter what my personal situation is, so I'd say there is more hope in being with someone than in being alone."

A forty-five-year-old single woman said, "I am hopeful every day that around the next corner I'll bump into a wonderful man. My friends in bad relationships feel trapped, not hopeful."

A divorced forty-year-old woman agreed. She said, "I felt hopeless when I was married. I used to sit on the patio on summer nights staring up at the sky wishing I could wish on a star. I wasn't able to wish and hope until I got out of the marriage first."

Interestingly, cohabiting couples typically expressed the least hope. They have rarely made the same level of commitment as married couples, but living together limits their dating options as much as being married does. If the relationship has problems, it's easier for them to get out and move on than for the married to divorce. For this reason, I expected they might be more hopeful in the face of unhappiness than their married counterparts. Surprisingly, they weren't. The pessimists I encountered were either unhappily cohabiting or recently divorced. There were, however, some notable exceptions.

The Survey Says

- 35 percent of Vietnam-generation men and 37 percent of women have cohabited with a lover. 11 percent of men and 14 percent of women currently cohabit.
- 41 percent of Watergate-generation men and 39 percent of women have cohabited with a lover. 15 percent of men and 17 percent of women currently cohabit.
- Among the Vietnam generation, there is little difference in the amount of sexual activity among cohabiting couples and married ones. But the cohabiting couples do have slightly more oral sex and are 20 percent more likely to participate in variations like anal sex, bondage, and spanking.
- Among the Watergate generation, the cohabiting couples report approximately 15 percent more sexual activity than married couples, approximately the same amount of oral sex, and 10 percent more participation in sexual variations.

But couples who have lived together for more than five years in both groups report the same levels and variations (or lack) of sexual activity.

I'M READY

"I'm ready for you and I hope you're ready for me."
(Recorded by Muddy Waters for MCA Records)

"My first big crush, when I was fifteen, was on my high school acting teacher," Joan says. "Maybe that crush set the tone for my sex life. He was twenty-five. The attraction was mutual, but he was too smart to do anything about it. I compared the boys my age to him, and they definitely suffered in the comparison. I had a very romantic, idealized view of life, love, and men. I was too romantic to have a typical sweaty teenage relationship with a boy my own age."

Now forty, Joan is living with an older man. Has she finally realized her romantic fantasy? Not exactly. Every workday she edits graphic sex articles, and almost every night she does not have sex.

"We have almost no sex life," she says. "There are two big reasons for that. We're sharing a house with my mother, and we work at opposite ends of the clock. I have a day job; he tends bar at night and plays in a band. Most nights he works until four A.M., then meets friends for breakfast. He's coming home at seven when I'm getting ready to leave for the office. Where do you fit sex into that?"

Joan, who lives in Westchester County and commutes to a magazine job in Manhattan, was born in Chicago. Her family moved to Upstate New York when she was five. The next year her father's career took off. He became a prominent advertising executive with major national accounts. Joan remembers a comfortable childhood, where creativity was encouraged, until her parents "inevitably" divorced, when she was in high school.

"My mother was an artist. After the divorce, she taught drawing classes in our living room. The first time I walked in on a group of women sketching a nude man was a little disconcerting, but I adjusted to it fast. Their favorite model was a beautiful black man. I still have fantasies about him.

"The pop-psych explanation for my huge crush on the teacher would be that I was looking for a father figure but he wasn't fatherly at all," she says. "He was handsome, sophisticated, worldly, suave. The boys my age weren't as interesting to me. I didn't have sex until I was one month shy of my twentieth birthday. It took me that long to have a first real boyfriend. After the crush, I didn't meet anyone who was interested in me if I was interested in them.

"I did have some romanticized cerebral attachments without physical contact. Maybe I'm weird. Maybe that's why I overcompensated and became a pornographer when I grew up."

Joan, while not really a "pornographer," did edit a magazine for women featuring photos of nude men for several years before taking an editorial job at a men's sex magazine. She laughs about "cock and pussy copy," but feels no shame or embarrassment about her work. Like many people with artistic goals, she meant to end up elsewhere, but considers herself fortunate to be working in the magazine industry at all.

"When I was an almost-twenty-year-old virgin, I never would have guessed I'd see so many penises in my life," she says. "I met my first lover in a notions store in San Diego. My father had moved to the West Coast after the divorce. He was living in San Diego with his second wife, and he was dying of cancer. I was running some errands for my grandmother, who needed a button. I saw this attractive man who was looking for a button to match one he'd lost. We struck up a conversation and talked until the store closed. He was older, twenty-eight. I didn't want to be with a little boy, especially the first time I made love, and I knew he was going to be my first right there in the notions store.

"We made love on our first date. My father was in the next room, slowly dying. The sex was wonderful. I didn't have any idea that not all men were going to be that wonderful in bed. Oh my God, if I'd known then what I know now! He took his time making love, and he was very skilled. His penis was large, and he got so hard.

"I liked him a lot. He was a kind man. We broke up because I lived in New York and he lived in San Diego. I felt like an emotional faucet, turning my feelings off and on when we got together and separated again. Age, geography, and fate came between us. It wasn't a great love, but it was great sex."

Joan has been in love with "a lot of men." She met the love of her life when she was twenty-five—and he was twenty. They came from similar family backgrounds, were facing similar "growing-up issues," and shared the strongest physical attraction she's ever felt for a man.

"If I'd had the choice, I would never have gone to bed with anyone else," she says. "He was not that good in bed, but I really wanted him. He was hung. When a man is big, you can always find a way to be satisfied with him. He came too fast, but it didn't matter. He was so big I could hold him inside me, flex my muscles around him, and use him that way to make myself come. And he smelled right. I knew when I smelled him, he was mine."

For ten years, they had a tempestuous relationship, breaking up, going back together. She saw other men. He saw other women.

"I remember the other men in my life during those ten years as threads woven into the fabric of me and him. He always broke up with me. The one time I broke up with him, he went off and got married to a poodle-headed woman. She has one of those bad perms that makes a woman look like a poodle. At least she's tall and thin. I can never remember her name. I have successfully blanked it out.

"I wouldn't go back to him, to the way it was. I'm glad I got off that bus. But nobody since him has smelled right, and he had that elephant penis, more than ten inches long. And girth—there was girth, too. In the early days, I called him 'Elephant Boy.' "

After Elephant Boy, Joan had a relationship with a man who was her "spiritual, intellectual" match. She remembers him as "someone not interesting." She says, "I didn't take it hard when he got married." Then came a series of men, including one she almost married. Following that breakup, she landed the job editing a woman's sex magazine.

"I was surrounded by penis shots, responsible for picking the centerfold of the month, and I wasn't having sex. It was bizarre."

Did the job have an impact on her subsequent relationships with men?

"No. I got a lot of flak from women about it, but very little from men. Most men found it amusing. Women were always lecturing me about the offensiveness of pornography. I did have sex with a couple of the center-folds, and admitting that to some women was a mistake. I asked for the grief they gave me. Maybe my background was conducive to this job. There's nothing wrong with nudity. We all have our lines we won't cross. Some people wouldn't work with pornographic material. I draw my lines in other places.

"Interestingly, I've only been sexually harassed by a woman. She was my boss at the time, before I got her job; she kept asking about my sex life at editorial meetings. I refused to talk or write about my own sex life as many editors and writers in this business do, and she wouldn't let it rest."

Shortly after getting her nemesis's job, Joan met the man with whom she now lives, "Mr. Joe Average." She was with girlfriends in a dark little Irish bar in Brooklyn. The owner and bartender, Joe, who had a girlfriend of his own, had a big Irish smile. He told her about his band. A few weeks later she went back to hear the band. Friends of his girlfriend's met her in the ladies' room and threatened to "tear [her] head off."

Joan says, "I asked myself, 'What's a nice Jewish girl like me doing in a scene like this?' I was determined to avoid him, but a few weeks later, I went back with my friends to the bar. He told me he was breaking up with his girlfriend and apologized for her friends. He said, 'You'll get used to the Irish.' I'm not sure I ever have. He is Irish, not Irish-American, and there is a big difference. They really hang together like expatriates in a land where no one speaks their language.

"We didn't date for a long time, but we knew we would be dating. He had to handle the breakup in the right way and not rush into a relationship with me. We Americans are used to being frank and impulsive. Well, the Irish aren't like that. When we did start dating, we moved slowly. I did some stupid things. I always find a way of sabotaging relationships. I have self-defeating dating habits. Either I am desperate and clingy or I am sleeping with someone else. I played it both ways with Joe, but we stayed together anyway.

"It was a good relationship, with good sex, until he moved in with me. First, my mother and I bought a house together. Then I lost my job. A few months later he lost the bar and filed personal bankruptcy. Fast-forward to present time. He is living with me and my mother. As much as everyone tries, it doesn't work. Partly, it's this Irish attitude about mothers. He almost can't bring himself to have sex in a house where somebody's mother is sleeping. When I went to Dublin to meet his mother, we slept in separate beds. He never has told her we live together. If he had his own place again, he'd be happier, and we'd have sex. The irony of spending my days working at a sex magazine and my nights not having sex isn't lost on me. Mr. Shower Massage is my companion.

"I have crushes, physical attractions, but I haven't been with anyone else in a long time. There is nobody I want to go after. For now, I am waiting this out. I feel hopeful about the future. Last month I was in San Diego. I hated it there. I felt ugly. In New York, it's okay to be interesting looking. I have big breasts, a lot of red hair. I'm not beautiful, but I can be stunning. Here, it's okay. There if you aren't perfect and blonde and very young, it isn't okay. As I get older, I worry about what will happen to me. Will I lose a job and not be able to find another one? Lose a man and not be able to attract another one? I would worry a lot more about me in California.

"When I came home, I realized I was happy to be here. I did have a moment in San Diego when I considered looking up my first lover, the old boyfriend. I even looked for his name in the phone book. It represented the idea of going back in time. If you could go back, would you go back . . . that sort of thing. I wouldn't.

"I've learned a lot. I am satisfied with myself sexually. I know what I like. I know how to satisfy myself and how to get satisfied. And I could be satisfied with the relationship again. We could turn things around.

"Sex changes in a relationship all the time. In the beginning, it's good, or at least plentiful. If Joe hadn't lost his bar and had to move in with me, we'd be having sex now. I want more sex. Someday I'll have it."

SEX TIPS FOR BOOMERS

The Loco-Motion
(Recorded by Grand Funk Railroad for Capitol Records)

How to Make His Penis Feel Bigger
- Develop her PC muscles. See page 23 for Kegel directions. (If I could give only two pieces of sex advice to a man or woman, they would be: Get those PCs in shape and become proficient at oral sex.) Strong PC muscles enable her to grasp his penis firmly during intercourse, making his organ feel larger for both of them.
- Hold the thumb and first finger firmly around the base of his penis during intercourse. Cock rings serve the same purpose, maintaining a state of engorgement, but they can be painful.
- Tinker with intercourse positions, until you achieve maximum depth of penetration. For example, in the missionary position, wrap her legs around his neck, hooking her ankles over his shoulders. Experiment with rear entry while seated. He sits on a chair or the edge of the bed. She squats down on his erection, facing away from him. Pillows are an effective means of changing the angle and depth of penetration, creating the feeling of a larger penis.

NEVER GOING BACK AGAIN

"She broke down and let me in."
(Recorded by Fleetwood Mac for Warner Bros. Records)

"That we are together at all is a testament of faith—my wife's faith in me when I was screwing around on her and later my faith in her when she had withdrawn from me following her diagnosis of breast cancer," Tom says.

Brenda and Tom, who recently celebrated their thirtieth wedding anniversary, have been, like the song says down twice. Way down. Each time one or the other of them brought their relationship back up from the mat. They married when Brenda was eighteen and Tom nineteen. She was pregnant with their first child. A draftee, he had a four-day furlough between basic training and Vietnam. Raised a Catholic, Tom insisted they be married by a priest. He made Brenda promise to take instructions while he was gone and to have the baby baptized in the Church. They were married in a small ceremony with only their immediate families present, in the church where Tom had been baptized, in South Bend, Indiana. There wasn't a dry eye in the house. Even the groom cried.

"I didn't really expect to come back," he says. "I had a fatalistic attitude. Most guys went over there thinking they would come back. They didn't turn fatalist until they'd been there a few weeks. I blew my student deferment by flunking out my freshman year. My father was trying to get me in the National Guard through his political connections, but I got drafted before he could. I was sure I was going to die in that rotten sinkhole of a country. I came home after a twelve-month tour of duty without a scratch.

"I didn't find out I had a son until he was six weeks old. I must have had a fleeting thought about Bren, about what she'd had to go through without me, but I don't remember. When I came home, I had the little convert Catholic wife anxious to do the right things in her new faith and a six-month-old baby. I thought she was on the Pill. Why? I thought every woman in America was on the Pill. I didn't know how to talk to her. I didn't know how to be married. And I absolutely didn't want to talk about the war. I built a wall around what I saw in Vietnam, and I wouldn't let anyone inside the wall. We didn't talk much at all. I found a job, enrolled in night classes to work toward my degree, and generally avoided being home with her in our little, cramped, and 'cute' apartment. Two months after I got back, she told me she was pregnant again."

Brenda gave birth to a daughter that year and another son the following year. The day they brought the third baby home from the hospital, Tom told her he would leave her if she got pregnant again. She went to the parish priest, who called Tom and asked him to come in for counseling.

"I was so angry at her. I'd never been that angry at anyone in my life, even the Vietcong. It wasn't personal with them. It was with Bren. I couldn't understand her. Why was she doing this to me? Saddling me with mouths to feed. I couldn't relate to the babies. She was little more than a baby-making machine in those days. There was always spit-up on her clothes. She smelled like breast milk. I was furious."

The consultation with the priest led to a later confrontation between

Brenda and Tom. Hurt and confused, she told him she was doing what he wanted, had told her he expected of her before leaving for Vietnam. He didn't know what she was talking about. She persisted. Didn't he, she asked, remember telling her to take instruction, become a Catholic, and promise to raise their children in the church?

"I thought I was going to die," he told her. "Don't you understand that? I thought I was going to die."

Brenda went on the birth-control pill, but she and Tom rarely had sex anyway. He was afraid she would get pregnant, pill or no pill. When her children were three, two, and one, she enrolled in college. Her mother, Tom's mother, and her best friend were her baby-sitters. She continued to attend mass, taking the children with her. Tom joined them only on Christmas and Easter.

"I guessed he was having affairs," she said, "long before I knew it. I didn't want to deal with it if he was. I found out the hard way. I was having heavy periods, a lot of pain. I was pretty sure there was something seriously wrong, maybe even cancer. That scared me, as much for the kids as myself. Tom wasn't that interested in being a parent. What would happen to my babies if something happened to me?"

With trepidation, she made a doctor's appointment. She had PIDS, or pelvic inflammatory disease, caused by undiagnosed and untreated gonorrhea. The scarring of her ovaries and tubes had left her sterile. Birth control was now a moot point.

"Tom had given me an STD," she says. "It had to be Tom, because I'd never been with another man since I lost my virginity to him in my senior year of high school." Even now, more than twenty-five years later, the memory of her pain brings tears to her eyes. "It gets worse," she says. "I'd never had an orgasm with Tom at that point in our marriage. I had orgasms alone when I masturbated, which I did infrequently, because I was so rarely alone. Never with Tom. I'd had three babies and no orgasms during lovemaking."

Tom was startled when Brenda told him what was wrong with her. When she said he had infected her, he didn't argue.

"I never doubted Bren's faithfulness," he says, holding her hand tightly as they sit side by side on a chintz covered sofa in their spacious living room. "When I was in 'Nam, other guys wondered about their wives and girlfriends. I didn't." He takes her hand to his mouth and presses his lips against her palm. "I gave her gonorrhea. If I could have died on the spot, I would have."

The discovery of Brenda's PIDS was a turning point in their marriage.

She told him he could stop cheating on her and work on the marriage—or get out. "I've been doing this pretty much without your help anyway," she said. He chose to stay. The next four years were difficult, they both acknowledge. They had little money, three small children, and almost no time for each other. He got his degree first and surprised her by saying he would take over some of the child-care duties in the evenings when she was at school.

"I had been depending on our mothers and my best friend, who couldn't stand Tom, by the way, for help," she says. "When he got involved with his own kids, things really began to turn around for us. We got closer to each other. One snowy winter night, I got home late from class because the roads were so bad. He was standing at the window waiting for me. My heart skipped a beat. He had bathed the kids and put them to bed. They were sleeping like little angels. He'd cleaned out the fireplace, built a fire, and had leftover pizza warming in the oven for me. I cried I was so happy. We made love that night, more tenderly and passionately than we had since the first weeks he was home from 'Nam."

After the children started school, Brenda earned her degree and found a good job. She bought sex advice books, learned how to have an orgasm during lovemaking, and began having them regularly. With two incomes, they were able to buy a four-bedroom home with a big backyard in a suburb outside South Bend.

"I woke up one day and realized I was happy," she says. "Life was good."

He says, "It was. Somehow we had gotten past all the terrible things we'd done to each other, especially me to her, and we were happy together. While I've never had as close a relationship with any of the kids as she's had with all of them, I had evolved into a decent father. We were lucky that we didn't have any big problems with them, not even in high school. They were good kids. We had planned a trip for the two of us to Hawaii the summer the last one graduated from high school. It was going to be the honeymoon we never had. Then Bren found the lump in her breast."

Brenda's doctor insisted on performing a lumpectomy before they booked their Hawaiian trip. The lump, he told her, was probably benign, as most were. She would, he said, enjoy her vacation a lot more if she knew there was nothing to worry about before she left. But the lump was cancerous; and the cancer had spread to her lymph nodes. She had a partial mastectomy, followed by chemotherapy treatments. The trip was postponed indefinitely.

"Brenda has always been a fighter," Tom says. "She fought for our marriage. She fought to earn a degree against heavy odds. When cancer hit her, she folded. She withdrew into a shell. I had to make her fight. I felt like I climbed a mountain every day just to reach her. It was the hardest work of my life."

"Tom pulled me back," she says. "I was sure I was going to die. I hated the way my body looked. I could barely hold my head up when I was on chemo. Working part time was all I could manage. I couldn't think sex. I didn't even want him to look at my body."

"I persisted," he says. "I kept after her. I even yelled at her sometimes and broke down and cried in front of her. I wasn't going to let her go. And I finally won her back."

A few weeks after her last chemotherapy treatment, Brenda let Tom make love to her. When he touched her wounded breast, she cried. He kissed the tears away, then kissed her breast. That kiss, she said, opened her heart wider than it had ever been opened.

"I took him utterly and completely inside me, body and soul," she says. "For the first time, I understood the true meaning of the phrase 'And two shall be made as one.'"

The Boomers Facts

- The Boomers, both generations, have not lost their erotic hope. Even if they aren't having good sex, they believe that they will (or could). Sex is still important to the Boomers. They have not written it off.

- In some marriages an erotic stalemate seems to exist. It is still possible for the participants to find their way back to a satisfying sexual relationship with each other. Whether they do or not probably depends more on the strength of their connection than the allure of other partners.

- Couples who have lived together for more than five years behave like married couples in terms of sexual frequency. The greater ease with which their commitment can be dissolved does compromise their ability to overcome serious difficulties within the relationship. They are, perhaps surprisingly, the least hopeful Boomers.

- In spite of the ubiquitous advice on how to communicate, most couples who have problems fail to initiate or sustain helpful dialogues with each other.

From the Pill
to the Pill

When the first members of this significant demographical group, the Baby Boom generation, turned forty, in 1986, *Time* magazine ran a cover story. The vanguard Boomers received similar attention upon the occasion of their fiftieth birthday, in 1996. Every newspaper and magazine article, every segment on the nightly news or in a newsmagazine trumpeted these passages in effusively positive terms. In February 1999 the published results of a ten-year study on "midlife development" by the MacArthur Foundation reinforced the message: Midlife is a happy place to be now that Boomers have moved in. We may be forty, then fifty, but we're still "youthful," "vital," "sexy." The birth-control pill was our ticket to ride, and Viagra will become our lifetime pass.

"We're seeing that fifty means all kinds of very vibrant, alive, sexy, dynamic people," June Reinisch, the director of the Kinsey Institute, told *Newsweek* magazine.

It would be politically incorrect to say anything else.

The defining characteristic of Boomers younger and older is the refusal to grow old, to commit, as it were, to acknowledging our place on the moving pathway leading inexorably to the end. Our parents and grandparents were better able to accept their mortality than we have been. *New York Times* columnist Russell Baker has labeled *Seinfeld* the comedy not of "nothing," but of "staying eternally young." Though not the first to make the connection, he makes it concisely, leaving little quibble room. Jerry,

George, Elaine, and Kramer, icons of prolonged adolescence, will date forever, and to those of us born after World War II, that does not seem an impossible state. We are the target market segment for the new generation of afterlife movies, where the undead continue to have romantic adventures. Life is not over; it's more beautiful and sexier. Many of us have dated longer than humans were surely meant to date, and still feel cheated when the opportunities for dinner and a movie with a virtual stranger are slim to none at all. Our mothers might well ask: "And what did you expect?" More. We have always expected more. And more again.

Sex may not necessarily be part of dating, but it is part of the concept of eternal youth. Cybill Shepherd, the actress labeled "sultry" at forty-eight, claims she's having the "best sex" of her life, and tabloid readers of a certain age want to believe her. In fact, boasts of midlife sexual power are not limited to the rich and famous. Ordinary women with little pot bellies say they've never been sexier than they are at forty. Chubby bald men talk about their increased technical proficiency, their ability "at last" to be well and truly intimate, making better sex possible at forty-five.

Every generation must secretly believe it invented sex. We Boomers didn't keep the belief a secret. The leading edge of us were the frontline troops in the sexual revolution. We lowered the age for first intercourse, raised the numbers of average lifetime partners, enormously inflated the statistics on the practice of oral sex, anal sex, and various kinky practices such as bondage and spanking—and put "living together" and "cheating" on the behavioral map. The last platoon of Boomers mainstreamed S&M, brought the videotape into the bedroom, and took homosexuals out of the closet and put their names together on joint bank accounts and deeds to shared property. "Don't ask, don't tell," may be the Army's motto. It has not been ours.

And now that we are past what only a few years ago we touted as our sexual prime, we're quick to let others know we've found something better: the deeper orgasm, the more intimate relationship, the uniting of sexuality and spirituality. That the increase in sales of books on Eastern lovemaking techniques, less dependent on erections than patience, coincides with the aging of the Boomer male is not a coincidence. Someday sexual historians may say that the two significant Boomer contributions are expanding the practice of oral sex and reviving interest in Tantra. Certainly it is better to be remembered for that than for designing the chastity belt.

Of all the themes of our lives, no matter the generation into which we were born, sex is a predominant one, and the theme is generally considered to be played most resoundingly by the young. In our minds, at least, that is no longer true. We now believe older is better. But we don't want to look older. No, anything but that.

The Boomers were less inclined to hide our sexual proclivities than our elders, but more apt to cover up the physical signs of aging, perhaps in part because liver spots and protruding veins, wrinkles, sags, bags, and protruding bellies are not desirable. The older celebrities labeled still sexy, like grandmothers Suzanne Somers, Raquel Welch, and Loni Anderson clearly do not look their age, and they are still sexy because they don't, not because they have made the appearance of "old" sexy. Jonathan Swift reportedly said that everyone wants to live forever, but nobody wants to grow old, and he could not have imagined the level of youth obsession in modern society. Cosmetic surgery is a growth industry now that the Boomers are aging. In 1996, people aged thirty-five to fifty accounted for fifty-one percent of cosmetic surgeries. The greatest leap for us will be across the caverns of our wrinkles into each other's freckled arms—without closing our eyes.

How will we make the leap? Will there be more partners for singles as the ranks of the widowed grow? What will sex be like for us in the next phase of our lives? Will sex still be important to us? The questions may not have mattered so much to the generation who fought and endured World War II, but they matter to us. Those people had the security of being right—and not only right, but noble. However hard their lives might have been, they had their stunning victories as well as their unassailable moral convictions to see them through the twilight years. We do not age "gracefully," if grace means letting our physical appearances and pleasures go by. And we do not give up sexual hope. In Columbus, Ohio, I had breakfast with a group of women in their forties—single and celibate, not by choice—who drive once a month to another city to watch nude male dancers perform. "We may not be touching it, but we still want to look," one explained. Another added, "I believe I will have a sexual relationship again soon and probably with a younger man."

Breathes there a Boomer who doesn't believe she or he looks, feels, and acts younger than her or his years—and can still have the sex/love of his or her life? In a national survey conducted by *Family Circle* magazine, on average, the women in their forties said they felt and looked ten years younger than they were while the men gave themselves an eight-year bonus. Other surveys have found similar results. There is a disparity between the chronological ages of Boomers and their images of how "young" they look, feel, and behave. Age denial is rampant. In her book on midlife, *New Passages*, Gail Sheehy wrote: "From my interviews and surveys [examined], I find that the image they carry around in their inner eye usually falls somewhere between twenty-eight and thirty-five." Or, thirtysomething forever: old enough to know how and young enough to keep doing it.

In truth, we may only look "younger" than our parents and grandparents did at the same ages because 60 percent of female Boomers dye their hair, many have had cosmetic surgery, and clothing styles are not as rigidly age-defined as they were in Mom's and Grandma's days. In spite of our strenuous exercise claims, we are fatter than our parents were in their forties and fifties.

"Our only genuine claim to better health habits rests on the fact that we (at least those who belong to the middle class)are much less likely to smoke than our parents were," wrote Susan Jacoby in the *Washington Post*.

Through the miracles of computer photo-shop technology, put Mom in modern clothes, make-up, and hairstyle at the same age you are now, and she may look younger than you do. Playwright and author Oscar Wilde said, "Thirty-five is a very attractive age. London society is full of women who have of their own free choice remained thirty-five for years." No doubt, the women of Wilde's acquaintance also thought they looked younger than their age, younger than their mothers had looked at their age. We want to look young, remain sexually desirable, and have as much sex as everyone else is having, too. Lucky for us, we believe that we can.

Ironically, the married among us have the best chance of living out their sexual dreams. According to *American Demographics* magazine, the statistical authority, Americans have sex on average fifty-eight times per year, or just over once a week. The frequency declines, precipitously, but unevenly, with age. Wealthier Boomers, particularly men, have more sex than their poorer counterparts. Married Boomers have, as they age, more sex than their single counterparts.

Still, I believe that we Boomers, married and single, younger and older, will retain an interest in sex throughout our lifetimes. At the very end of our days, we'll be protesting for the closed-door policy in nursing homes and a vibrator in every drawer. Viagra, or a derivative thereof, will be ground up in the breakfast gruel.

We will go on.

If you believe the Boomers are losing interest in sex, you probably believe we're all working out four times a week, too.

Appendix A

The Questionnaire

In search of the answers to universal Boomer sex questions, I conducted hundreds of interviews, backed by a brief survey with results not meant to be taken as science. One of my pet peeves: journalists, sociologists, psychologists, and others who extrapolate data (which they label "scientific evidence") backing up their theses from samplings of people willing to talk about their sex lives. Masters and Johnson did scientific sexual research in a laboratory setting. No one else has done anything approaching their work on a significant scale. Surveys are like snapshots, capturing a moment in our lives. They are not the archives of our lives.

I distributed the questionnaire through friends and professional associates. One book club in St. Louis County generated 112 responses. The ten women in the club made copies and distributed them nationwide to friends and relatives, including one enterprising Boomer who scanned the questionnaire into his computer and E-mailed it to a few hundred of his closest cyber friends.

Obviously, my respondents do not represent the rainbow coalition that is America. They are disproportionately white, middle- and upper-middle-class professionals, 60 percent women, and largely heterosexual.

THE QUESTIONNAIRE

Please make your answers as long and detailed as you like. If you want to comment on some aspect of sexuality not listed on the questionnaire, do so on separate paper.

Age: Gender: Race: Marital Status: # Of marriages:

RELIGIOUS AFFILIATION:
POLITICAL AFFILIATION:
GEOGRAPHICAL LOCATION:
ANNUAL INCOME, INDIVIDUAL: FAMILY (IF APPLIES):

1. At what age did you become sexually active? Lose your virginity? Was your first partner a romantic interest? A one-night stand? Other?

2. How frequently do you have sexual relations with a partner now? How does that frequency compare to past levels of sexual activity?

3. How many partners have you had?

4. Are you currently involved in a monogamous relationship? If so, for how long?

5. Have you ever had an affair while involved in a committed relationship?

6. If the answer is yes, was the affair serious? How long did it last? How did it affect your relationship? Was the affair discovered by your partner or not?

7. Was there more than one affair? How many more?

8. If heterosexual, have you ever had a homosexual experience?

9. If homosexual, have you ever had a heterosexual experience?

10. If homosexual, at what age and in what circumstances did you "come out?"

11. Have you ever experienced any of the following (if so, describe):

Sex abuse?

Rape?

Incest?

Sexual harassment?

Sexual addiction?

12. Have you had sex therapy? If so, describe the circumstances that propelled you into therapy as well as the process and the outcome.

13. Look over the following list of sex practices. How many have you tried? Practice occasionally or frequently? Would you like to try some of them if your partner were interested?

Fellatio

Cunnilingus

Anal stimulation

Anal intercourse

Spanking

Bondage

S&M

Ménage à trois or group sex

Phone sex

Fantasy playacting

Sex-toy play

Viewing X-rated videos

14. Have you ever had sex in a place where you might have been observed?

15. How frequently do you have sexual fantasies? And how have your fantasies changed over the years?

16. At what age did you first masturbate?

17. Do you masturbate now? How frequently?

18. Have you ever had a sexually transmitted disease? If so, describe.

19. If not in a monogamous relationship, do you regularly use condoms?

20. Have you lived with a sexual partner outside of marriage?

21. What is the age difference between you and your current partner? Between you and past partners?

22. What are your sexual fears, concerns, problems?

23. What do you like best about your sex life?

24. What is your orgasm profile? (Do you reach orgasm never, rarely, sometimes, often, always, or nearly always?) How have orgasms changed, if they have, over the years? Do you fake orgasms? Does your partner fake orgasms? Are orgasms as important to you now as they were in the past?

25. How would you rate your overall sexual satisfaction? How would you rate your overall life satisfaction?

APPENDIX B
Resources

Mail order sources for sex toys, books, videos:

Good Vibrations, 1210 Valencia St., San Francisco, CA 94110.
(800) 289-8423
goodvibe@well.com

Xandria Collection, Box 319005, San Francisco, CA 94131.
(800) 242-2833
www.Xandria.com

Focus International, 1160 E. Jericho Turnpike, Huntington, NY 11743.
ms@focusint.com

Sinclair Institute, Box 8865, Chapel Hill, NC 27515.
www.bettersex.com

For help in choosing a therapist:

The Society for the Scientific Study of Sexuality (SSSS); American Association of Sex Educators, Counselors, and Therapists (AASECT)
Box 208
Mt. Vernon, IA 52314
(319) 895-8407

Suggested Reading:
Anand, Margo, *The Art of Sexual Ecstasy.* Tarcher Books, 1991 (paper).
Bechtal, Stefan, Laurence Roy Stains, and the editors of *Men's Health* magazine, *Sex: A Man's Guide.* Berkeley, 1998 (paper).
Berkowitz, Bob, *His Secret Life: Male Sexual Fantasies.* Pocket Books, 1998 (paper).
Block, Joel, Ph.D., *Secrets of Better Sex.* Prentice Hall, 1996 (paper).
Gilbert, Harriet, ed., *Fetishes, Florentine Girdles, and Other Explorations into the Sexual Imagination.* HarperCollins (paper).
Keesling, Barbara, Ph.D., *Super Sexual Orgasm.* HarperCollins, 1997. *The Penguin Book of Erotic Short Stories by Women.* Viking Penguin, 1996 (paper).
Sheehy, Gail, *New Passages.* Perennial Library, 1996 (paper).